This book belongs to:
HOLMBERG - MARCH

Haunted by the
Archaic Shaman

Haunted by the Archaic Shaman

Himalayan *Jhãkris* and the Discourse on Shamanism

H. Sidky

LEXINGTON BOOKS
A division of
ROWMAN & LITTLEFIELD PUBLISHERS, INC.
Lanham • Boulder • New York • Toronto • Plymouth, UK

LEXINGTON BOOKS

A division of Rowman & Littlefield Publishers, Inc.
A wholly owned subsidiary of The Rowman & Littlefield Publishing Group, Inc.
4501 Forbes Boulevard, Suite 200
Lanham, MD 20706

Estover Road
Plymouth PL6 7PY
United Kingdom

British Library Cataloguing in Publication Information Available

Library of Congress Cataloging-in-Publication Data

Sidky, H., 1956-
    Haunted by the archaic shaman : Himalayan Jhakris and the discourse on
shamanism / H. Sidky.
        p. cm.
    Includes bibliographical references and index.
    ISBN-13: 978-0-7391-2621-9 (cloth : alk. paper)
    ISBN-10: 0-7391-2621-0 (cloth : alk. paper)
    1. Shamanism--Nepal. 2. Nepal--Religion. 3. Nepal--Social life and customs.
I. Title. BL2033.5.S52S53 2008
299'.1495--dc22   2008001514

Printed in the United States of America

♾️™ The paper used in this publication meets the minimum requirements of
American National Standard for Information Sciences—Permanence of Paper for
Printed Library Materials, ANSI/NISO Z39.48–1992.

To the *jhākris* of Nepal, indomitable spirit masters who are engaged in a perpetual cosmic struggle against the forces of chaos and disorder

Contents

Acknowledgments

I would like to express my gratitude to my friends Dilip Gurung, Shubhash Karki, Ranjan "Ranaam" Adhikari (Mount Everest Films) for their help over the years in the video documentation of numerous night-long *jhākri* healing ceremonies. My thanks also go to Dr. Lawrence Downes of the Miami University College of Arts and Science IT department for his help and technical advice with the images reproduced in this book. I alone assume responsibility for any errors or problems and for the opinions expressed in this book.

Introduction

S hamanism has long fascinated scholars and popular audiences in the West. The literature on the subject is immense and centers upon the figure of the Paleolithic or "archaic" shaman. An ostensible explorer of the potentials of the human consciousness, inventor of art, and originator of humankind's ancient "ur-religion," this mysterious figure haunts us from cave walls and rock faces on which ancient people drew his enigmatic images. Reports written by eighteenth- and nineteenth-century Western travelers to Siberia, where the ancient shamanistic complex purportedly survived into historic times, provide additional clues about the archaic shaman.

Researchers in the field of shamanic studies are drawn from numerous disciplines, including archaeology, comparative religion, history, medicine, psychology, psychiatry, neuroscience, and interdisciplinary studies, among others. However, although scholars and scientists have devoted considerable time and effort to the study of shamanism, as evidenced by the voluminous output of books and articles from diverse disciplinary perspectives, a number of seemingly intractable conceptual problems beset this area of research. This has resulted in marked divergences of opinion over such basic issues as the definition of shamanism, its origins, history and prehistory, and its geographical frame of reference.

Views articulated in the shamanic studies literature are at variance with the ethnographic picture of shamanism in places such as Nepal, where I have been conducting field research since 1999 (Sidky et al. 2002). The shamanistic pattern in Nepal is remarkably similar to Siberian shamanism, which Euro-American scholars have long considered as the prototypical example of the practice. The cultural configuration in Nepal is therefore pertinent to the field of shamanic studies. This book developed out of an effort to resolve the discrepancy between my ethnographic findings and conventional understandings of shamanism. I do not treat this discrepancy as a confirmation of the facile conclusion by anthropologists who have disengaged from the topic that shamanism is an academic illusion (Atkinson 1992: 307; Boddy 1994; Holmberg 1989; Humphrey 1994; Taussig 1989). Instead, I see this as an opportunity for reassessment and analytical refinement of key issues pertaining to an important area of anthropological concern.

Using Nepalese ethnography it is possible not only to address some of the contentious issues that underlie the conceptual quandaries related to the study of shamanism, but also to call into question long-standing assumptions regarding the antiquity of shamanism, its role as humanity's archaic religion, and the experiential and phenomenological nature of the shaman's states of consciousness. In this book, the archaic shaman who has haunted Western imagination since the eighteenth century comes face to face with his ethnographic counterpart, the Nepalese spirit-master called *jhākri*.

My first encounter with *jhākri*s took place in 1999, while I was conducting ethnographic fieldwork in eastern Nepal. Although the original focus of my research was altogether different, my interest in the subject matter grew after observing an all-night *jhākri* healing ritual. Thereafter, I attended as many healing ceremonies as possible, observing these magicoreligious practitioners beating their drums, trembling, and shaking violently as they grappled with invisible forces. I participated as observer and assistant in numerous ceremonies and in several instances I was also the subject of the *jhākri* healing rites, although my intention has never been to provide an "experiential" ethnography in which the anthropologist's personal experiences are offered as ethnographic data (cf. Hamayon 2001: 3).

Over the course of the next seven years, I spent long hours in the Dolakha District in eastern Nepal, in and around the Kathmandu Valley, in Kabhre District, and Chitwan talking to various practitioners about their lives and profession. I worked closely with shamans belonging to different social and ethnic groups, including Chetri, Gurung, Jirel, Rāi, Sherpa, and Tamang practitioners. I recorded the songs and mantras that *jhākri*s carefully and painstakingly commit to memory and compiled video footage and photographs of their ritual activities and demonstrations of paranormal feats of power, or *śakti*, such as eating fire, walking on hot coals with bare feet, and immersing their hands in boiling liquids. For comparative purposes, I also interviewed other ritual intercessors, such as oracles, mediums, priests, and astrologers (*dhāmi*s, *mātā*s, *lāmā*s,

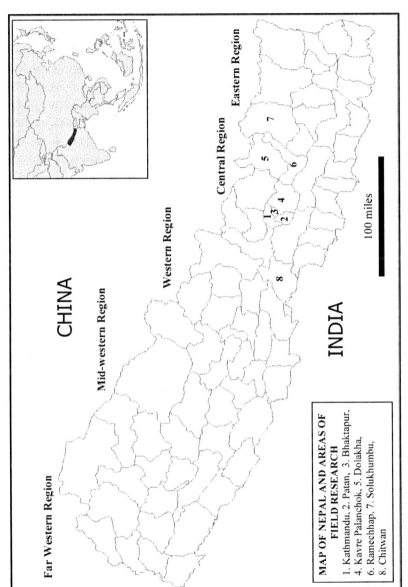

CHINA

Far Western Region

Mid-western Region

Western Region

Central Region

Eastern Region

5

7

6

3 4

1 2

8

INDIA

100 miles

MAP OF NEPAL AND AREAS OF
FIELD RESEARCH

1. Kathmandu, 2. Patan, 3. Bhaktapur,
4. Kavre Palanchok, 5. Dolakha,
6. Ramechhap, 7. Solukhumbu,
8. Chitwan

Map

and *jōtisi*s). My findings reveal that *jhākri*s across the country belong to a distinct category of ritual intercessors and are easily distinguishable from other magicoreligious practitioners. Moreover, there is a remarkable unity of beliefs and practices among the *jhākri*s, making shamanism a pan-Nepalese phenomenon. As a widespread, dynamic, and flourishing tradition, Nepalese shamanism can provide many insights into the broader picture of Asiatic shamanism as well as shamanism in general.

In the present study, I discuss in detail various aspects of the *jhākri* beliefs and practices as well as pointing out the similarities and differences between Nepalese and Siberian shamanism. Where appropriate I juxtapose the Nepalese ethnographic material against current understandings of shamanism to illustrate or address relevant theoretical issues and problems.

My work in Nepal was not only intellectually rewarding, it also allowed me to develop close personal friendships with a number of *jhākri*s, whom I found to be highly intelligent, confident, charismatic, and extremely perceptive individuals who possess profound mystical knowledge and are masters of a large corpus of oral narratives. My perseverance in this project was due in large part to their gracious help, active encouragement, and superhuman patience for my many impositions, including attentively listening and providing feedback while I read draft chapters of this book to them for commentary. *Mitraharu, ma tapāīharu prati krītagya ra abhar chhu* (My friends, you have my utmost gratitude and thanks).

1

From Siberia to Nepal:
The Discourse on Shamanism

This book examines shamanistic beliefs and practices in the small land-locked Himalayan kingdom of Nepal. Nepalese shamanism is a thriving tradition, as rich as any on earth. The ethnographic materials from Nepal are therefore highly relevant to any discussion of shamans and shamanism. Before discussing Nepalese shamans and their craft, I shall address some of the theoretical issues within the broader scholarly discourse on shamanism. Such an overview is necessary for two reasons: first, the general discourse on shamanism is fraught with a number of methodological and conceptual problems that have a bearing on ethnographic cases; second, ethnographic research can constructively contribute to the general debate on shamanism beyond self-referential particularistic ethnographic narratives. It is my contention that the debate on shamanism, which initially began within the discipline of anthropology itself, was needlessly abandoned by cultural anthropologists under the influence of theoretical fads and phobia of general theories associated with the so-called deconstructionist movement of the 1980s (for a full discussion see Sidky 2006; 2004; 2003a). The present study is an attempt to reengage in the general discourse on shamanism using empirical ethnographic data to address key conceptual issues and problems in this area of research.

Shamanism has interested Western scholars from a variety of fields since at least the eighteenth century (Flaherty 1992; Narby and Huxley 2001; Znamenski 2004). The term shaman originally derives from the word *šaman* used by Tungus speakers of Siberia to denote a particular type of magicoreligious practitioner (see Balzer 1996; Eliade 1964:

495–496; Hultkrantz 1973: 26; Rogers 1982: vii-xii; Shirokogoroff 1935: 276; Walter and Fridman 2004: xxii; Znamenski 2003: 1). Religious scholar and shamanism expert Åke Hultkrantz (1973: 26) suggests that the root of the word *šaman*, "*ša-*," means "to know"; a shaman is therefore "one who knows" (cf. Czaplicka 1914: 144). Anthropologist Ioan Lewis (2003: 35) maintains that the root "signifies the idea of violent movement and of dancing exuberantly, throwing one's body about."

The Tungus (Evenki) themselves appear to have borrowed the word *šaman* from elsewhere. An interesting case has been made that the term may have originally derived from *samaṇa* (Sanskrit *šramaṇa*), the word for Buddhist monk in Pali, the ritual language of Buddhism (Gibson 1997: 50–52; Mironov and Shirokogoroff 1924; Morris 2006: 16). This word is identical to *sha-men*, the Chinese word for Buddhist monk (Hutton 2001: 114–115; Maskarinec 1995: 97). However, some writers disagree with this etymology (Hultkrantz 1973; Laufer 1917; Siikala 1992a: 2). The word shaman became part of the Russian language through the descriptions of the peoples and customs of Siberia by Western explorers and it subsequently entered English and other languages (Flaherty 1992: 6; Hutton 1993: 10; Shirokogoroff 1935: 268–270; Townsend 1997: 431; Znamenski 2004: xxi). As historian Ronald Hutton (2001: vii) has put it:

> By the late eighteenth century [the word "shaman"] was current among authors from Russia westward to Britain to denote a phenomenon which was encountered in Siberia and impressed western writers as both dramatic and alien: an individual who claimed to contact spirits through an often spectacular public performance and to use this power to help or blight other human beings.

Heavily impacted by hostile encounters with Islam in the southwest, Buddhism in the southeast, and Christianity elsewhere during the historic period (Hutton 1993: 17; Morris 2006: 28), by the time systematic data collection on Siberian shamanism got under way the indigenous cultures of the region had been profoundly altered. Tsarist imperialism and especially the hostile policies of the subsequent Soviet regime and its energetic efforts to suppress shamanism as a fraudulent and superstitious practice contributed to the systematic extermination of shamanism in Siberia during the first part of the twentieth century (see Balzer 1990: vii; 1997: xiii; Glavatskaya 2001; Hultkrantz 1998a; Humphrey and Onon 1996: 1; Hutton 2001: 3–44, 116; 1993: 17–18; Kehoe 2000: 16–19; Siikala 1992b: 17). Thus as the Soviet-era ethnographer Vilmos Diószegi (1960: 10) put it, "Today, shamanism already belongs to the past. . . .it [is] extinct."

In spite of these circumstances, Western writers consider Siberia as the locality where shamanism had survived in its ancient and pristine form to the present. Moreover, for many scholars shamanism has become synonymous with the indigenous religions of Siberia, although the practices to which this label is attached were only one and seldom the most salient element of those religions (Hutton 2001: 47). Despite assertions by many writers (e.g., Diószegi 1960: 8; Furst 1977: 21; Hedges 1992: 70; McClenon 2001: 63, 80–81; Ripinsky-Naxon 1992; 1998), shamanism is not a religion, although it can be embedded in the wider ritual field and religious configuration of a society (Böckman and Hultkrantz 1978: 10–11; Hultkrantz 1988; Townsend 1997: 431). The shaman is not a religious leader in the sense of representing the cosmic and moral orders of society (cf. Krader 1978: 185) and, unlike most religions, shamanism has no soteriology.

Sometime during the late nineteenth century, shamanism, a concept that initially referred to a geographically circumscribed phenomenon, was transformed into an analytical category to be applied to similar assemblages of beliefs and practices elsewhere around the globe (Hutton 2001: vii; Krader 1978: 231; Znamenski 2004). In the hands of the Romanian scholar Mircea Eliade (1907–1986), who attempted to synthesize the published material on shamanism in the 1940s, this approach received new impetus and seeming precision (Hutton 2001: 124). Interestingly, Eliade started out with the objective of adding precision to the concept of shamanism and correcting the facile use of the terms *shaman* and *shamanism*:

> If the word "shaman" is taken to mean any magician, sorcerer, medicine man, or ecstatic found throughout the history of religions and religious ethnology, we arrive at a notion at once extremely complex and extremely vague; it seems, furthermore, to serve no purpose, for we already have the terms "magician" or "sorcerer" to express notions as unlike and as ill-defined as "primitive magic" or "primitive mysticism." (Eliade 1964: 3)

Eliade (1961: 153) integrated into a coherent picture the available ethnographic monographs and thousands of pages of facts and observations "published," as he put it, "in the hope that they would be read, thought about, and used not only by specialists but also by scholars in adjacent disciplines and by those whose function can be called 'generalizing.'" His concern was what anthropologist Jane Atkinson (1992) calls "shamanism writ large."

Eliade approached the problem from the perspective of the history of religions, emphasizing that shamanism could be treated as a subject matter in the same way as classic world religions. By situating the problem "in the context of the history of religions," as Eliade (1981: 117) explained, he in effect modernized the study of shamanism, which had been relegated to the category of ethnographic oddities, and gave it a new sense of significance, legitimacy, and relevance (Znamenski 2003: 34; 2004: xlvi–lii). Eliade's book, *Shamanism: Archaic Techniques of Ecstasy* (1964), first published in French in 1951, presented a staggering compilation of data from an equally staggering array of sources. The book appeared to be an exhaustively researched, meticulously documented, and erudite piece of scholarship. It was received as the definitive study on the subject during the last quarter of the twentieth century that had a profound and lasting intellectual impact on Western European and North American academic and popular audiences (Bowie 2000: 176; Knecht 2003: 6–7; Morris 2006: 17). Hultkrantz (1991: 9) has described Eliade "as the foremost shaman scholar of modern times." Aside from influencing anthropologists and scholars in other fields, Eliade's views of shamanism had a profound impact upon Carl Jung, the founder of analytical psychology (see TePaske 1997). Jung's ideas have, in turn, informed the works of those writing on shamanism and related "transpersonal" phenomena.

Eliade's construal of shamanism, which is fraught with methodological problems and ethnographic errors, laid the ground work for subsequent studies and continues to inform the works of those interested in the subject matter (Hamayon 1998: 180; Hultkrantz 1998b: 164; Le Quellec 2001: 148; Price 2001: 5; Winzeler 2008: 208). Eliade's methodology, as archeologist Henri-Paul Francfort (2001a: 34) has pointed out, consisted of "creative hermeneutics," an approach that is akin to what a novelist does in order to create plausible narratives without validation or verification (see Sidky 2003a: 215, 241). For these reasons, Eliade's work requires scrutiny.

Eliade began his study by stating the importance of Siberia, the so-called *locus classicus* of shamanism. However, he never claimed that shamanism is a religion, although he noted that it could coexist alongside various forms of magic and religion. Instead, he classified shamanism as a form of mysticism (Eliade 1964: 5, 8). Shamans, in Eliade's vision, were spiritual elites who achieved mastery of ecstatic trance states through a rigorous initiation process involving illness, death, and resurrection. Thus empowered, their ultimate role was to act as the guardians of the "psychic integrity" of their communities. These "specialists in the sacred," who could "see" the spirits, "go up into the sky and meet the gods," and "descend into the netherworld and fight demons, sickness, and death," articulated the "knowledge of death," and reassured people that they were not alone and helpless in a "foreign world" beleaguered by demons and "the forces of evil" (Eliade 1961: 184–185). The shaman's world therefore promised freedom and endless possibilities "where the dead return to life and the living die only to live again, where one can disappear and reappear instantaneously, where 'the laws of nature' are abolished and a certain human 'freedom' is exemplified and made dazzlingly present" (Eliade 1964: 511).

For Eliade (1964: 227–228; 1961: 155) the Siberian shaman's soul journey (magic flight) or "ascension to Heaven" and "descension to the netherworld" while in a "trance" was the defining characteristic of genuine or "classic shamanism." It was through the soul journey that the adept acquired power over spirits, the ability to heal the sick, and the capacity to escort the souls of the dead to their final destinations, i.e., the capacity to function as a psychopomp. By traveling through the multitiered cosmos, the shaman communed with the celestial "Supreme Being" in person. Belief in a "Supreme Being," Eliade (1964: 507) maintained, was the "original underlying ideology" of shamanism. In his view, it was only after the complex degenerated that interaction with lesser supernatural entities replaced communion with God. A dubious supposition here—which is akin to the idea of *Urmonotheismus*, or primordial monotheism, of Wilhelm Schmidt of the German diffusionist school of anthropology—is that the belief in a supreme deity preceded beliefs in multiple lesser gods (see Sidky 2004: 100–103; see also Swanson 1964).

Eliade referred to the shaman's communion with God as an "archaic technique of ecstasy." The ecstatic experience is a manifestation of the timeless "sacred" (what he termed hierophany) and was to Eliade the defining attribute and essence of human religiosity. "Ecstasy" is not the product of any historical or cultural factors, but is a fundamental aspect of the human condition (a universal human psychological attribute) found in the present as it was in ancient times, although valued differently in separate historical and cultural settings (Eliade 1964: xv, 504; 1978: 19). This postulate of an innate timeless universal spirituality enabled Eliade to disclose to his readers the states of consciousness of Paleolithic peoples and to talk about their "deep spirituality" using information from extant or recently extant societies. This aspect of his work became the basis for what anthropologist Peter Jones (2006: 7) describes as "spatiotemporally free theories of neurophenomenology and neuroepistemology" (see d'Aquili and Newberg 1998; 1999; 2000; Krippner 2000; Laughlin et al. 1992; Winkelman 2000; 2002; 2004a).

Eliade's depiction of shamanism as an ancient, universal, and pristine form of spirituality, undistorted by institutional hierarchies and dogmas of conventional religions, with a promise of infinite possibilities, romanticized the subject for those in the pursuit of timeless human religiosity, self-healing, and a yearning to return to the eternal community of shamans as envisioned by the Romanian scholar. Shamanism thus became a part of everyone's heritage, rather than belonging to indigenous societies, a factor that later greatly facilitated the marketing of shamanic journeys to receptive audiences in the West. Eliade's work figures prominently in the literature of the popular self-discovery "core shamanism" and "neoshamanism" spiritual movements (Bahn 2001: 56; Noel 1999: 29). The underlying feature of this literature is the unmitigated conviction that shamanism encompasses miraculous, extraordinary, and paranormal forces and powers that are as relevant to human life today as they were to the lives of the ancient peoples among whom the practice is thought to have originated (see Jakobsen 1999: 147–207; Morris 2006: 34–36;Townsend 2001: 260; 1999).

A major defect in Eliade's work stems from his disregard for the sheer complexity and diversity of the phenomenon under study, the intricate ways practices labeled as shamanism articulated with other aspects of social and religious configuration, and his tendency to dismiss information that did not correspond to his theoretical constructs. Rather than adjust and fine-tune his model, Eliade treated variant practices (from his perspective) as subsequent transformations of the genuine form, syncretisms, peripheral innovations, or merely degenerations and distortions (cf. Eliade 1964: 499–500; Hutton 2001: 122). His "creative hermeneutics" gave him the liberty to selectively choose and assemble bits and pieces of information to support his vision without regard to context (Francfort 2001a: 34). A number of problems, such as the place of spirit possession in shamanism, discussed in chapter 2, were thus needlessly created that could have easily been avoided by attending to ethnographic complexities and honest appraisal of the implications of data conflicting with a proposed model or generalization.

Eliade's work on shamanism stands as a testament to the follies of opting for the hermeneutic approach to the analysis of cultural phenomena over approaches based upon the rigorous testing of propositions against empirical data. What distinguishes scientific approaches from hermeneutic, meaning-centered, context-dependent narrative ethnographic writing is that scientific approaches attempt to enhance knowledge through the rigorous analysis of sociocultural phenomena and the systematic measurement of premises against the obdurate matrix of empirical data. Scientific knowledge changes in relation to empirical findings and science postulates procedures to discriminate between alternative hypotheses (see Sidky 2004: 13–33; 2006).

Eliade (1964: xix, 503–504) traced the origins of shamanism back to the Upper Paleolithic period some 25,000–30,000 years ago and argued that shamanism was the foundation of all religions, or what some anthropologists later called the "ur-religion" of humankind (Furst 1977: 4–7; Harner 1980: 53; La Barre 1972a; Ripinsky-Naxon 1993: 9; Winzeler 2008: 17, 214). Other writers push the date as far back as 50,000 to 100,000 years or more (Furst 1977: 4; Hayden 2003: 118; Halifax 1991: 3; Ripinsky-Naxon 1993: 70). The anthropologist Weston La Barre (1972a: 161) goes as far as to assert that:

the ancestor of the god is the shaman himself, both historically and psychologically. There were shamans before there were gods. The very earliest religious data we know from archaeology show dancing masked sorcerers or shamans at Lascaux, Trois Frères, and other Old Stone Age caves.

The idea that shamanism is an ancient religious phenomenon was inspired entirely by the speculative nineteenth-century evolutionary schemes of armchair anthropologists that treated extant aboriginal peoples and their belief systems as surviving representatives (living fossils) of earlier and "lower" and "primitive" stages of human evolutionary development. In other words, Eliade accepted the conjecture that extant small-scale non-Western populations at the extreme fringes of the "civilized world" have preserved aspects of culture long ago displaced by civilization in the West (Kehoe 2000: 39). Many writers still maintain this view today. For example, Ripinsky-Naxon (1993: 219) asserts that, "the aboriginal religions in the New World may be viewed as the archaeological present of the Mesolithic horizon." It followed from this supposition that the magicoreligious practices recorded by travelers and ethnologists in far-off and remote places such as Siberia during the eighteenth and nineteenth centuries were similar to the beliefs and practices of Paleolithic hunter-gatherers living millennia ago (Kehoe 2000: 39).

The other criterion Eliade used for the antiquity of shamanism was the postulate that the more widely a phenomenon is distributed, the older it must be (cf. Reinhard 1976: 15), based on the "age area hypothesis" of the defunct early-twentieth-century school of diffusionist anthropology. Unfortunately, this postulate is hopelessly flawed. If we apply it to a contemporary example, we would conclude that the invention of personal computers preceded the development of mechanical typewriters (Sidky 2004: 135, 137).

To demonstrate shamanism as a global phenomenon, Eliade sifted and arranged available ethnographic and historical information in the manner of James Frazer's dubious selective pick-and-choose/cut-and-paste approach to the comparative study of religion, pointing to the presence of "ecstatic" practitioners resembling Siberian shamans elsewhere in Asia and the Americas (Hutton 2001: 120–121). This procedure yielded shamans in vast quantities. Shamanism, it appeared, was indeed widespread. It followed that if shamanism was widespread then it had to be very ancient. Eliade concluded, therefore, that shamanism was humankind's heritage from Paleolithic hunter-gatherers. Ever since this bit of scholarly ingenuity, the ghost of Eliade's archaic shaman has been haunting anthropology and related fields and refuses to be exorcised.

All of this, however, is rank speculation for which there is little or no convincing evidence. As Hutton (2001: 113–149) has shown, the history of shamanism in Siberia is unknown. There are no records prior to the sixteenth century and whatever of its prehistory might be deduced from petroglyphs—highly problematic sources of information for deducing the presence of shamanism to begin with (Jacobson 2001; Francfort 2001b)—is equally hazy and is probably no more than a few thousand years old (Hutton 2001: 114). Given that shamanism is an oral tradition, the question of historical origins is nearly impossible to solve even where an abundance of high-quality ethnographic information exists, such as in Nepal (see chapter 3).

Paleolithic cave art in Europe depicting costumed or therianthropic (half-animal and half-human) figures (see Dickson 1990: 131; Breuil 1952: 149–151,165–167), such as the so-called sorcerers or shamans at Trois Frères, which are open to numerous equally plausible and not so plausible interpretations (magician, master of animals, mythical being, divinity, monster, prehistoric clown, hunter in camouflage, ancient astronaut, Martian, etc.), is hardly conclusive evidence (see Bahn and Vertut 1997: 182–183; Díaz-Andreu 2001; Francfort et al. 2001). Moreover, sorcerers and shamans are entirely different kinds of ritual intercessors. So which is it? An alternative interpretation is provided by prehistorian Steven Mithen (1996: 164–165, 178–179) who suggests that Paleolithic images of humans with animal attributes could reflect anthropomorphic (animals and plants as people) and totemistic (people as animals) thinking and that these representations give us clues about the emergence of human cognitive fluidity. Mithen does not go on to postulate the presence of shamans based on these images.

Another line of archaeological research necessitates some comment. Beginning with Eliade's (1978: 19) postulate that shamanistic trance is universal in time and space and is based on neurognostic structures (i.e., archetypes) of the human mind, some scholars have attempted to identify evidence of these visionary experiences, and hence shamanism itself, in prehistoric rock art. According to the proposed neurophysiological model upon which this approach is based (Lewis-Williams and Dowson 1998; Pearson 2002: 87–89), trance is characterized by a universal sequence of visual effects, beginning with the phenomenon of phosphenes (images, such as dots and lines internal to the eye) that result in the formation of geometric patterns, called entoptics. These include spirals, circles, zigzags, honeycombs, undulating parallel lines, and more complex transformational motifs, such as human-animal-human images (Clottes and Lewis-Williams 2001: 218). Identification of these images in ancient art, proponents assume, is evidence of shamanism in prehistory. Shamans, according to this perspective, also become the inventors of art, prehistoric art being an outcome of shamanistic practice (cf. Lommel 1967: 128; Smith 1992: 35–36).

In this line of reasoning, Paleolithic cave paintings in Europe and rock art associated with ancient hunting-gathering peoples elsewhere represent shamanistic trance states and hallucinations (see Bednarik et al. 1990; Clottes and Lewis-Williams 1998; Francfort et al. 2001; Lommel 1967;

Figure 1.1. The "sorcerer or shaman" at Trois Frères, France (drawn after Breuil 1952: 166)

Lewis-Williams and Dowson 1988; Lewis-Williams 2003; Pearson 2002; Price 2001; Wellmann 1981). One problem here is that one does not need to be in a trance to see entoptic forms, which can be experienced during migraine headaches or simply by pressing the eyeball (Bahn and Vertut 1997: 183; see Neher 1990: 12–13). Also, even if we grant that the suggested approach enables us to discover images by entranced artists, which is highly debatable (see Francfort et al. 2001; Helvenstone and Bahn 2003; 2004; Hodgson 2006), being entranced does not mean that someone is a shaman. This is because the range of altered states of consciousness is considerable (cf. Tart 1980: 243) and shamanism does not encompass the entire range (cf.

de Beaune 1998; see chapter 6). This point is demonstrated in the comparison of different ritual intercessors in Nepal in chapter 2.

Moreover, there is no documentation of entranced shamans, Siberian, South African, or otherwise, ever making rock art based on their visions (Bahn and Vertut 1997: 183; Kehoe 2000: 4, 71–80). Thus, as archaeologist Paul Bahn has observed, "we have absolutely no evidence whatsoever to link any Ice Age art to something like shamanism except as a simple assumption" (Bahn and Vertut 1997: 182). Nepalese shamans depict images on their drums and on the ground during certain rituals, but never while they are in altered states of consciousness (see chapters 5 and 10). Shamanic art, where it occurs, functions to convey symbolic messages in the context of ritual performances rather than being a medium for the representation of the shaman's psychic states.

Archaeological evidence of a different type cited as evidence for the archaic shaman is the "flower burial" in Shanidar Cave in Iraq, dated to be over fifty thousand years old (Pearson 2002: 65–66). This was a male Neanderthal burial covered with species of flowers (identified from the pollen) with medicinal properties (Pearson 2002: 65–66, 113; Leroi-Gourhan 1975; Solecki 1971). The burial is interpreted as evidence of a Paleolithic healer at work. This too is decidedly problematic. Even if the palynological evidence is indisputable, which it is not (Gargett 1989; Sommer 1999), what the Shanidar burial possibly suggests is that Neanderthals had acquired skills as herbalists, this does not indicate the handiwork of a shaman. Humans get sick and cure themselves through various techniques, but this does not mean that every time we encounter curers we are in the presence of shamans.

Archaeological evidence for shamanism in general (e.g., Hayden 2003: 147–153: Pearson 2002: 113–143) is meager and the interpretations are untestable and unfalsifiable (Bahn and Vertut 1997: 183). Some experts even doubt that archaeological data alone can determine the prehistory of shamanism (e.g., Leroi-Gourhan 1987). Take one famous and often cited example, "the Scene in the Shaft at Lascaux" (see Dickson 1990: 135; Breuil 1952: 149–151), which depicts a prostrate bird-headed man in front of a speared charging bison and a staff with a bird image at one end and a spur or hook at the other end, probably an *atlatl*, or spear-thrower. Wild hunches, sheer speculations about motive, content, and meaning (Bahn and Vertut 1997: 182), and extraordinary inferential leaps render this scene of a probable hunting accident into a "flying shaman" in a trance, complete with an erection, which we are told, "sometimes occurs in ecstasy" (Davenport and Jochim 1988; Hayden 2003: 149; Joseph 2003a: 333; Lommel 1967: 128). To make the interpretation seem plausible, the prostrate figure and the staff with the bird are often reproduced in publications without the wounded charging bison, eliminating the hunting elements of the painted

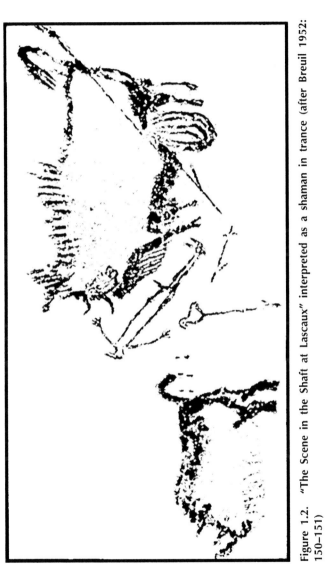

Figure 1.2. "The Scene in the Shaft at Lascaux" interpreted as a shaman in trance (after Breuil 1952: 150–151)

scene. The spear thrower, a Paleolithic implement that often had bird and animal images carved at one end (Lechler 1951), is described as "a bird on a staff [that] indicates shamanic flight" (Hayden 2003: 149). Ornithological symbolism, which for Eliade (1964: 156–158, 177) and those influenced by him always means "shamanic flight," can have various meanings, soul journeys not necessarily being among them, as in the case of Nepalese shamanism (see chapter 5).

What makes such fantastic interpretive exercises even more problematic is that they are guided by Eliade's flawed vision of shamanism, which is unsupported by ethnographic and historical evidence. In other words, writers in pursuit of the archaic shaman are chasing a phantom whose ritual enactments belong not to the hidden alcoves of Paleolithic labyrinths, but to the inner recesses of Eliade's free-flowing imagination. What is more remarkable is that what initially inspired a number of scholars (e.g., Giedion 1962; Kirchner 1952; Narr 1959) to interpret Paleolithic archaeological materials as evidence of shamanism was Eliade's (1951) work itself (contra Znamenski 2004: xlix, Lommel 1967 was not the first to utilize Eliade's ideas). Eliade presented these studies in the 1964 English edition of his book as archaeological support that shamanism is humanity's archaic religious system (Eliade 1964: 503; on the circularity of this position see Hutton 2001: 130–131). Others continue to cite these sources as evidence for the antiquity of shamanism (e.g., Pearson 2002: 65).

Arguments for the extreme age of shamanism based on ethnographic analogies (e.g., Dickson 1990: 135–136), which are also inspired by Eliade's (1978: 19) speculations, are problematic as well. This is because prehistoric hunter-gatherer societies do not fit the examples of hunter-gatherers in the ethnographic record. Prehistoric hunter-gatherers operated in resource-rich ecological settings, unlike contemporary foragers who exist in extremely marginal environments, are in contact with farming and herding societies (Stiles 1992), and are affected by regional, national, and global forces and processes. Moreover, some prehistoric hunting-gathering societies had characteristics such as social ranking and hierarchy, large sedentary populations, developed political leadership, and occupational specialization, not found among contemporary hunter-gatherers (Price and Brown 1985). In other words, the sociocultural systems of the Paleolithic period were unlike any hunter-gatherer societies documented in the ethnographic record. The ecological, economic, and sociopolitical differences between contemporary and prehistoric hunter-gatherers make arguments by analogy dubious.

Thus, like the evidence for the age of Siberian shamanism, the evidence for the antiquity of shamanism in general is highly questionable. This by no means detracts from the significance of shamanism as a sociocultural, neuropsychological, and neurophysiological phenomenon and by no means diminishes its importance as a topic of investigation; it merely highlights extremely bad scholarship. The dubious nature of the evidence and uncertainty regarding the antiquity of shamanism casts serious doubt upon scholarly works that treat shamanism as humankind's so-called archaic heritage and the basis of human religiosity. Scholars who are inattentive to the scientific rules of evidence and who do no critically appraise the data with which they are working are in danger, as anthropologist William Arens (1979: 7) put it in another context, of becoming nothing more than the "erudite purveyors of attractive pedestrian myths."

The noted ethnographer of Siberian shamanism Sergei Shirokogoroff (1935: 282–286) forwarded a compelling alternative hypothesis—at least no less compelling than the idea of shamanism as a surviving Paleolithic religious phenomenon—that Tungus shamanism is a relatively recent development. Shirokogoroff suggested that shamanism developed during the medieval period through a blending of indigenous beliefs and Buddhist Lamaism, itself heavily influenced by the "folk religion" of Tibet (cf. Samuel 1993: 177). In this connection, we might recall the association of the Tungus word *šaman* with the Pali word *samaṇa* for Buddhist monk. More recently, Tibetan Buddhism specialist Todd Gibson (1997: 50) has developed this thesis further, by suggesting a Buddhist source for the term for shaman among the Turkic-speaking peoples of Inner Asia, such as the Turkmen, Karakalpaks, Kazakh, Kirghiz, and Uzbeks. As Gibson (1997: 50) points out:

> The use of these words must be seen as indicating that, at a certain point in the history of these cultural groups, shamans were predominantly if not exclusively Buddhist shamans, or at least that the most essential of the shaman's functions had derived from Buddhism. . . . Such an assertion has important implications for both the history of the shamanic and that of Buddhism. First and most basically, the parallels in the Turkic languages add weight to the case for a derivation of the Tunguz *shaman* from *śramana*. Secondly, that several different Buddhist words are used to refer to the shaman (*śramana—shaman, vira—dpa'.bo, burxan,* and *bakshi*) indicated that Buddhism's effect cannot be explained by positing a single wave of cultural influence, but must be seen as a process that was repeated several times.

Eliade (1964: 495–500) acknowledged the influence of Buddhism on parts of Siberia, and appears to concede its broader diachronic and geographic impact, but he seems to have been convinced that the near-global distribution of shamanistic practices proves that the origins of shamanism go back to the prehistoric culture of Siberian hunters.

Critics have observed that the defining ethnographic features of Siberian and circumnorthern shamans do not occur in other parts of the world and question the validity of extending the term "shaman" to the magicoreligious/medicoreligious practitioners in these places (Kehoe 2000: 4).

In other words, the phenomena described as shamanism around the world do not resemble the Siberian pattern. For this reason, some writers suggest limiting the use of the term *shamanism* either to Siberia and the Arctic regions (Bowie 2000: 194) or to the source areas in Siberia and some parts of North America (Bahn 2001: 57).

For Hutton (1993: 15), Siberian-style shamanism existed only in Siberia and the Arctic regions of the globe, with traces in southeastern Europe. The Americas, western and southern Europe, Africa, southern Asia, and Australasia fall outside the geographic limits of the Siberian configuration. Hutton acknowledges the somewhat subjective nature of his effort to delimit the geographical extent of Siberian-style shamanism. Moreover, there are clusters of practices within the areas excluded by Hutton that are similar in some ways to Siberian practices. Hutton mentions, for example, the practices of the Araucanians of southern Chile (see Métraux 1967). However, the issue that divides many scholars when considering such cases is whether these are "survivals" of the presumed global shamanistic religion of the Paleolithic period or instances of parallel cultural development (Hutton 1993: 15). The question of geographical frame of reference thus remains a contentious issue in the academic discourse on shamanism (Price 2001: 6).

Despite the substantial uncertainties pointed out here, Eliade's vision of the Siberian shaman as the model of the quintessential spiritual human being and the master of the "archaic technique of ecstasy" has been widely accepted. Siberia itself has been dubbed the "classic" homeland of shamanism where the basic blueprint of humankind's once widely diffused pristine religion survived to modern times. Some even believe that shamanism originated in Siberia (Riboli 2000: 56).

However, using Siberia as a model for archaic shamanism is highly problematic. In addition to the issue of the effects of contact from Islam, Buddhism, and Christianity during the historic period, there is another problem pertaining to the use of Siberia as model for Paleolithic shamanism, namely the type of social formations found there. As Hutton (2001: 126) has queried, how can Siberian societies, with subsistence patterns based mostly on reindeer, horse, cattle, or sheep herding, represent the pristine or "classic" example of the shamanism of Paleolithic hunting-gathering cultures? The symbolic human-animal relations, in which Paleolithic shamans purportedly played a crucial role as mediators, are strikingly different between herding and hunting-gathering societies (cf. Fukui 1994: 139; Watanabe 1994; Yamada 1994; see also Irimoto and Yamada 1994). Non sequiturs such as this and other logical inconsistencies abound in this literature.

Nevertheless, the idea of shamanism as the religion of ancient hunting-gathering peoples has assumed the status of an incontrovertible fact (Clottes and Lewis-Williams 2001: 190; Furst 1977: 21; Hultkrantz 1989: 47;

1978: 27–28; Hedges 1992: 70; Morris 2006: 16; Pearson 2002: 115; von Gernet 1993: 73; Winkleman 2000: 58). As Hultkrantz (1989: 47) has put it, "shamanism is . . . a heritage from the ancient hunting cultures." Even Eliade's critics acknowledge that "shamanic practices are undoubtedly very ancient in north Asia" (Humphrey 1994: 191). Scholars from various fields not only construe shamanism as the universal "ancient religion" of hunter-gatherers, they also consider it to be the very foundation of human religiosity (Furst 1977; Hultkrantz 1989; 2001: 6; La Barre 1972a; 1972b; 1979; McClenon 2002: 6; Siikala 1992a: 2; Wallace 1966: 72; Walsh 1990: 13, 141–150, 161; 1996: 96; Winkelman 2000: xiii; 2002: 1873, 1875; 2006). Unfortunately, the high degree of certitude with which these assumptions are articulated is inversely proportional to the scanty amount of evidence available to support them.

The exclusive association of shamanism with hunting-gathering societies is sharply at odds with the presence of identical beliefs and practices among stratified village herders and farmers, such as for example in present-day Nepal (Hutton 2001: 126; Jones 2006: 8 has raised the same issue in reference to North America). There we find an assemblage of beliefs and practices that display nearly all the key attributes supposedly restricted to the shamanistic practices of pristine hunting gathering cultures (Townsend 1997: 436; Watters 1975; Thorpe 1993: 129–134). This is how the Siberian and Mongolian shamanism expert Roberte Hamayon (1993a: 200) attempts to explain away the problem:

> As everyone knows, shamanism is present as a symbolic all-embracing system only in non-centralized societies, whereas in centralized, state societies, shamanism is present only in the form of isolated, marginalized phenomena carried out by more or less marginal individuals. In other words, shamanism acts as a central religion in non-state societies, and is unable to act as a state religion, whereas it may combine as an inferior constituent with world religions.

Unfortunately, there is no conclusive evidence that shamanism was a central religion in politically decentralized unstratified societies. There is some evidence that shamans were not at the center of all religious life (Humphrey and Onon 1996: 50–51; Hutton 2001: 47; Morris 2006: 25). Moreover, as I have already pointed out, shamanism is not a religion. Also, Nepalese ethnographic materials do not support the idea that shamanism can only have subsidiary existence in more complex societies. As anthropologist John Hitchcock (1976b: xiv, xiii), one of the pioneers of Nepalese ethnography, pointed out, shamanism is a "vital aspect of Nepal's religious life . . . as thoroughly a part of the fabric of their lives as Hinduism and Buddhism, and just as intricately enmeshed with these two." This hardly describes "marginalized phenomena carried out by more or less marginal individuals."

Anthropologist Michael Winkelman (2000: 71–75; 2006) has attempted to deal with the issue of shamanism in complex societies by classifying such practitioners under a different designation. He uses the compound label "shamanistic/healers" (see chapter 2). This, however, does not adequately address the discrepancy because, as we shall see in the following chapters, the practitioners labeled as such, as in the case of Nepal, are indistinguishable from those Winkelman labels as "genuine" shamans.

Problems notwithstanding, Eliade convinced many scholars that one could legitimately use the concept of shamanism, as he defined it, to classify practices elsewhere into a single category for investigation (e.g., Glosecki 1989: 4; Torrance 1994: 139; Vitebsky 1995: 6, 50–51). Distortions and obfuscations mar this approach. Playing fast and loose with historical and ethnographic evidence, writers who believe in shamanism as a worldwide phenomenon have even recast the witch-hunts in early-modern Europe as the persecution of nature-worshipping "pagan" ecstatic shamans. European shamans, we are told, were targeted as witches by the logocentric, trance-hating church authorities who sought to crush the shaman's nonrational or rationally inexplicable wisdom and vision of the unity of all life forms (Harner 1999: 1; Winkelman 2000: 3), a view similar to one forwarded earlier by the postmodern guru Michel Foucault (1973: 44–52). The portrayal of European witches as shamans, inspired by the uncritical adoption of Eliade's faulty vision (e.g., Ginzburg 1990; Klaniczay 1984), is based on very shaky evidence and questionable methodology (see Sidky 1997: 13–14; Hutton 2001: 145–147). The victims of the witch-hunts in Europe were ordinary and helpless individuals, not shamans! The only trance or altered state of consciousness most of the accused witches experienced was the psychochemical torture they were subjected to in jails, and the persecutions were anything but the concern for the predominance of a logocentric worldview (see Sidky 1997: 208–221).

The extension of the idea of shamanism based on the Siberian model to a universal global scale has, not surprisingly, resulted in the incorporation of diverse magicoreligious practitioners and others who enter into "trance" and commune with spirits under the category of "shaman" (Jakobsen 1999: 3). As the archaeologist Neil Price (2001: 6) has summed it up:

In its broadest and most popular understanding "shamanism" has latterly come to cover virtually any kind of belief in "spirits" and the existence of other worlds, states of being, or planes of consciousness—a definition that of course encompasses the majority of the world's religions, organised or otherwise, ancient and modern. In this context the term "shaman" has been similarly used to refer to almost any kind of mediator, in any kind of medium, between one perception of the world and another. As a result, those popularly described as shamans have included an astonishing variety of individuals ranging from Jesus to Jim Morrison.

Critics note that such broad application of the term has led to the misinterpretation of ethnographic cases and mistranslation of indigenous words that have other meanings than "shamanism" (Bahn 2001: 57; Hamayon 2001: 2; Kehoe 2000: 40; Le Quellec 2001: 147–148). These objections are not new. As early as 1903, the eminent ethnographer/folklorist Arnold Van Gennep (2001: 52) called for a restriction of the term *shaman* to the religions of Siberia. He decried the then current usage of the label "shamanism," noting that researchers were playing with "a dangerously vague word" uncritically adopted from eighteenth- and nineteenth-century travelers to Siberia, who:

> knew almost nothing about ethnography and general ethnopsychology and thought they had found a special, characteristic form of religious belief and practice. Then the word gained favor among the ignorant, general public and among amateurs of exotic euphonism.

The global application of the term *shaman* has caused considerable ambiguity and confusion in the scholarly literature (Gibson 1997: 40; Klein et al. 2002; Klein et al. 2005; Klein and Stanfield-Mazzi 2004; Lindholm 1997: 424; Maskarinec 1995: 97; Price-Williams and Hughes 1994: 3–5; Sullivan 1994: 29). Although several hundred books and many more articles have been published on the topic, no commonly accepted definition of shamanism has been formulated (see Gibson 1997: 44; Gilberg 1984; Hultkrantz 1989; Hutton 2001: vii, 126; Jolly 2005; Lewis 1984; Lewis-Williams 2004; Rank 1967; Reinhard 1976; Siikala and Hoppál 1998; Sidky 2003b: 544–546; Townsend 1997: 430; Voigt 1984). The resurgence of scholarship on shamanism that began in the 1980s because of multidisciplinary interests in states of human consciousness and healing (Atkinson 1992: 307; for an overview see Znamenski 2004) has added to the ambiguity (Furst 1994: 4; Hamayon 2001: 2; Hutton 2001: vii; Jones 2006: 5; Kehoe 2000: 2). As Hultkrantz summed it up in the late 1980s, "[there] is a chaos in the understanding of what shamanism is: most authors dealing with the subject never give any definitions. . . . Those who define the subject differ widely."

Still there are scholars who, while acknowledging the constructed nature of the concept of shamanism and its limited scope of applicability, believe in its usefulness and wish to retain it. As Price (2001: 6) has put it:

> the concept of shamanism has always been an externally imposed construction, and does not exist anywhere at all other than in the minds of its students. . . As both a term and a notion, shamanism is entirely an academic creation, and as such it is certainly a useful tool serving to describe a pattern of ritual behavior and belief found in strikingly similar form across much of the arctic and subarctic regions of the world. Even within this broad understanding, the meaning of shamanism is entirely a matter of consensus, discussion and continuing redefinition.

The stance taken with respect to the study of shamanism by certain cultural anthropologists is interesting. Operating under the banner of "postmodern deconstructionism" during the late 1980s, these anthropologists expressed deep suspicions of general theories, "master narratives," "transcultural" categories, rationality, and scientific model building (see below). They rejected shamanism as a vestige of a discredited and defunct twentieth-century evolutionary religious typology, a reification, a contrived Western category, an inversion of the Western self, a trope, essentialism, an illusion, and a false category to be deconstructed (Atkinson 1992: 307: Boddy 1994; Taussig 1989; Humphrey 1994). However, some anthropologists writing in the 1960s had already declared shamanism an outdated concept, an "insipid" category that belongs in the garbage heap of nineteenth-century evolutionism rather than in modern anthropological discourse (Geertz 1966: 39; Spencer 1968: 396).

However, one may note, as Hamayon (2001: 5) has pointed out, that field anthropologists abandoned the debate on shamanism without really achieving a conclusive "theoretical deconstruction of the concept." The main obstacle seems to be the apparent universality of the phenomena subsumed under the label of shamanism. For this reason, critics themselves fall into flagrant conceptual quandaries when attempting to discuss the topic as a historically situated phenomenon. Take, for example, anthropologist Caroline Humphrey's (1994) work. Advocating a particularistic perspective, she treats shamanism as "discourse" and writes that "shamanism is not one thing but many" (Humphrey 1994: 192, 208). While disdainfully dismissing "context-free," "static models" of shamanism as forwarded by Eliade and his followers who ignore the multiplicity of ritual intercessors on the ground, Humphrey (1994: 194, 197–198) needlessly conflates distinct ritual specialists of all sorts. She talks about shamans in state bureaucracies, court shamans, patriarchal shamans, transformational shamans, and priest-like shamans, and so on, when in reality she has "inspirational specialists" in mind. Humphrey even talks about the existence of ritual specialists who are identical to Eliade's construal, while denying the validity of his model:

> [Daur shamans called *yagdan* or *saman*] were "chosen" by spirits; experienced initiatory death and rebirth; were capable of mastering spirits, transforming them from one kind to another, and renewing their powers; they were able to travel to the "other world" to rescue souls. Most of their activities were concerned with curing people of physical and psychological troubles, but they also held a complex ritual every few years for the revitalization of the relation between society and the entire range of spirits. (Humphrey 1994: 218)

If "shamanism" is an "insipid" category, a trope, essentialism, an illusion, not one thing but many things, why continue to use the word? What does anthropologist David Holmberg (1989: 142–143) mean when he talks about "Tamang shamanic practices" and "shamanic soundings" in Nepal? What does anthropologist Michael Taussig (1987: 237) mean when he writes about "Putumayo shamanism" or says that "shamans are the shock absorbers of history"? Are ritual specialists in southwest Colombia shamans? Clearly they are not, not if we adopt the point of view espoused by these writers themselves. Then who are the shock absorber of history? What are the Tamang specialists in Nepal who "sound" their drums? What about ritual specialists or ecstatic practitioners in Central America, Africa, or Australia, are they shamans? Again, the answer is no, not if we adopt the point of view espoused by these writers themselves. That such writers continue to use the term *shaman* is indicative of their failure to dismantle the concept theoretically. Anthropologist Brian Morris's (2006: 14) comments on these points are relevant:

> In recent years . . . postmodern anthropologists have been telling us that as shamanism is a "made-up, modern, western category" (in case you didn't know it!) and as it does not exist as a "unitary and homogeneous" phenomenon, we should stop talking about "shamanism" and instead write only of "shamanisms" or "shamanry" or shamanizing. By these criteria they themselves should stop writing about "anthropology," "western," "time," and the Evenki. Such semantic quibbles and banal nominalism seem to be unnecessary and stultifying and cannot be sustained even by their advocates.

Critics of shamanistic studies have in particular targeted Eliade himself, disparagingly calling him an ivory tower intellectual, an armchair savant, a metaphysician who failed to attend to empirical rigor and ethnographic facts, a new age guru, and a "cultural primitivist." His work has been described as mysticism, "religious revelation," and creative fiction, rather than "scholarly conclusion" (Kehoe 1997; 2000). Some of these criticisms are justified. Eliade's work, as discussed above, is fraught with problems. Moreover, the concept of shamanism has been grossly misapplied and misused both by scholars and those writing for the popular press. However, something that a number of critics have lost sight of is that Eliade's failings and his misuse of the comparative method do not invalidate the important anthropological task of developing generalizations to account for cross-cultural similarities and differences.

With a few exceptions, cultural anthropologists have relinquished general theorizing about shamanism to researchers in the fields of comparative religion, psychology, medicine, neuroscience, transpersonal psychiatry, archaeology, and multidisciplinary studies. The new agenda in cultural anthropology is ethnographic particularism (see below), hermeneutic approaches ironically akin to Eliade's "sacred fiction" writing, and an all-abiding concern with local practices and local knowledge in their particular historically situated sociocultural contexts (Thomas and Humphrey 1994: 4). Expressing this particularistic focus is the use of the term "shamanisms" in place of "shamanism" as a unitary phenomenon (Holmberg 1984: 41; Thomas and Humphrey 1994). As Atkinson (1992: 321) points out, the theoretical focus of this research is on topics such as aesthetics, local politics, gender and power, and colonialism, rather than on shamanism per se (e.g., Taussig 1987; Mumford 1989; Holmberg 1989; Desjarlais 1992), and much of this work is antithetical to the universalizing aims of shamanic studies.

The perspectives in question are labeled variously as postmodern, post-structuralist, phenomenological, hermeneutic, textual, dialogic, interpretive, and cultural constructionist. Although ostensibly distinct from the point of view of their particular adherents, these perspectives are based upon comparable epistemological and ontological assumptions. They tend to draw heavily upon the works of writers such as Jacques Derrida, Michel Foucault, Roland Barthes, and other French philosophers and literary critics, place great emphasis on narratives, texts, and tropes, advocate *epistemological relativism* (i.e., the view that all ways of knowing are equally valid and impossible to distinguish by means of any criteria), and rely upon intuitive subjective orientations incompatible with the epistemology of science (for a full critique see Appell 1989; Gellner 1992; Kuznar 1997; Lett 1997a; Sangren 1988; Sidky 2006; 2004: 394–411; 2003a; Sokal and Bricmont 1998). The idea that it is possible to distinguish between different or contending claims to knowledge—the premise upon which science is based—is dismissed by these writers as an aspect of the West's hegemonic discourse (Sidky 2006). Antiscience writers reject the rules of logic, empirical evidence, validation, and standards of proof and disproof (see Reyna 1994: 576). Science is thus portrayed merely as a culturally constructed set of beliefs or a story with no more validity, universality, or authority than any other way of knowing (e.g., Clifford 1986: 2–3; Herzfeld 2001: x, 2, 5, 9, 10, 22; Marcus 1986: 263). In this view, the epistemological status of claims to knowledge is irrelevant in determining the veracity of such claims. This is because to the coterie of antiscience writers under discussion everything is "culturally constructed," there are multiple realities, multiple equally valid truths (except science) and ethnography is "fiction" (for a full discussion see Sidky 2006).

My critique of these antiscience, meaning-centered, hermeneutic, or interpretive perspectives does not suggest that "meaning" is unimportant in scientific anthropological analysis or that personal narratives and empirical data are mutually exclusive, as one theoretically myopic commentator has imprudently implied. The understanding of systems of meaning and interpretation are essential components of many forms of anthropological analysis, including scientific ones. Indeed, ethnographic understanding depends upon fathoming the insider's point of view, or the emic perspective, which is interpretive in nature. What is problematic with the perspectives in question is the exclusive reliance on subjective approaches that are immune to verification, a vehement but unfounded rejection of the epistemology of science, the insistence that meaning encompasses the whole of culture and hence everything is culturally constituted (for a critique see Cerroni-Long 1996: 52; D'Andrade 1999: 88), and the emphasis on the individual case (also known as the ideographic approach). The outcome of all of this is the production of context-dependent, self-referential accounts, which I refer to as *ethnographic particularism*. Such accounts are inimical to nomothetic cross-cultural generalizing perspectives.

One permutation of ethnographic particularism has been the effort by some to write "narrative ethnographies of the particular" (e.g., Abu-Lughod 1991: 150–151), which amounts to the production of cleverly and experimentally written, subjective, idiosyncratic stories from the "bottom up." This trajectory has redirected the anthropological enterprise toward the same dreary dead-end road embarked upon years ago by Franz Boas and his students and later by Clifford Geertz and his acolytes with equally disappointing and dismal results (see Sidky 2003: 91–140; 199–242; 2004: 111–129, 132–163, 305–333). What this shift toward "narrative ethnographies of the particular" has amounted to has been the replacement of systematic and rigorous analysis with impressionistic anecdotal accounts (e.g., West 2007). As pointed out elsewhere, narratives and anecdotes do not enhance knowledge (Sidky 2006). They are laden with bias aimed at swaying audiences by appeal to emotion rather than evidence (Dawes 2001: 113).

My criticism of ethnographic particularism is not a rejection of ethnographic research, as the two are entirely different endeavors, and my use of ethnographic data from particular places to engage the discourse on shamanism does not constitute ethnographic particularism and is by no means at odds with my theoretical stance. The points of contention are the epistemological and ontological assumptions upon which hermeneutic, meaning-centered approaches are based, not ethnographic research and the application of ethnographic data from specific field site areas toward the construction and refinement of general models.

Recent anthropological research in Nepal reflects the particularistic trajectory I have mentioned. Work by professional anthropologists in Nepal began in 1953 (Fürer-Haimendorf 1974: 1). Many among the first group of researchers to work there treated the topic of shamanism in detail in relation to their respective ethnographic field areas (Allen 1974; 1976a; Fournier 1976; 1978; Hitchcock 1967; Höfer 1974a; 1974b; Macdonald 1975; 1976a; Peters 1979; 1982; 1987; Sagant 1982; 1988; Watters 1975; also the volumes edited by Fürer-Haimendorf 1974, and Hitchcock and Jones

1976). Rather than eschew nomothetic formulations, these anthropologists sought to refine the concept of shamanism by exploring its various dimensions and attempted to provide more ethnographically grounded perspectives.

Works by a subsequent generation of field researchers touching upon shamanistic practices tended to focus on the wider systems of ideas and performances in which such practices are embedded, rather than on shamanism itself. These studies may be described as "dialogic," and are concerned with the interplay of perspectives within and between local communities (see McHugh 1992). The studies by anthropologists Stan Mumford (1989) and David Holmberg (1989) are good examples of this trend. Mumford focuses on the dialogic interchange and conflicting discourses between Gurung shamans, whose practices he associates with "the 'classic' shamanism of the Siberian type" and Tibetan *lāmās* (Mumford 1989: 6). Holmberg's research concentrates on the dialogic interchange among Tamang *bọmbos* (shamans), *lámbus* (nonecstatic exorcists), and *lāmās*. Holmberg reiterates Geertz's (1966: 39) characterization of shamanism as an "insipid" category and points out that shamanism as a general topic is "intractable" and as an isolate is "an artifact of anthropological history and an illusion" (Holmberg 1989: 144–145; 1983: 41). Shamanism is an illusion, Holmberg (1984: 697) observes, in the sense that close scrutiny invariably reveals something else, such as "multiple specialists" or "multiple types of ritual practice."

It does not require a disengagement from theorizing or the adoption of "dialogic" or other so-called experimental approaches to arrive at such realizations. As anthropologist Rex Jones (1976a: 53) pointed out three decades ago in the context of Nepalese ethnography, "It is probable that shamanism, as defined by Eliade, never existed in reality but merely as abstraction of the comparative analyst." Similarly, anthropologist Johan Reinhard (1976) astutely pointed out the considerable variation in shamanistic practices in Siberia markedly at odds with Eliade's construal. Reinhard (1976: 14) provided his own, more nuanced definition of shamanism. These examples suggest that shamanism is not as intractable as we are led to believe. Jones (1976: 53) made a point worth listening to today as it was thirty years ago, which is that anthropologists "have much to offer the comparative study of religion" and that empirical ethnographic analysis can correct "simplistic notions of what a shaman is and does."

Despite anthropology's disengagement from comparative research on shamanism, the presence of similar practices in numerous traditional societies around the world is an incontrovertible fact (Hutton 2001: 120) and the anthropological problem this poses remains unsolved. Studies that attempt to explain the ubiquity of shamanistic traditions worldwide by linking them to universal genetically based neurognostic structures within the human nervous system (see d'Aquili and Newberg 1998; 1999; 2000; Krippner 2000; Laughlin et al. 1992: 275; Winkelman 2000: 76; 2002; 2004a), rather than cultural diffusion, have made anthropology's concern with "shamanisms" and the local perspective irrelevant in the broader interdisciplinary debate on shamanism. This is ironic because, as already noted, the works of anthropologists themselves underlie general academic and popular interests in shamanism (cf. Jones 2006: 9–10). Focused, empirically grounded ethnographic research on shamanistic practices can provide an invaluable counterbalance to the debates within the wider field of shamanic studies and, as Atkinson (1992: 321) has commented, anthropologists have the obligation to pay attention to this wider discourse, although her own relativistic theoretical stance rules this out.

It is my contention that one can productively address many of the central issues in the discourse on shamanism, including the problem of definition, through an examination of the rich body of information on shamanistic practices in Nepal. Unlike the problematic, secondhand, and often sketchy and decontextualized nature of much of the Siberian ethnographic data (Diószegi 1960: 10; Hutton 2001: 43–44, 151–156; Siikala 1992: 17), the Nepalese materials are solid and extensive and include a remarkable assemblage of fastidiously transcribed oral texts (Hitchcock 1974a; 1974b; Höfer 1981; 1994; Maskarinec 1992; 1995; 1998).

Shamanism in Nepal, which bears many similarities to Siberian and northern and central Asiatic practices, is part of a wide regional interethnic magicoreligious tradition recorded among many distinct ethnic groups and lower Hindu castes extending from eastern to western Nepal (Höfer 1994: 18; Hitchcock and Jones 1976: Riboli 2000: 56–57; Watters 1975). The Nepāli word for shaman is *jhākri*. The *jhākri* is a part-time practitioner whose calling is involuntary and encompasses a transformative initiatory crisis. He operates as a ritual intercessor, healer, and in some places, officiates in clan-god rituals (Nicoletti 2004; Sidky et al., 2002: 97–114). Among some groups, *jhākris* officiate over funerals in the capacity of psychopomp, as well as serving as intermediaries between humans and the god of hunting and nature spirits (Messerschmidt 1976; Riboli 2000: 125, 178–190).

Nepalese shamanistic practices do display certain distinct permutations within particular local cultural contexts. However, the cosmology that underlies it is a pan-Nepalese phenomenon (cf. Allen 1976a: 124, 1976b: 514; Desjarlais 1989: 304; Fournier 1976: 118; Hitchcock 1976: 171; Jones 1976: 52; Macdonald 1975: 113; Miller 1997: 20; Ortner 1995: 359; Paul 1976: 145; Peters 1981: 68; Townsend 1997: 44). Moreover, overall there is a remarkable unity of belief and practice even though there are no formalized fraternities of shamans as such in Nepal. As ethnographer Casper Miller (1997: 4) has succinctly put it, these practitioners, "no matter what their ethnic group, all have a basic unity of approach to the world, a world-view, which they share in common with their patients." The ethnographic data I collected working with practitioners from different ethnic groups and communities reveal a striking correspondence of beliefs and practices. There are also notable similarities in the costumes, the ritual paraphernalia, and techniques used by shamans throughout the country (see chapter 5). The emphasis on "shamanisms" overlooks this unity in belief and practice among Nepalese shamans.

Jhākris comprise one of several categories of ritual intercessors, such as for example the *dhāmi* (oracle), *jhārphuke* (nonecstatic healer who "blows" mantras and sweeps illnesses away), and *janne manche* (literally, "he who knows," healers who use mantras and dispense charms), among others (see chapter 2). Ethnographers and their consultants may, and sometimes have, conflated these categories (see Okada 1976; Stone 1976; Walter 2001), but this does not necessarily support the assertion that shamanism in Nepal is a mirage that turns out to be something else upon detailed scrutiny. As the materials presented in the following chapters demonstrate, shamanism is a unitary, pan-Nepalese phenomenon with striking similarities to the so-called classic shamanism thought by many shamanic studies scholars to be exclusively associated with pristine foraging cultures. Many insights regarding the subject matter may be gained by the examination of the Nepalese configuration, a task that I shall undertake in the following chapters.

The aims of this study are twofold: (1) to explore the relevance of the Nepalese ethnographic material to the wider discourse on shamanism; and (2) to explore the relevance of findings in the broader field of shamanic studies to the Nepalese context. In the process, I shall use Nepalese ethnographic materials to address some of the key assumptions about shamans and shamanism that underlie the conceptual quandaries in the field of shamanic studies.

2

Jhãkris and Other Intercessors: The Problems of Defining Shamanism

In an article originally published in 1962, Alexander Macdonald, one of the first anthropologists to discuss the topic systematically, referred to the *jhãkri* as "an interpreter of the world" (Macdonald 1976a, 1975). He offered this description in preference to designations with pejorative connotations of fraud or deception, such as "conjurer" or "wizard," provided in Turner's (1931) dictionary of the Nepāli language. Macdonald (1976a: 310) pointed out that these latter terms "are generally associated with irregular activities that either stray from the societal norms or . . . are blatantly anti-social. The *jhãkri*, however, is the very vehicle of a certain Nepali traditionalism." According to Macdonald (1976a: 310), the *jhãkri*:

> is a person who falls into a trance, during which time voices speak through his person, thereby enabling him to diagnose illnesses and sometimes cure them, give advice for the future and clarify present events in terms of their relationship to the past. He is therefore both a privileged intermediary between spirits (who cause and cure illness) and men; between the past, present and future; between life and death, and most importantly between the individual and a certain social mythology . . . he may belong to any *jāt* [caste, clan, tribe] and may take as a pupil from any other caste; a Lepcha may play the role of guru for a Nepali and vice versa.

Credit for providing a definitive and still unsurpassed description of the *jhãkri* must go to Macdonald. His account is completely consistent with the field data I collected while working with Chetri, Jirel, Sherpa, Rāi, Gurung, and Tamang shamans in the Dolakha District, in and around the Kathmandu Valley, and in Kabhre District between 1999 and 2006.

Spirit possession, as noted by Macdonald, is an important feature of *jhākri* beliefs and practices (on the appropriateness of using the term *spirit* over the jargon term *dividual*, see Morris 2006: 14–16). Gellner (1994: 29–30) is in error when he draws a distinction between *jhākris*, as practitioners who "go" to the gods (i.e., soul journey), which he associates with a "Himalayan and Central Asian shamanic tradition," and mediums, adepts who are possessed by gods, ancestors, and ghosts that "come" to them, which he links to a South Asian tradition. That spirits and gods come to the *jhākris* is evident from their recitations:

> Come my guru, come!
> Śrī Gorkhānath, teacher
> Gauri Pārbati, Lord Mahādev!
> Change into fire and flames
> Come
> Jhākri Spirit
> Come
> (Jhākri Shukra Bahādur Tamang)

What should be immediately evident is the discrepancy with Eliade's construal of soul flight or soul journey as constituting the universal and essential feature of genuine or "classic" shamanism, to the exclusion of the phenomenon of "spirit possession," that is, the practices of adepts who become voluntarily possessed by spirits and act as the mouthpieces of the possessing supernatural beings. As Eliade (1964: 506) put it:

> familiar relations with "Spirits" that result in their "embodiment" or in the shaman's being "possessed" by "spirits" are innovations, most of them recent, to be ascribed to the general change in the religious complex.

According to Eliade (1964: 505–506), this change happened when beliefs in lesser gods who come down to people displaced the idea of a celestial Supreme Being.

In this view, the *jhākri's* beliefs and practices are merely the lingering odds and ends of an ancient and authentic prototype transformed into something else, at best something shamanistic, but a mere echo of the genuine phenomenon. Not so, however, if we turn to the work of the British social anthropologist Ioan Lewis (1971: 55; 2003: 34), who considers the control practitioners exercise over the spirits incarnate in their bodies as the defining feature of shamanism, which he described as an "ecstatic religion." According to Lewis (1984: 9), "a shaman is an inspired prophet and healer, a charismatic religious figure, with the power to control the spirits, usually by incarnating them."

Why is there this discrepancy? Is this confirmation that shamanism is intractable as a subject matter? As noted previously, the lack of consensus on what the phenomenon in question "really is" continues to characterize the general literature on shamanism "writ large" (cf. Walter and Fridman 2004: xxii; Jones 2006). The shift in the direction of general ethnography in the United States from empirical field research toward increasingly particularistic narratives or story writing has not helped the situation. As a result, construals of shamanism have remained largely dependent upon the discretion or decisions of individual "authorities" in the field. Thus, as Hutton (2001: 126) has noted, "entire continents may appear in or be deleted from the ledger of admissible data" on shamanism. In Eliade's view, for example, shamanism is ubiquitous in Asia, Australia, and the Americas, but not in Africa. Hultkrantz (1989: 47) excludes Australia and Africa. Lewis (1971), who is familiar with the spirit possession cults in Africa, where he conducted field research, contests Eliade's conclusion and argues for a central place for spirit-possession and Africa in the discussion of shamanism. Anthropologist Piers Vitebsky (1995: 50–51) includes, in addition to Siberia, the Arctic region, the Americas, Europe, Asia, Africa, and New Guinea.

In my view, many of the ambiguities and inconsistencies in the general discourse on shamanism relate to the nature and quality of the original Siberian ethnographic data, the manner in which Eliade handled those materials, and his general inattentiveness to the complexities of ethnographic reality in relation to proposed models. He was no fieldworker and did not have firsthand experience with practitioners on the ground, as is the case with many today who write on the subject. For example, the ethnographic materials on Siberia clearly indicate the co-occurrence of "soul journey shamanism" and "possession shamanism" (Reinhard 1976: 15) amply documented by the eminent Russian ethnologist Waldemar Jochelson (1908: 49–52; 1926: 196–199). By dismissing this, Eliade (1964: 500) needlessly created a theoretical quandary easily avoidable had he bothered to reconcile his model with the ethnographic facts. This error of juxtaposing "true shamanism" against spirit possession has been perpetuated by others, including anthropologists interested in states of consciousness and healing (e.g., Gombrich 1988: 36–37;Hamayon 1990: 32; 1995: 450; Heinze 1991: 15; Heusch 1965; Le Quellec 2001: 148; Rouget 1985: 20; Winkelman 2000: 88; 2006: 143, 146).

Ethnologist and prehistorian Jean-Loïc Le Quellec (2001: 148), who treats spirit possession and true shamanism as binary opposites, maintains that "the shaman is not the instrument of the spirits, but their master . . . he is the taker and not the taken, tamer of spirits and not a mount of the gods." Le Quellec's characterization of the spirit possessed as "taken" and "tamed," as we shall see below, does not fit the ethnographic picture of the *jhākris*. Folklorist and shamanism expert Anna-Leena Siikala's (1992b: 21) position, which avoids such binarisms, is to treat soul journey and the embodiment of spirits as "alternatives describing the communication between the shaman and the other world." Lewis (1984: 9) also attempts to deal with this problem by suggesting that, "If spirits speak through [the shaman], he is also likely to have the capacity to engage in mystical flight and other 'out-of-body experiences.'" This, however, overlooks the phenomenological and experiential dimensions of the shaman's ASC, which does not easily fit either category, as I shall point out below.

The discrepancy between Eliade's construal of the shaman and the Nepalese *jhākri* is deceptive because spirit possession was an aspect of Siberian shamanism. Shirokogoroff (1923; 1924; 1935) emphasized spirit possession as the key attribute of Tungus shamanism. As he puts it, "the most important and characteristic condition which makes an ordinary man a shaman is that he is *a master of spirits*, at least of a group of spirits" (Shirokogoroff 1935: 71). He reiterates this point:

> In all Tungus languages the term [shaman] refers to *persons of both sexes who have mastered spirits, who at their will can introduce these spirits into themselves and use their power over the spirits in their own interests, particularly helping other people, who suffer from spirits.* (Shirokogoroff 1935: 269)

Eliade (1964: 500) dismissed Shirokogoroff's data as irrelevant to his soul-journey model by attributing the Tungus pattern to a later historical development, a degeneration of the pristine complex due to the impact of outside influences. This position has been take more recently by Gibson (1997: 40), who considers Shirokogoroff's definition as accurate only for "the Tunguzic people, and only for the modern period." This view is incorrect because Shirokogoroff's description fits the Nepalese context perfectly. Here is how one practitioner characterized the *jhākri*'s interaction with spirits:

> We purify ourselves and call the gods, ancestors, our spirit helpers (*guru-deutā*), and other supernatural beings. We convince them to enter our bodies. They cling to us and make us tremble (*kāmnu*). This is how we get power. The spirits are under our control. We ask them to come and go as we wish. We call the gods and spirits to protect us, give us strength, help us perform miracles, and to cure sick people. We sing particular songs for particular powers. When the spirits are with us we become fearless and can face and defeat witches, evil spirits, and ghosts (*boksī, picās, bāyu*) that cause people troubles and sickness. (Jhākri Rabindra Rāi)

At intervals throughout the course of a ritual performance, supernatural beings of sundry classes are beckoned, manifest themselves in various combinations, and enter the *jhākri's* body, causing it to tremble, which is a sign that the spirits and gods have come (*deutā aayo*). In some cases, this process is quite dramatic, with the *jhākri* bouncing several inches off the floor where he sits in a cross-legged position. The spirits are embodied, vigorously reined in and brought under control, and the trembling subsides. The *jhākri* is not "the instrument of the spirits" or a passive vessel compelled to "endure" the force of the possessing entities, but controls and puts them to use (cf. Höfer 1974a: 150). Control is mastery (for further discussion see chapters 4 and 6).

In terms of the Siberian material assembled by Jochelson and Shirokogoroff, there is some justification to refer to the *jhākris* of Nepal as shamans. This, however, would be at odds with the widely accepted assertion that genuine shamanism is restricted to hunting-gathering societies. As Winkelman (2000: 77) speculates, "Shamanistic traditions have arisen throughout the world because of the interaction of innate structures of the human brain-mind with the ecological and social conditions of hunter-gatherer societies." One must be cautious with such assertions because the "ecological and social conditions of hunter-gatherer societies" in prehistoric times were quite variable in comparison to contemporary or recently extant foraging societies. In the literature on shamanism, such

Figure 2.1   A *jhākri* embodying spirits
(Photo by H. Sidky)

statements regarding hunter-gatherers and shamanism abound and are often accepted as self-evident, without any evidence to support them.

To explain the presence of shamanism in other kinds of societies, Winkelman (2000: 88; 2006) proposes an evolutionary typology that distinguishes between shamans, shaman/healers, healers, and mediums in terms of variations in socioeconomic patterns and levels of sociopolitical integration (cf. Wallace 1966: 86–88). Following Eliade, who is still considered the foremost authority on the subject by many (e.g., Achterberg 2002: 12–13; Hayden 2003: 50, 84; Hultkrantz 1991: 9; Knecht 2003: 2; Siikala 1992b: 22–25), Winkelman (2000: 71–75; 2002: 1837; 2003: 387; Winzeler 2008: 208) maintains that while these other practitioners share "the core characteristics of shamanism"—"the use of ASC [altered states of consciousness] for their communities and interaction with spirits"— they do not share soul flight, death-rebirth, animal transformations, animal spirits, and hunting magic of genuine shamanism. In Winkelman's model, shamans proper exist exclusively in hunting-gathering societies, shaman/healers appear in agrarian societies, and healers and mediums are present in agrarian societies with political integration beyond the level of the local community.

This typology is highly problematic not only because it perpetuates Eliade's unwarranted binarism between "soul journey" and "spirit possession" shamanism, but also because in Nepal, which is a stratified agrarian state-level society, we find shamans, shaman/healers, mediums, oracles, and healers operating side by side. Moreover, as we shall see in subsequent chapters, the cosmos of the Nepalese shaman does not exclude the themes of spirit journey, ascension and descent, or death and rebirth (see Hitchcock 1976: 167; Holmberg 1989: 147; Jones 1976: 37; Maskarinec 1989: 205; Mastromattei 1989: 229–230; Oppitz 1981; Peters 1981: 81, 89; 1996: 208; Riboli 2000: 113–123). Nor does Nepalese shamanism exclude the concepts of animal transformations and animal spirits. At least two practitioners with whom I worked (Jhãkri Kami Singh Tamang and Jhãkri Nir Bahãdur Jirel) asserted their abilities to incarnate tiger spirits and to transform themselves into tigers. Among some groups, such as the Chepang, shamans can also turn themselves into birds and insects (Riboli 2000: 121). In addition, before the government of Nepal banned hunting, shamans served as intermediaries between humans and the god of hunting (Riboli 2000: 125).

Indeed, the *jhãkri* stands in a particular relationship to the wild animals and dangerous and hungry nature spirits, such as *ban-deutā* (gods of the forest and owners of the creatures dwelling therein) and *sikāri* (hunter spirits who take the form of wolves), who stand ready to strike those who defile their domain. "Evil and dangerous spirits of the wilderness that *jhãkri*s must fight and control," Jhãkri Dul Temba Sherpa once told me, "emanate from the jungle." There is also an important relationship between Nepalese shamans and *ban-jhākri*, a therianthropic forest god, master of animals, and primordial shaman, whom I will discuss in chapter 9. Finally, Lord Śiva, the archetypal figure in Nepalese shamanism, in his form as Paśupati, is the "Lord of the Beasts."

Using the characteristics Winkelman associates with core shamanism, that is, "the use of ASC for their communities and interaction with spirits," is problematic and results in the erroneous conflation of distinct spirit intercessors. Such a conception of shamanism led me in my earlier fieldwork erroneously to label ritual intercessors in the Karakoram Mountains and elsewhere in Central and South Asia as shamans (Sidky 1990; 1994; 2003b).

The construal of shamanism in Winkelman's terms is certainly problematic in the context of Nepalese ethnography. Anthropologist Gregory Maskarinec (1995: 97–113) raises this issue with respect to the *jhākris* and the *dhāmis*, or oracles in western Nepal (Gaborieau 1976: 225). Both *jhākri* and *dhāmi*, who are often male, employ ASC, become spirit possessed, and undertake soul journeys and thus fit the stated definition of a shaman (Maskarinec 1995: 98). Many Nepalese people are unclear about the differences between the two specialists and sometimes use the two terms interchangeably (Macdonald 1976b: 367, 382; see Okada 1976; Stone 1976; Walter 2001). However, these practitioners are distinct in many respects, such as the kinds of spirits with which they interact and the nature and consequences of that interaction. Examining the differences between these ritual intercessors is highly instructive in reference to suggestions that shamanism is an illusion that upon close scrutiny turns out to be something else, such as, "multiple specialists" or "multiple types of ritual practice," (Holmberg 1984: 697), or that it is impossible to provide "reliable criteria for diagnosing shamanism cross-culturally" (Klein et al. 2002; 2004; Klein et al. 2005).

As Reinhard (1976: 16) pointed out, the shaman is able to become spirit possessed at will, whereas the *dhāmi* is unable to exercise such control. A specific recognized tutelary god chooses and regularly possesses the *dhāmi*. Their possession events are spontaneous, that is, they are brought on by the god's will, take place at specific occasions according to the lunar calendar, and happen with or without the presence of worshippers (Gaborieau 1976: 225). The *dhāmi* is attached to a particular shrine or temple dedicated to the deity in question. He is thus linked to a hierarchical pantheon. The *dhāmi* does not have a specialized ritual costume and does not play a drum or dance. Members of a musician caste provide the drumming that induces the spirit possession event. Moreover, the *dhāmi*'s ceremonies are always the same, unlike the fluid and highly dynamic performances of the *jhākri*.

While possessed, the *dhāmi* sits on a throne and remains there as long as the god is present. Unlike the *jhākri*, the *dhāmi* does not undergo training or text memorization (Maskarinec 1995: 106). Occasionally, he may recite the possessing deity's personal history, using a known text that does not vary. His repertoire includes dispensing several grains of uncooked blessed rice (*achētā*) and placing a *ṭikā* or red spot on the foreheads of supplicants who come to worship the god and seek its advice. Worshippers consult the god on issues involving interpersonal disputes and injustice. Outside the context of the shrine these practitioners act as healers relying on "their aura of godhood" (Hitchcock 1976b: xxv), rather than utilizing ASC.

The *jhākri*, by contrast, to use Gilbert Rouget's (1985: 126) phrase in characterizing the shaman, is "the musicant of his own entry into trance." Moreover, the *jhākri* beckons spirits belonging to a variety of classes "to come and go" as he wishes (cf. Maskarinec 1995: 106). The entities with which the *jhākri* traffics and which he embodies include protective beings, tutelary spirits, gods, harmful beings, such as *bir*, *picās*, *pret* (see chapter 7), and numerous other nonspecific paranormal entities. The *jhākri* deliberately embodies these beings, controls them, and puts them to strategic use. South Asian specialist Frederick Smith (2006: 63), the author of a recent volume on spirit possession in South Asia, is incorrect when he states that shamans do not make a distinction between spirits and deities, according to which he erroneously defines South Asian shamans as "deity mediums."

The *jhākri*'s possession takes place at night on a date of his choosing, usually in the patient's house. He employs specialized paraphernalia, such as a ritual costume and a specific type of drum, which he plays during the course of the ceremony in order to beckon spirits and gods (see chapter 5). While in a state of possession, the *jhākri* will dance, jump, and act out dramatic movements, such as fighting with invisible beings (see chapter 10). Unlike the *dhāmi*, he undergoes years of apprenticeship to acquire specialist knowledge, which entails memorizing lengthy oral texts and mantras pertaining to specific topics and ritual activities, as well as learning drumming techniques and dance sequences (see chapter 4). The *jhākri* conducts a variety of dynamic and flexible ceremonies for which he possesses specific texts (Maskarinec 1995: 106) that are arranged in various combinations according to the occasion and around which he structures his performances (cf. Schmid 1967: 85). This body of information constitutes a form of private specialized knowledge that provides the theoretical underpinning of Nepalese shamanism (Maskarinec 1995: 111) and serves to validate the shaman's activities and social role. Thus, it is perfectly clear that the *jhākri* and the *dhāmi* are two very different types of magicoreligious practitioners.

Elsewhere in Nepal, such as for example in the Kathmandu, Nagarkot, and Panauti, Kavre, ordinary people use the term *dhāmi* somewhat imprecisely, often in the compound form of *dhāmi-jhākri*. However, the *dhāmis* themselves are emphatic that their profession is distinct from that of the *jhākris*. As Dhāmi Bal Bahādur Gurung insisted:

> yes, there is a certain overlap in our techniques, such as rice divination and the use of mantras, but we [*dhāmis*] do not memorize long songs, wear a special costume, or use the types of instruments *jhākris* have, such as the drum, *ghaṇṭa-mālā* [bandoliers with attached bells], and the *phurba* [ritual knife].

Dhāmis do not conduct dramatic public performances involving drumming, singing, dancing, and the manipulation of supernatural beings, which, in addition to a distinctive mode of interaction with paranormal beings (see chapter 6), are all central elements of the *jhākri's* repertoire. Only one *dhāmi* I met claimed that he embodies spirits and shivers mildly, alluding to altered states of consciousness, and that sometimes spirits attacking his patients will turn on him and enter his body. As Krishna Bahādur Humagain, a Chetri (Kshetri) *dhāmi* from Panauti, Kavre, said, *dhāmis* go about their business without being "mounted by gods" (i.e., entering into altered states of consciousness).

Furthermore, the *dhāmi* vocation is not precipitated by illness or some initiatory psychological crisis characteristic of the *jhākri's* calling (see chapters 4 and 9). Often taught by a single guru, in contrast to the *jhākri*, who may have multiple teachers, the *dhāmi's* healing techniques consist of blowing mantras and brushing (*jhārphuke garnu*), fumigating with incense (*dhūpanam*), and the occasional use of herbal remedies. The *dhāmi's* activities do not extend beyond the treatment of minor ailments in adults and diseases of children and domestic animals attributed to minor spirits. Finally, unlike the *jhākri*, the *dhāmi* does not deal with cases of witchcraft. Several *dhāmis* I

Figure 2.2.   A *dhāmi* healing a patient without entering into altered states of consciousness (Photo by H. Sidky)

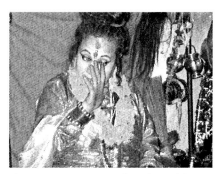

Figure 2.3.   A *mātā* undergoing spirit possession (Photo by H. Sidky)

interviewed adamantly refused to discuss the subject of witchcraft, stating merely that such circumstances were outside their area of expertise.

Winkelman's (2000: 71–72; 2006: 145–146) category of "shamanistic/ healer" seems to apply to mediums, or mother goddesses (*mātā* in Nepāli, *deo-mā* in Newari) in the Kathmandu Valley, but even here a number of problems arise with such usage. Mediums are primarily female. Like the *dhāmi* of western Nepal, they too are regularly possessed by an identified tutelary deity, the principal one being Hārītī, the protector of children (Dougherty 1986). A medium's career begins when a possessing deity chooses her. Mediums do not exercise mastery over the spirits they embody. Infrequently, other known divinities may briefly possess the medium as well. Gellner (1994: 32) mentions an instance he observed in which a medium was possessed successively by twenty-eight known deities, including Hārītī's eight children. Mediums are therefore connected to a hierarchical pantheon, as are the oracles in western Nepal.

The possessing *deutā* of one of the mediums whose healing sessions I attended in Kathmandu is Mahalakṣmī, the goddess of wealth and fortune. This medium's career began twelve years ago when she moved to her husband's house upon marriage. The goddess came to her while she was making offerings at a temple, whereby she acquired healing powers. She regularly worships and embodies Mahalakṣmī.

While the medium is possessed supplicants worship her as a goddess and cults may form around successful ones (Gellner 1994). The healing techniques of the mediums involve offering *ṭikā*, divination (*jokhānā hernu*) by examining the pattern of grains of rice (*achetā*) on a plate or on the palm of their hand, brushing (*jhārnu*) to remove evil influences, blowing (*phuknu*) mantras for protection, along with sermons on morality, making them, in Gellner's (1994: 39) words, "religious traditionalists." Using Lewis's categories of peripheral and central spirit possession, Gellner offers an interesting analysis of the mediums in Kathmandu, focusing upon

Figure 2.4. A *mātā* healing a patient by brushing (Photo by H. Sidky)

the function of spirit possession as a means for women to transcend the sociocultural constraints upon their gender. Applying the term "shamanistic/healer" to such practitioners is unnecessary and confusing because it implies that any individual who communicates with the spiritual world in an altered state of consciousness is somehow connected with shamanism.

Religious studies and Tibetan Buddhism specialist Geoffrey Samuel (1993: 8), whose view of shamanism is similar to Winkelman's characterization of the core features of shamanism—"the use of ASC for their communities and interaction with spirits"—not only considers the practices of Tibetan "spirit-mediums" as shamanic, but goes on to create an entire category he calls "shamanic Buddhism." Samuel (1993: 8) defines shamanic practices as:

> the regulation and transformation of human life and human society through the use (or purported use) of altered states of consciousness by means of which specialist practitioners are held to communicate with a mode of reality alternative to, and more fundamental than, the world of ordinary experience.

Such a broad designation neglects the shaman's concrete and distinctive ethnographic attributes. To reiterate, these include transformative initiatory crisis, dramatic public performances involving drumming, singing, and dancing in which he is the musicant, the ability to access ASC at will, a distinctive mode of interaction with paranormal beings of various classes, the mastery/manipulation of spirit helpers for the benefit of clients, distinctive specialized paraphernalia, and command of a body of specialized knowledge transmitted from teacher to pupil. One may raise the same objection regarding Gibson's (1997: 44) definition of the shaman:

> If a person is recognized by his own society as being in direct contact with the divine or extrahuman (however society defines it) by virtue of concrete demonstrations of unusual or unique capabilities, then he or she is a shaman.

Moreover, reliance on the criteria of recognition by members of the shaman's society, that is, the emic perspective, in defining who is or is not a shaman is problematic because members of society are often unclear about the various ritual intercessors, as in the case of the *dhāmi* and *jhākri* in Nepal.

Morris (2006: 19), following Lewis and Shirokogoroff, defines shamanism in terms of control over spirits:

> a shaman is a person who is able to control spirits. What is crucial is not the "ecstatic magical flight," as a visionary journey, but the ability to contact and possess spirits, so that a dialogue or relationship can be established between the spirit and the local community. He or she is therefore a specific kind of spirit-medium.

This designation is problematic because it also neglects the shaman's concrete and distinctive ethnographic attributes and leads to the needless conflation of different ritual intercessors, such as mediums, oracles, and shamans.

Based upon the material presented in this chapter, it should be evident that the *jhākri* belongs to a distinct category of magicoritual practitioner whose beliefs and practices are distinguishable according to concrete ethnographic criteria from those of various other Nepalese ritual intercessors, such as oracles and mediums. Smith's (2006: 64, 77, 143) categorization of *jhākri*s, whom he erroneously labels as "jhamkri" (the variant of *jhākri* is *jhankri*, not jhamkri!), as spirit or "deity mediums" and his treatment of the possession events associated with these practitioners as "oracular possession" is untenable and leads to the conflation of distinct ritual intercessors. Gibson (1997: 48) also conflates distinct practitioners when he talks about Tibetan *tertöns* ("treasure revealers"), *dpa'.bo/pawo* (mediums), and the Tibetan state oracle as different types of shamans. Also unwarranted is the facile acquiescence to the intractability of the definition problem and reliance on interchangeable usage of the terms medium, oracle, and shaman, as Srinivasa (1998: 178) has done in the context of her analysis of spirit possession among the Buddhists of Ladakh.

An incredibly confusing and misleading picture emerges if one fails to differentiate between distinct ritual practitioners, such as the *jhākri*, *dhāmi*, and *mātā*, among others. Conflating these specialists would result in the picture of a "shaman" that is possessed by either ancestral spirits, known deities, or neither. In some contexts, people will worship this shaman while he or she is incarnating gods and cults would form around successful ones. In some cases, the shaman would be associated with particular temples or shrines, while in other cases there may be no such association. This shaman would conduct healing rites with or without altered states, either in people's homes or at shrines, during specific dates, or at

Figure 2.5. A Tibetan medium in a state of deity possession. These ritual intercessors are erroneously viewed by some scholars as a type of shaman (Photo by H. Sidky)

any time during the day or night. The shaman's equipment may or may not include a drum and distinct ritual garb. Some of these shamans would undergo extensive training under several teachers and memorize extensive oral narratives, while others would operate solely through divine inspiration, and so on. Using the concept of "shamanisms" in place of "shamanism" as a unitary phenomenon, as some advocate (e.g., Holmberg 1984: 41; Thomas and Humphrey 1994), to accommodate variations adds to the difficulties because it perpetuates the conflation of distinct practitioners by subsuming all of them under the category of "shamanisms," that is, different kinds of shamans.

Making distinctions between magicoreligious practitioners is only possible if we pay particular attention to the ethnographic details when comparing categories within and between cultures. With respect to the Siberian ethnographic materials, this would have been extremely difficult given the uneven quality of the information and loss of context (cf. Diószegi 1960: 10; Siikala 1992b: 17). On the basis of this body of information, outside observers assumed that Siberian cultures possessed only one kind of ritual intercessor and that the varied indigenous names for magicoreligious practitioners recorded among different groups referred to the same thing (Siikala 1992a: 1). Humphrey and Onon (1996: 4, 46–47) have called attention to this issue in their critique of shamanistic studies. It is very possible that the sources were describing and treating as equivalents ritual intercessors as distinct as the *jhākri* and *dhāmi*. Compounding the problem was the vision of shaman presented by Eliade, a collage based on Siberian materials and evidence drawn from elsewhere, including related and unrelated features. The linkage with a hypothesized Paleolithic magicoreligious tradition simply added to the conceptual morass. Attempts to get around the confusing picture that developed by opting for the minimal definition of shamanism, that is, the use of ASC to contact the supernatural world for the benefit of communities (e.g., Pandian 1991: 94), has led to additional difficulties.

If these observations are correct, then we have a partial explanation for the seemingly insurmountable problem of defining shamanism with which scholars have been struggling for so long. Hamayon (2001: 3) has commented on the lack of agreement as to what shamanism is or is not: "This absence results from the very fact that 'shamanism' is a conceptual category abstracted from realities while it cannot be set apart as such in reality." Hamayon's observations do not necessarily mean that shamanism does not exist or it is an illusion that upon close scrutiny turns out to be something else, such as "multiple specialists" or "multiple types of ritual practice," as Holmberg (1984: 697) maintains. It means simply that the widely popularized construal of shamanism since Eliade involves the conflation of distinct ritual intercessors and an ethnographically and historically unrelated configuration of behaviors/beliefs. The Nepalese materials raise serious doubts regarding the appropriateness of classificatory and conceptual schemes based upon Eliade's suppositions about shamans and shamanism (e.g., Winkelman 2000: 71–72). Whether shamanism exists or not is an empirical question (although empirical knowledge and verification are becoming less of a concern to many writers these days, see Sidky 2003a; 2006) and one can indeed find an answer to this question in places like Nepal, where shamans are clearly and easily distinguishable from other practitioners in terms of their activities, sphere of operations, and rituals.

In the following chapters, I describe in detail various aspects of the *jhākri* beliefs and practices, pointing out the similarities and differences between Nepalese and Siberian shamanism. Where appropriate I juxtapose the Nepalese ethnographic material against the current understandings of shamans and shamanism. I shall also revisit the problem of definition, and related issues pertaining to geographical frame of reference, the antiquity of shamanism, the nature of the shaman's inner psychic states, and whether the term *shaman* should or should not be retained in its global coverage in light of the ethnographic evidence from Nepal.

3

Myths, Narratives, and Ethnography: Clues for the Origins of the *Jhãkri*

My research on the *jhãkri*s began in 1999 while I was conducting field-work in the Jiri Valley in the Dolakha District in eastern Nepal. Very early on, the inevitable and perhaps not unreasonable comparison with Asiatic shamanism arose in my mind. How did the *jhãkri* tradition develop? How old is it? Is it an extreme southerly example of a shamanistic tradition connected to "classic" Asiatic shamanism, as Hitchcock (1967: 158) suspects? Is it diffusion, migration, or an ancient "proto-tradition" predating the intrusion of Hinduism and Buddhism, as anthropologist David Watters (1975: 155) queries? If so, "at what point [had] Hinduism and Buddhism began to insinuate themselves into the existing shamanic system" as anthropologists Sara Shneiderman and Mark Turin (2005) have asked more recently in a discussion of the Thangmi (Thami) people in Dolakha and Sindhupalcok districts of eastern Nepal. Are we looking merely at an accidental pattern, "not a system of balance, nor a system of contradiction, nor a system of paradoxes—simply not a system," as Maskarinec (1995: 73) suggests? Are we looking at "an accretion of separable strands," as Nepalese religions are sometimes portrayed or, as Holmberg (1984: 698) asks, are the patterns observable today the outcome of centuries of "dynamic intercommunication among groups" in a process that has altered prior practices beyond recognition?

Some anthropologists are in agreement with Holmberg, affirming that the history of documented religious rituals makes it clear that "nowhere do these persist unchanged" (Kehoe 2000: 48). If this is the case, anthropologist Alice Kehoe (2000: 38, 48) asks, why should we expect the religions of indigenous people—"people of color," characterized as "people

without history, semi-naked people, people with long hair drumming"—
to persist unchanged? The problem of cultural origins and cultural reconstruction is therefore a daunting one, especially when working with oral
traditions, as in the case of Nepalese shamanism.

Nepalese shamanism, unlike Siberian practices recorded during the last
two centuries, is a thriving and dynamic tradition. One can find and consult its practitioners throughout the country. Are we in a better position to
ascertain the questions of origins in this context? What do the *jhākri* themselves have to say? *Jhākri* oral narratives detail the creation of the universe, the origins of men and beasts, the birth of culture, laws, and customs, the beginnings of agriculture, the development of metallurgy, and
the genesis of the supernatural beings who populate the space between
the celestial world of the gods and the watery netherworld inhabited by
snake spirits. These narratives also recount the genesis of demons and
witches, why evil intrudes upon humans, and the reasons for human suffering and death. These beliefs rightly constitute a shamanic cosmology
(see chapter 7). Among these narratives are also accounts of the first
jhākris, their struggle against the forces of evil, their journeys to the sky
and underworld, how they obtained their drums and ritual paraphernalia, the rationale for their rituals, and their relations to witches. These stories create for those versed in them a common vision of reality and, as
Maskarinec (1995: 75) has put it, a "common culture." Analysis of this material will not necessarily solve the question of the origins of Nepalese
shamanism as an historical event, but it does highlight the complex and
dynamic interrelationships of juxtaposed elements from several cultural
traditions. Therein, perhaps, one might glean some insights regarding the
sources of *jhākri* beliefs and practices.

A recurring figure in *jhākri* origin myths is Śiva, also known as
Mahāguru or Mahādev ("the Great God"), one of the major deities of Hinduism. Mahādev, the cosmic dancer, is at once a fearsome destroyer and a
symbol of regeneration, the guardian of souls and wrathful avenger, a
dreadful god who joyfully dances in the cemeteries and cremation
grounds (*masān-ghāṭ*) and supreme healer (god of medicine), lord of the
beasts and protector of humans. Mahādev is also the great master of yoga
and tantra, a symbol of sensuality and embodiment of asceticism. As
ethnographer Martino Nicoletti (2004: 26–28) has pointed out, Mahādev's
ambivalent attributes and his numerous deeds as the destroyer of demons
lend themselves to shamanistic interpretation. Śiva as master of cemeteries and cremation grounds from whence emanate many of the particularly
dangerous spirits with which *jhākris* must contend is especially significant
in Nepalese shamanistic practices. As ethnographer Diana Riboli (2000:
134–135) has observed:

Figure 3.1. Lord Śiva, also known as Mahāguru or Mahādev ("the Great God"), a recurring figure in jhākri origin myths (Chamundi Temple, Himachel Pradesh, photo by H. Sidky)

Shiva is certainly an ancient divinity who precedes the Hindu religion itself and has many characteristics that could fit a proto-shamanic figure and for this reason he is respected by all the *jhākri* in Nepal and known by the name Mahādev or great god.

The following account, presented in a preliminary form earlier (Sidky et al. 2002), was provided by a Jirel shaman (called *phombo* in the Jirel language) in the Jiri-Shikri Valley in eastern Nepal. It is similar to the narratives collected from Nepalese *jhākri*s by Macdonald (1976a: 319–22, 336–338) in Kalimpong, in West Bengal, and by Nicoletti (2004: 26–28) from Kulunge Rāi shamans in eastern Nepal.

> Mahādeu was the first *jhākri*, the original one, who performed all the services we perform today. It was he who created the *ri-phombo* (*ban-jhākri*), who lives in the forest, to be his first disciple. He then created other *jhākris* and taught them tantra-mantra [spells] and magical skills to heal people when demons and witches strike. He sent them to the four corners of the world. What Mahādeu the healer did is now the task of the human *jhākris*, whose body becomes the vessel for the gods and spirits. This is why *jhākris* worship (*pujā garnu*) Lord Śiva, wear his *rudrācche mālā* (string of *rudrācche* beads) when they perform, and paint his trident (*triśūl*) on their drums (*dhyāgro*). (Jhākri Nir Bahādur Jirel)

In Macdonald's account, Mahādev, the first *jhākri*, encounters a Tibetan *lāmā* on Mt. Kailas (Tisé) in Tibet, which is the abode of Śiva and a place of great religious significance to Hindus, Buddhists, and followers of the Bön religion. A fierce contest of magical prowess ensues in which the shaman, represented by the Hindu god, is set in opposition to a Tibetan monk, represented by a *lāmā*. Macdonald's text is highly interesting because it reflects certain elements of the cosmology that underlies Nepalese shamanism, which developed in the context of centuries of historic interaction, encapsulation, and mutual accommodation between aspects of Hindu, Buddhist, and indigenous beliefs and practices.

With mantras alone, the contestants bring from the jungle various items (Macdonald 1976a: 319). Mahādev brings forth *rudrācche mālā* (beads worn by shamans); the *lāmā* produces prayer beads. Mahādev draws out porcupine quills (*dumsi ko kāro/ kānda*, a shamanic ritual item), and the *lāmā* produces a Tibetan prayer wheel. Mahādev fills a copper pot with water and the *lāmā* brings out a book of mantras and sacrificial rice dough images (*torma*). It is important to note, that Mahādev produces articles connected to the shaman's practice, while the *lāmā*'s objects pertain to Buddhist practice. The book of mantras, which signifies the *lāmā*'s textual authority, and the *torma*, his rejection of blood sacrifice, are central elements of the Buddhist discourse of opposition regarding shamanism (Ortner 1995: 357). The story continues with the protagonists engaged in a race to the sun:

Mahādeu arrived halfway to the sun, but everything became dark and he could no longer follow the path; the lama arrived at the sun. Since the lama had caused additional objects and a greater number of objects to come forth from the jungle, and since Mahādeu had not succeeded in reaching the sun, the latter became angry and constructed a drum [the *jhākri*'s instrument of power]. With this drum he would be able to reach the sun. It was agreed that henceforth the lama would perform their *pujā* during the day, whereas Mahādeu would perform his at night. Mahādeu and the lama separated and each settled down in different parts of Mount Kailas. (Macdonald 1976a: 319)

The contest thus ends with a division of labor between the shaman, who performs at night, and the *lāmā*, who performs in the day. Although the *lāmā* seems to triumph, Mahādev fashions the magical drum, the shaman's principal ritual implement on which he flies to the sun, thereby replicating his adversary's feat. Mahādev goes on to create, in addition to the *ban-jhākri*, and six other *jhākris*, who represent the mythical prototypes of present-day practitioners (see chapter 9). The god then scattered these *jhākris* across the land, East, West, South, and North, with the mandate to heal the sick and to recruit worthy candidates and train them as *jhākris* (Macdonald 1976a: 337–338). Shamanism is thus established on earth.

Macdonald (1976a: 355) notes that this narrative is not a result of direct Tibetan influence, but rather indicates a "desire to copy" Tibetan tradition. However, it is far more than that. Texts such as this have been produced through a process of free and unmitigated borrowing, sharing, synthesis, and incorporation of material among *jhākris* belonging to different ethnic groups. This process has led to the development of a collective tradition or corpus of esoteric knowledge in the form of oral narratives that is the basis of a common vision of reality among Nepalese shamans (see chapter 4). The shamanic tradition is transmitted from generation to generation through these oral texts.

Similar stories in the form of *lāmā*-shaman contests exist among many Tibeto-Burmese and Tibetan groups in the hills of Nepal, such as the Gurung (Mumford 1989: 51–43; Pignède 1966: 387–388), Tamang (Höfer 1981, 1985, 1994; Holmberg 1989: 218–220; 1984; Peters 1981: 57), Sherpa (Oppitz 1968; Ortner 1995: 357; Paul 1976: 148), Chepang (Riboli 2000: 105), and Thakali (Vinding and Gauchan 1977). These stories draw on an old and well-known legend in Tibetan Buddhism about the inferiority of shamanism (Ortner 1995: 357). If the thesis that the essential features of shamanism derived from Buddhism is correct, then that influence must have been from an earlier esoteric nonscriptural Buddhism and the opposition between shamanism and Buddhism depicted in the legends under discussion represents a later historical development.

The Tibetan version of these legends is the dramatic confrontation between Milarepa, the eleventh-century Tibetan *lāmā* and saint, and Naro Bön-Chung, a Bönpo magician, whose practices, some say, represent pre-Buddhist Tibetan shamanism similar to that in north and central Asia (cf. Chang 1977: 220–221; Hoffmann 1979: 25; but see Samuel 1993: 10–13). Again, the location of the encounter is Mount Tisé (Kailas) where Milarepa has gone to meditate. He encounters a Bönpo, who claims that the mountain is the property of the Bönpos (Stein 1972: 240). They begin a contest that includes magic, ingenuity, and a race, not to the sun, but to the mountain's summit, with the prize being ownership of the sacred mountain itself (Hoffmann 1979: 25).

> Early in the morning, Naro Bon-Chung wearing a blue fur cloak, ringing [a bell], mounted his drum and went flying into the sky. . . . Then, as the sun was rising, Milarepa snapped his fingers once; and flying by spreading his robes like wings, he instantly arrived at Ti-se's peak just as the sun arose. Then, when Naro Bon-Chung arrived . . . he was unable to stand the sight; he fell out of the sky, and his drum went rolling down the south slope of Ti-se. His pride and arrogance subdued, he begged permission to stay at the foot of Ti-se and practice his rites, which Milarepa let him do. (in Ellingson-Waugh 1974)

In some versions of the legend, Naro Bön-Chung's drum, the symbol of shamanic power, breaks into pieces, and in some, the *lāmā* flies on a ray of sunlight to reach the summit ahead of his rival (Dás 1881: 210–211; Mumford 1989: 52; Ortner 1995: 357). In other versions, the Bönpo's double-sided drum splits down the middle into two pieces (cf. Mumford 1989: 52; Riboli 2000: 105), which is why the shaman's drum is one-sided (as is the case in central and western Nepal). The ethnologist and Tibetan specialist René de Nebesky-Wojkowitz (1956: 423) noted the resemblance between the story of Naro Bön-Chung's drum and a Buryat legend, which relates that originally the shaman's drum was double-sided, until a shaman foolishly snatched a soul taken by the heavenly Tengri (Sky-Father/Sky-God), and the enraged deity diminished the power of shamans by cleaving their drums in half (see also Lot-Falck 1961: 26). In another legend, it is the Dalai Lama rather than Tengri who reduced the power of the shamans by dividing their drums (Riboli 2000: 106).

In a Tamang rendering of this story recorded by anthropologist Larry Peters (1981), the shaman's opponent is not Milarepa, but the legendary Padmasambhava, also known as Guru Rinpoche, the eighth-century founder of the Tantric school of Buddhism in Tibet. Padmasambhava is known as the "second Buddha," who defeated shamanism, vanquished the local gods of Tibet, and made them protectors of Buddhism. This narrative again encapsulates the tensions between the *lāmā* and shaman (*bǫmbo* in the Tamang language) and relates the basis for the present-day division of ritual tasks between them.

At one time, the *bombo* had all the religious responsibilities. They cured the sick and conducted souls to heaven during the funeral ceremony. However, the souls of the deceased were not reaching heaven so Guru Rinpoche . . . decided to investigate. He went to the village where Nara Bon Chen (the first human shaman) was conducting a funeral service. Nara played the drum and called the deceased's spirit to enter a wooden effigy dressed in the dead man's clothes. The effigy began to shake (indicating that the soul had entered it) and Nara questioned it about the causes of death, afterworld existence, etc. The effigy responded by nodding yes or no. Disguised as a beggar, Guru Rinpoche watched the proceedings and then flashed his *dorje* [the ritual object, "thunderbolt of enlightenment," used by lamas while conducting religious ceremonies] at the effigy causing it to fall to the ground. Nara tried in vain to animate the effigy but the ceremony ended. (Peters 1981: 57)

In the biography of Milarepa, on which this story is based (Chang 1977: 220–221; Stein 1972: 239–240), the saint demonstrates that the spirit raised is actually a demon that the Bönpos are nefariously using to steal human souls. He chases the demon out of the village and it finally reveals its true form, a creature resembling a wolf. Milarepa says to the Bönpos, "You people, you show the road to the . . . demons that carry off souls, but me, I show the [actual] road to the dead" (Stein 1972: 239–240). In the Tamang version, Guru Rinpoche declares to the villagers, "Your souls are not reaching heaven because Nara [makes blood sacrifices]" (Peters 1981: 57). The shaman's dubious nature and his deception are exposed and the *lāmās* appropriate funerary rites among Buddhists in Nepal. The one exception is the funeral rites of shamans, which are officiated over by other shamans.

Aside from depicting a clash between the divergent ritual practices of *lāmās* and shamans, this narrative highlights the tension between shamanistic sacrificial rites and the Buddhist rejection of blood sacrifice. It is for this reason that Tamang shamans are not supposed to kill animals during their rituals (Höfer 1994: 19; Holmberg 1989: 120). In actual practice, however, this tension regarding blood sacrifice is more apparent than real. The Tamang *bǫmbo*s with whom I work frequently slaughter sacrificial animals during their performances. They do this by slitting the animal's throat in order to collect the blood for offerings, rather than the customary Nepalese method of decapitation with a swift blow to the back of the neck with a large *khukurī* knife. Nor does the interchange between *lāmās* and shamans result in paradoxical situations everywhere in Nepal. It is not unheard of for the same person to officiate as shaman and *lāmā* in different contexts, without philosophical dilemmas. Among the Jirels, for example, a noted shaman underwent training and assumed the role of *lāmā*, but continued to train new shamans and conduct shamanistic healing rituals (Sidky et al. 2002: 143).

Returning to the story of the contest, we find the humiliated Naro Bön-Chung challenging Guru Rinpoche to a race to the top of the mountain, declaring that whoever wins will assume all religious duties. Naro Bön-Chung flies on his drum toward the summit, but Guru Rinpoche transforms himself into a vulture, overtakes, and trips him. The angry Naro Bön-Chung utters a mantra creating a swarm of bees that sting Guru Rinpoche in the face and neck (Peters 1981: 57). The Bönpo's magical attack that threatens his rival's eyes and hence his ability to see and read may be an indirect allusion to the opposition between the *lāmā*'s authority, which is based on reading books, and the shaman's authority, which derives from an oral tradition (cf. Höfer 1994: 335). In a story of a battle between a powerful *lāmā* and the *dhāmic* spirit Mahākāl, referred to by Maskarinec (1995: 92), the *lāmā* is blinded by stings to the eyes by Mahākāl in the form of a wasp and is rendered powerless because he is no longer able to read his books. Guru Rinpoche is therefore in danger of losing his powers if blinded. However, he is unable to harm the bees because of his Buddhist vows not to take life. He therefore offers the following compromise:

> "Send away the bees and retain some of your powers." So Nara dispatched the bees and healed Guru Rinpoche's wounds, whereupon it was decided that Nara would retain his healing abilities. Thus, among the Tamang, the *bombo* still cures the sick. (Peters 1981: 57)

In Holmberg's (1989: 219) version, the division of labor amounts to the *lāmā* taking care of the dead and the shaman attending to the needs of the living. In Höfer's version, the primordial shaman is Dunsur Bön (Tusur Bön), who is defeated and killed. It is the four sons or students of the defeated Dunsur Bön whom, according to Höfer (1974b: 173; 1981: 34), present-day *bombo*s revere as their spiritual ancestor.

Here again, in actual practice matters are not as clear-cut. For example, Jhākri Bir Bahādur Tamang and his associates mentioned Guru Rinpoche, who defeated the false shamans, as the original *jhākri* and spiritual ancestor of all present-day practitioners. This association linking shamanism and the founder of Tibetan Buddhism somewhat obscures the *lāmā-bombo* division of labor. The tensions or paradoxes arising from the juxtaposition of contrary orders involving *lāmā*s, *lámbu*s, and *bombo*s in the Tamang ritual field that are central to Holmberg's (1989: 222) study are thereby defused in practice in some contexts.

Höfer (1994: 2) suggests that the term *bombo* was imposed on Tamang shamans by *lāmā*s in order to associate their practices with heresy. However, given the de facto situation, Höfer (1994: 18) adds, this represents an "accommodated" rather than stigmatized heresy justified in terms of the resolution of the contest with a division of labor between the *lāmā* and shaman. Not all variants of the story support the inferiority of shamanism in relation to Buddhist practice. In an account I collected in Jiri, not only are the two protagonists evenly matched, but the *lāmā* is bested and has to resort to deception. Also addressed in this account is the *lāmā's* claim to superiority because of textual authority over the shaman who has no books.

> The *jhākri* and *lāmā* competed for a long time. But the *jhākri's* powers were greater. So the *lāmā* decided to cheat (*chalnu*). He pretended to throw his book of mantras into a fire, declaring that his powers are so great that books were unnecessary. Goaded in this way by the *lāmā*, the *jhākri* (whose knowledge was at that time was also based on books) threw his book in the fire. The *lāmā* then revealed his book to prove that he had fooled his opponent. But the *jhākri* snatched the ashes from the fire and ate them, saying, "My powers are greater because everything [ritual knowledge] is now inside me and books are useless." This is why *jhākris* sing their songs and utter their mantras from memory and can operate at night when evil spirits are all around, but the *lāmās* have to read books, without which they are powerless and can only operate during the daytime. (Jhākri Narsing Jirel)

The *lāmā* who resorts to trickery is depicted here as the charlatan, while the view that "doing it by the book" is less likely to lead to deception is the general impression in everyday life (Ortner 1995: 361; Paul 1976: 147; Peters 1981: 60–61).

Holmberg (1984, 1989) has analyzed the *lāmā*-shaman contest in terms of "ritual paradoxes" created by the coexistence of multiple ritual specialists and forms of practice. Mumford (1989) looks at it in the context of the interchange between Gurung shamans and Tibetan *lāmās* in terms of "opposed narrative memories." Höfer views these narratives as the basis for a de facto acceptance of shamanism as an "accommodated heresy." My concerns focus around methodological questions. Can the origins or antiquity of shamanism in Nepal be determined using the type of ethnographic material discussed in this chapter? Can ethnographic research in general answer this question? Is it possible to clear away layers of beliefs and practices in a kind of semantic archaeological exercises to uncover what lies beneath the Hindu or Buddhist elements?

There is a remarkable heterodoxy in the Nepalese shamanic cosmology reflecting the influence of diverse religious beliefs and practices over centuries, a process that occurred under Hindu religious and cultural hegemony (Sidky et al. 2002: 75). Practitioners in some communities do not have narratives concerning an archetypal shaman (Allen 1976a: 128).

Some mention human ancestors (Fournier 1976: 103), others have stories that suggest that the first shamans descended from the sky on a mission from a deity not identified as Hindu or Buddhist (Jones 1976: 32), while still others identify the original *jhākri* with Mahādev or Guru Rinpoche. The heterodoxy in Nepalese shamanism is well illustrated by the *jhākri* pilgrimages of power to holy sites and the range of deities, Hindu, Buddhist, and of local origins, associated with them in the Dolakha district, as described by Miller (1997). The *jhākri*'s ritual objects (see chapter 5), which derive from both Hinduism and Tibetan Buddhism, also attest to this heterodoxy. The *jhākri*'s double-sided drum (*ḍhyāgro*) with the exterior wooden handle is identical to the one used by Tibetan *lāmās*. Shirokogoroff (1935: 299) and several other scholars (see Eliade 1964: 502) believed that the Tibetan double-sided drum mentioned here was in fact the prototype of the shamanic drum used by groups in Central and North Asia, including the Chukchi and Eskimo. This southerly influence may be the basis of the Buryat legend regarding the shaman's original double-sided drum discussed by Nebesky-Wojkowitz (1956: 423). The *jhākri*'s ritual dagger, or *phurba*, and human thighbone trumpet are implements used by *lāmās* (Höfer 1981: 32). Finally, the trident and *rudrācche mālā* and the snake vertebrae necklace (*nāg mālā*) used by *jhākris*, which are highly reminiscent of Śiva's ritual paraphernalia, are of Hindu derivation (see chapter 5).

The identification of Mahādev as the primordial shaman in *jhākri* narratives may represent nothing more than the appropriation of a deity from a "high-religion" who possesses attributes that lend themselves to interpretation as shamanistic, a reflection of the influence of Hinduism on Nepalese society as a whole. These narratives validate the *jhākri*'s practices and beliefs by associating them with major deities and a mythic past, a Golden Age of long ago, when the universe was new and when deities such as Mahādev were accessible and responsive to intercession (cf. Maskarinec 1995: 120). As one *jhākri* explained:

> In the past, the gods came down in person. Mahādeu used to cure the sick himself. But now, in this present age of disorder, the gods have turned to stone statues and so their spirits must now enter the bodies of human beings. What Mahādeu used to do, is now done by humans, whose bodies become the receptacles of the gods (in Sidky et al. 2002: 146).

In connection with Hinduism, Höfer (1994: 19) raises the possibility of influence from Śaivite asceticism on Nepalese shamanism:

> With a certain degree of variation, the *jhākri* shares his "ornaments of the gods" with a number of other specialists who are in a sense marginal: ascetics, exorcists and artists, the latter often of low-caste affiliation. Thus, the long hairlock and the rosary of *rudrācche* beads, both common to *jhākris* in

Nepal, might have derived, ultimately and indirectly, from Shaiva asceticism. Suffice it here to refer to the "topknot" of Śiva in his representation as an ascetic, or the *rudrākṣa* rosaries worn by Śiva himself and Shaiva ascetics. Again, the long white robe as a ceremonial dress, small bells attached to the strap of their drum among the bards of Kumaon and Far Western Nepal—whose tradition and practices are firmly rooted in Shaiva asceticism, and some of whom also act as exorcists inducing possession in secondary mediums—are reminiscent of the *jhākri's* robe and bell-strings respectively (Höfer 1994: 70).

Höfer (1994: 19) adds, however, that elements of Nepalese shamanism have apparently evolved from ancient "tribal" and "regional" traditions. He does not specify what these older traditions are. As anthropologist Romano Mastromattei (1989: 228–228) has commented in this connection:

> The cases observed . . . indicate strong Sivaite elements. . . . Such elements, however, raise a problem that is not at all easy to solve: whether it is a question of authentic "protosivaismo" with intense shamanistic traits or of Sivaite myths and cult aspects as an expression of the dominant culture, adopted as an ideological ritual corset for ancient autochthonous and purely shamanistic practices and beliefs. One thing is certain, however, the *jhākri*, like the shamans of the north, move the pieces of their magic chess-board, selecting them with the greatest freedom and nonchalance.

The identification of the archetypal shaman with a Tibetan Bönpo magician, whether Naro Bön-Chung, Dunsur Bön, or someone else, may be the handiwork of the *lāmās* in Nepal in recent times, as noted above, rather than evidence of a direct historical connections with the pre-Buddhist folk religion of Tibet. Lay communities and shamans themselves (cf. Höfer 1973: 173; 1981: 34; Mumford 1989: 6, 30–31; Paul 1976: 144) nevertheless accept the association.

One must also consider the noteworthy similarities between the pantheon of Nepalese shamans and the cult of local gods associated with the pre-Buddhist religion of Tibet, which included earth deities, gods of the soil, spirits of cliffs, caves, groves, serpent spirits of the water, mountain gods, hearth gods, personal tutelary gods, and clan gods and goddesses (Ekvall 1964: 25). Although referred to as Bön, the system to which these beliefs belong has nothing to do with the contemporary religious order of Bön, which replicates the religious orders of orthodox Tibetan Buddhism (Samuel 1993: 12; Stein 1972: 19; on the various usage of the term Bön see Kværne 2001: 9–10).

Central to the Old Bön worldview was the attribution of sickness and suffering to the malice of local gods, demons, and various spirits. These beings therefore had to be worshiped and propitiated in order to avert misfortunes and cure illnesses. Prognosticating the identity of the gods, spirits, or demons causing the problems and "ransom-offerings" characterized human relations with the supernatural world (Snellgrove and Richardson 1968: 55). One could describe Nepalese shamanism in these very terms. Luring the spirits and capturing them in ritual devices, structures, or objects was one method used by Bön magicians to address the problem (Snellgrove and Richardson 1968: 55). Once the spirit was caught in the device, ransom was offered, and the device was deposited elsewhere or destroyed. The underlying beliefs as well as the techniques themselves are similar to those of Nepalese shamanism (see Allen 1976a: 135–135; Hitchcock 1976: 191; Nicoletti 2004: 57).

The two traditions also share similar views of the universe as constituting several levels corresponding to an upper world, the world of people, and an underworld, although the notion of a tiered cosmos is not exclusively shamanistic (Kehoe 2000: 73). There is also a similarity in orientation. Like Bön, Nepalese shamanism is concerned almost exclusively with well-being, success, and protection in this life, rather than with the affairs of an afterlife, or salvation (cf. Ekvall 1964: 30).

There are other parallels. Nebesky-Wojkowitz (1956: 425) describes a particular category of Tibetan ritual specialists, called *dpa'bo* and *bsnyen jo mo* in the Chumbi Valley, at the intersection of Sikkim, Bhutan, and Tibet, who are alleged to be representative of the Old Bön. Gibson (1997: 49–50), however, links the *dpa'bo* (also known as *pawo*) to esoteric nonscriptural Buddhism. These practitioners, who wear the five-paneled *rigs lnga* crown as part of their ritual apparel (Gibson 1997: 50), are remarkably similar to some Nepalese shamans. According to Nebesky-Wojkowitz (1956: 425):

> The *dpa'bo* and *bsnyen jo mo* are believed to be sorcerers and sorceresses who become possessed by the spirits of the dead, and who are able to communicate, while in the trances, with their protective deities. Their main task is to perform divinations and to cure illnesses. Just like other Tibetan mediums also the *dpa'bo* and *bsnyen jo mo* are supposed to have been forced by one or the other supernatural beings to assume this position. In most cases only people who belong to families in which some members had already exercised such functions become possessed by the spirits visiting these two particular groups of mediums. It is customary to call then an experienced *dpa'bo* or *bsnyen jo mo*, who will first propitiate the spirit and establish his identity; the same person also usually takes over the initiation of the novice.

Nebesky-Wojkowitz (1956: 425–426) adds:

> After the period of instruction have been successfully completed, the new *dpa'bo* or *bsnyen jo mo* will have to perform a so-called *Bon Khrus gsol* [Bön pu-

rification rite using water], which is carried out in the following way: a few flowers and official herbs are laid in a small bumpa [*bumba*, a brass ritual vase] which is then filled with ordinary water. The bumpa is wrapped in a white ceremonial scarf, and strings of white wool are tied around its mouth. The novice has to place this vessel on the left hand, and while whirling a small sand-glass shaped drum with his right hand he invokes all the *bon skyong* [Bön deities] requesting them to descend upon the bumpa. After a while the vessel is supposed to start shaking, the indication that the multitude of the *bon skyong* has arrived. The ceremony ends by pouring some of the water contained in the bumpa on the head of the newly initiated, and subsequently also on the heads of all those present. Some people drink this water, or they wash their eyes with it, since it is supposed to have turned in the course of the ceremony into an efficacious medication.

This account is very similar to the initiation of the Jirel shamans (see chapter 4). The latter also wear the five-paneled *rigs lnga* crown as part of their ritual outfit and beckon gods and spirits to manifest themselves in the *bumba*, which shakes when the deities arrive. These practitioners dance holding the *bumba*, balance it on their heads, and use the sanctified water inside the container in their healing rituals, pouring it on their patients' heads and asking them to drink it as a form of medicine.

Nebesky-Wojkowitz's (1956: 538–553) discussion of shamanistic elements of Bön in relation to the Asiatic variety suggests additional similarities with Nepalese practice. These include: the association of the shaman's calling with involuntary selection by spirits, initiation involving illness, death and rebirth, abduction and initiation of potential candidates as children by spirits, the belief that the spirits of suicides and murder and accident victims return to harm the living, and the idea that mentioning the name of a spirit evokes its immediate presence. Other similarities include the shaman holding his drum close to the face with drumsticks oriented upward when chanting and evoking spirits, feather headdresses, and the attribution of magical powers to the shaman's ritual outfit.

An important and rather striking likeness between Bön and Nepalese shamanism, both of which are wholly oral traditions, is the central place of memorized texts recited to elicit desired outcomes. As Tibetan specialists David Snellgrove and Hugh Richardson (1968: 55) observe:

An essential part of theses rites was the "exposition" of a sacred archetype in the form of myth. These "expositions" consisted in the recitation by the invoking priest (Bon) of ancient myths recounting the origins of existence, of gods, demons, genies and the rest. The exposition "intoned with ululation" served to invoke the powerful beings whose nature and functions might be described.

Recitation of oral texts and evocation of "sacred archetypes" to invoke paranormal powers whose nature and functions are depicted in the texts is one of the defining characteristics of Nepalese shamanism (see Maskarinec 1998; 1995).

There are also similarities in some of the texts recited. For example, the Nepalese "Song of the Nine Witches" (see chapter 8), parallels the story of Dongba Shilo, the ancestral shaman of the Nakhi. An indigenous people of Tibetan origin, the Nakhi live in the foothills of the Himalayas, in the northwestern part of Yunnan Province and southwestern part of Sichuan Province in China. Their religion has supposedly preserved many elements of the pre-Buddhist Tibetan Bön (Greve 1989: 220; Meredith 1967: 240; Rock et al. 1963). Ethnologist Reinhard Greve (1989: 220) identifies Dongba Shilo as Shenrab Mibo (gShen-rab Mi-bo) the founder of the Bön religion. Like the Nepalese "Song of the Nine Witches," the story of Dongba Shilo describes the encounter between the primordial witch and the original shaman and figures prominently in shamanic healing rituals (Greve 1989: 221).

These similarities are intriguing and raise the following question: Is it possible that a pre-Buddhist shamanistic tradition once found in Tibet could have persisted in a recognizable form in Nepal? Snellgrove and Richardson (1968: 55) forward just such a view:

> Similar rituals with exactly similar recitations of ancient myths survive to this day among peoples of old Tibetan stock who penetrated the Himalayas in pre-Buddhist times and have since escaped the full impact of the later Tibetan Buddhist culture. Thus, from a Nepalese people like the Gurung we can probably even nowadays gain some impression of the workings of such rituals in early Tibet.

However, shamanistic beliefs and practices were also part of the folk beliefs of many other Tibeto-Burmese speaking peoples, such as the Limbu, Rāi, Jirel, Sunwar, Tamang, Thakali, Chantel, and Magar who settled in Nepal as part of a broad demographic shift spanning several centuries.

The point raised by Mastromattei (1989: 228–228) concerning Sivaite elements as the source of Nepalese shamanism may be raised with respect to a pre-Buddhist Tibetan influence as well. That is, are we looking at a source, or merely an ideological veneer for an ancient autochthonous shamanistic configuration? The possibility that I would like to highlight is the presence of an indigenous shamanistic tradition specific to the area that is now Nepal. This tradition, centered on the figure of *ban-jhākri*, an autochthonous forest deity, may have been the more direct basis of Nepalese shamanism (see chapter 9). Certainly, for some groups in Nepal, such as the Shorung Sherpa, this tradition has been the more perceptible model of shamanism than their own distant Tibetan tradition (Paul 1976: 145). *Ban-jhākri* tradition plays a similar role for Chetri villagers in Solu Khumbu, the Jirels and Kulunge Rāi in eastern Nepal, and the Chepang in southern and central Nepal (Nicoletti 2004; Riboli 2000: 84; Sidky et al. 2002; Walter 2001).

This is about all that one can reasonably say about the origins of Nepalese shamanism. As indicated at the start of this chapter, oral narratives of the type analyzed are not suitable for resolving the question of origins as an historical event, but they do underscore the complex historic interrelationships of juxtaposed elements from several cultural sources. The shamanistic configuration in Nepal is clearly a dynamic and evolving tradition rather than an ossified relic from the Stone Age. Based upon the discussion above, it is clear that one must exercise extreme caution when attempting to reconstruct chronologies or address questions of historical origins, as Eliade and others have attempted to do working with far more fragmentary evidence from Siberia. Indeed, the Nepalese materials raise serious doubts regarding any conclusive determinations based upon such efforts. The antiquity of shamanism in Nepal, as of shamanism in Siberia and elsewhere, is unknown.

4

✣

Seized by Spirits: The *Jhãkri*'s Calling, Initiation, and Training

ot anyone can become a *jhãkri*," Jhãkri Dul Temba Sherpa said, "it is only possible if you are seized by a god or goddess or ancestor spirit and shaken. The gods and spirits choose candidates. Then you have to find a teacher and train for a long time before you can practice." This is the common pattern of the shamanic call among many ethnic groups in Nepal (Allen 1976a; de Sales 1991; Hitchcock 1976a; Höfer 1994; Holmberg 1989; Nicoletti 2004; Oppitz 1981; Riboli 2000; Sagant 1976; Steinmann 1987; Watters 1975). The process through which an ordinary individual is transformed into a *jhãkri* generally takes place in three stages, as it did in the case of shamans in Siberia (cf. Hutton 1993: 18–19; Grim 1983: 169): being selected by the spirits; training under established practitioners; and acceptance by the community. Some writers treat the sequential transformative process that creates shamans as a rite of passage (Laughlin et al. 1992: 272), with its tripartite structure involving separation, liminality (or a stage of being "betwixt and between"), and reincorporation (see Turner 1967: 97; van Gennep 1960).

When a paranormal being such as a god or ancestral spirit descends upon an unwilling human being, who is chosen to become a *jhãkri*, there is disruption, disorder, and imbalance. It is an "unsolicited" or "involuntary" spirit possession. The force and violence of the supernatural world impinges upon the helpless human who is suddenly face-to-face with unexpected and unknown terrors and wonders beyond the ego that for some verges upon madness (Laughlin et al. 1992: 270, 272). The incipient shaman is plunged into his own psyche, the inner space from whence emanate visions and dreams that form an internally generated symbolic field, but is unaware that this space exists inside and that the transformative experiences are occurring within himself (Laughlin et al. 1992: 270).

The future *jhākri*, like the shamans of Siberia, experiences illness and is assailed by spirits who torment him (cf. Vasilevič 1996; Diószegi 1996; 1960: 58; Bogoras 1909: 421). Anomalous and terrifying experiences, such as torture and assaults by demons, are common elements of the shamanic initiatory motif. This is how Nir Bahādur Jirel described one of his encounters with the terrifying world of spirits and ghosts:

> I was walking home late one evening and passed by the cremation grounds. It was very dark. I became very nervous and began to walk faster and faster. Suddenly, I heard noises, as if someone was pushing or rolling rocks. Then everything began to move in the ground before me. Rocks and boulders began to fly out of the ground and came crashing down on the path nearly blocking it. All the trees began to swing back and forth. There was screeching, like the sound of a terrible wild beast, and corpses and graveyard demons appeared all around. The sound was their commander, *karbir-masān*, rallying them. Some had no eyeballs, only empty sockets, some had no heads, and others had eyes on their chests. They made motions for me to approach them. I was very afraid and ran away as fast as I could. Each time I turned to look behind, the dead people were still there right next to me. I did not stop running until I returned home. I shouted that there were dead people with me and for them to run away. My family looked surprised and replied, "What are you talking about?" I looked behind, but there was nothing there anymore. I became sick for many days. Afterward, I saw such apparitions repeatedly. Sometimes I saw them as I described, sometimes demons would attack me at night, seize me so that I could not move or speak (*aīthan* or sleep paralysis). The attacks were terrifying. Then they would release me.

This is what some writers have referred to as "the shamanic illness," "spiritual emergency," or "transpersonal crisis" (Gorf and Gorf 1986; Gorf 1998: 8-10; Walsh 1990: 99; 1996: 100), a period of suffering marked by seizures, hallucinations, visions of spirits, and other anomalous experiences. A more appropriate description of the encounter with spirits might be "ontological crisis," an experience that threatens to undermine and shatter the subject's hitherto taken for granted construal of reality. Anthropologist Charles Laughlin and his colleagues (1992: 272) interpret these pathological effects as "symbolic expressions of what is, over time, an expansive, developmental transformation of [the incipient shaman's] consciousness." The shaman's initiatory sickness involves "introversion and fragmentation of consciousness" (Laughlin et al. 1992: 272). The shamanic trajectory begins with anomalous experiences and a progression of such incidents, which characterize what sociologist James McClenon (1995: 113) refers to as the "shamanic biography," gradually wear down resistance and skepticism, and convince the incipient shamans of the authenticity of the calling, compelling them to acquiesce to the fate thrust upon them.

As already noted, in Nepal the physiological expression of spirit possession is the uncontrolled trembling of the body, called *kāmnu*. "Those who are possessed," as Jhākri Gau Bahādur Gurung put it, "shake under the weight of the spirits the same way a sacrificial goat shakes when it is doused with holy water before it is decapitated." In this context, as the *jhākris* put it, the term *kāmnu* is distinct from trembling or shivering experienced as a result of fear, shivering because of frigid temperatures (*siu-siu gārdai kāmnu*), trembling due to a fever (*kām-jaro*), or fits attributed to epilepsy (*mirgi*). *Kāmnu* refers specifically to the *jhākri's* state of mind and body, or his "trance state." Encapsulating this is the saying, "*nakāmne manchhe jhākri hoina*," which means, "if he does not tremble he is no *jhākri*' (cf. Nicoletti 2004: 86). Hamayon (1993b: 7) is patently wrong in stating that "shamanistic societies do no make use of native terms homologous to 'trance'" and do not refer to "a change of state [of consciousness] to designate the shaman's ritual action."

The shamanic calling is an onerous fate. The *jhākris*, like their Siberian counterparts, come to their calling under duress and against their will (cf. Krader 1978: 184). Refusal of the calling is not an option because to do so would invite disaster upon the candidate or his family (Eliade 1964: 18; Höfer 1994: 24; Pigg 1995: 22; Riboli 2000: 149; Watters 1975: 127). As Jhākri Shukra Bahādur Tamang put it:

> If someone is possessed by gods or spirits and does not follow their direction, if he does not seek to become a *jhākri*, he will go mad (*baulāunu*). He must learn to control the spirits or he will lose his mind.

Spirits of ancestral *jhākris* select candidates. As in the case of the Buryat shaman, as Krader (1978: 195) noted, "the most important is the possession of (and possession by) a shaman ancestral spirit." It is believed that when a *jhākri* dies, his spirit does not move on to be reincarnated, but lingers on an ethereal plain until it can find a suitable candidate. These revenants appear to select people spontaneously. However, this process is not as random or haphazard as it might seem. *Jhākris* often come from the same descent group. Thus, candidates are the descendants of other practitioners, although the occupation does not necessarily pass on from father to son (cf. Krader 1978: 201). The hereditary principle is not unique to Nepalese shamanism, but was also an aspect of Siberian shamanism (Eliade 1964: 3–23; Diószegi 1996; Vasilevič 1996).

In the case of Jhākri Nir Bahādur Jirel, whose grandfather was a *jhākri*, it skipped one generation. In Dul Temba Sherpa's case, the vocation has been taken up in his family in an unbroken succession from father to son for four generations. Shukra Bahādur Tamang stated that his "is a hereditary vocation. Both my grandfather and father were *jhākri*s. When my father died, the gods and spirits entered into my body." Peters (1981: 79) reports that among the Tamang he studied, when a *jhākri* dies the *jhākri* officiating at the funeral entreats him to pass on his power to one of his relatives so that they may not be lost to the world. One among the mourners, a son or grandson, may then tremble, indicating the presence of the deceased *jhākri*'s spirit, and will inherit his ritual paraphernalia and take up the calling. This is how Shukra Bahādur described the process:

> When a *jhākri* dies, they hold a funeral procession (*mahlām*). Only *jhākri*s officiate, *lāmā*s cannot take part in the service. In the procession toward the cremation grounds, we beat our drums and one *jhākri* carries an urn full of holy water with *tite-pāti* [*Artemisia vulgaris*] and broom-grass dipped into it. We use this to sprinkle holy water on the body. Someone carrying a lit clay oil-lamp walks ahead of the procession. A family member carries the dead *jhākri*'s drum and ritual outfit. In the cremation grounds, we dance, beat our drums and burn incense. We pour libations with *chhyang* and *raksi* [local alcoholic drinks] and drink. Then we purify the dead *jhākri*'s body with *chhyang*, *raksi*, and holy water and cremate him. We burn his clothes [not costume] as well.
>
> Then, at the end of the ceremony, the soul of the dead *jhākri* possesses one of his sons or grandsons. The dead *jhākri*, through the possessed son or grandson, speaks about where he is and where he is going and the possessed one takes away his drum and the costume. In some cases, this possession does not happen in the cremation ground, but may occur within a week after the *jhākri*'s death. However, if the possession does not happen at all, the dead *jhākri*'s son or grandson may give away his drum and costume to some other *jhākri*s.

The vocation is also hereditary for Jhākri Narsing Jirel, although he noted that the recruitment of his grandfather was not through spirit possession, but through abduction by *ban-jhākri*, the primordial shaman of the forests. Kumar Thapa, a Chetri (Kshetri) *jhākri*, is also an abductee initiated by the forest shaman. *Ban-jhākri* abduction represents an alternate but culturally acknowledged path toward a career as a *jhākri* (see chapter 9). Spirit abduction is an avenue for certain individuals without *jhākri* ancestry to become shamans.

Anyone among the lineal descendants of an ancestral *jhākri* is a potential candidate and may be called upon when an ancestral spirit descends upon him. In contrast to ghosts, elemental spirits, and demons, ancestral spirits only assault their own male descendants. None of the *jhākri*s with whom I worked could recall a female being chosen, although they all acknowledged that this was possible. There certainly are some female *jhākris* in Nepal.

When a spirit seizes or "mounts" the candidate, as *jhākris* describe the experience, he acts as if he is "mad" (*baulāhā*), undergoes uncontrollable seizures and chronic illness, and has horrifying dreams and visual and auditory hallucinations. This is not a haunting or merely an encounter with ghosts because it culminates in a conversion experience that results in a fundamental alteration in values and lifestyle (cf. Evans 2001: 60).

The spirits that descend upon a potential *jhākri*, the beings he interacts with during his practice, and the paranormal realms to which his spiritual excursions will take him, fit in with his society's cosmology (cf. Bourguignon 1976a: 38; Laughlin et al. 1992: 270). Accounts provided by the *jhākris*, compiled from my field notes, provide a glimpse into the nature of the calling by spirits.

> I began to shiver when I was 11 years old. I was walking home from the fields with my father and brothers when it happened the first time. My body became tight and I felt tingling sensations in my stomach, just below my chest. Then I began to shake uncontrollably. I did not know what was going on. My father took me home and I became senseless. I was sick with fever for many days. I heard noises and had frightening dreams. When I awoke, I could not speak. Sometimes I saw people and spoke to them, but no one else could see or hear them. I was confused and terrified and could not understand what people said to me. I felt pain in my chest and my body would tremble. Spirits used to converge on me lashing with iron whips. Sometimes they took me high in the alpine forests and kept me there for days. They whispered in my ears. I resisted—they persisted. This would happen every few weeks. Those days are like a terrible dream. I did not get better until I found a guru who told me what was going on and how to control the spirits and gods (Jhākri Rabindra Rāi).

Escape into the mountains or forests results in personal encounters with numinous beings (cf. Eliade 1964: 21). Escape or "retreat to the forest," a recurrent theme in Nepalese shamanism, is one expression of the initial stage of the vocation (Sagant 1976: 68–70), and will be discussed in detail in chapter 9. This is the separation stage of the transformative process, in which "introversion and restructuring" not only dissociates the incipient shaman from mundane ego consciousness, but also from members of society, which is also expressed in the metaphor of escape into the wilderness, solitude, and capitulation into possession states (Laughlin et al. 1992: 272). Introversion and fragmentation of consciousness is often expressed through the metaphors of "dismemberment," madness, and death and dying (Diószegi 1960: 54).

The incipient *jhākri*, in Jungian terms, now confronts archetypal beings and realms, autonomous unconscious materials that burst forth and overwhelm him. The spirits encountered during this period of isolation provide instructions and reveal secret information, mantras, and the locations of materials with which to construct shamanic paraphernalia (cf. Riboli 1995: 81; Eliade 1964: 147, 168–169). Such transmission of knowledge takes place during intense dreams and visions that intrude on their waking hours. Anthropologist Erika Bourguignon (1973: 12–13) is correct to include other types of ASC, such as revelatory dreams, in the shaman's phases of consciousness (cf. Laughlin et al. 1992: 269).

Jhākri Narsing Jirel explained his initial encounter with the spirit world with considerable detail:

> When I was 14 years old I started to have frightening dreams. At other times, I lay in bed without moving. This went on for some time. People thought I had lost my mind, that I was mad (*pāgal*). I began hearing voices murmur to me, inside my head. I could not bear it. I would move aimlessly in the hills outside the villages. One night I went to the cremation grounds (*thursa* in Jirel) above Yersa village. I don't remember why I went there I felt attracted to the place. . . . I was there for hours and I fell asleep under a tree. I remember being unable to move. Then there were ghosts (*bhut*, *masān*), and spirits (*jakkhu*) all around . . . they were holding me down. I could not breathe and my chest felt like it would be crushed. The spirits attacked me . . . I felt pain and thought I was dead. I saw my body being ripped to pieces and I became unconscious . . . and then I heard voices. They said they were my ancestors and informed me I was to become a *jhākri*, like them. I told them no! I pleaded. However, they said if I refused, I would die that night. I gave in and they began to teach me mantras and *jhākri* songs. I could then see these spirits. I was alive again. Then they whispered in my ears the different mantras I would need.

Severe illness associated with the imagery of death and dying as part of the *jhākri* initiatory crisis is common in the ethnographic literature of Nepal (e.g., Holmberg 1989: 147; Watters 1975: 126). The sensation of dying, or believing oneself to have died, is a familiar shamanistic motif and is a part of a psychological transformative process that happens in times of great emotional stress (Walsh 1990: 63). Narsing's account is also reminiscent of the "near death experience" phenomenon in the West, which according to some writers has "shamanic themes," including emerging from the experience endowed with healing powers and a sense of a new identity (see Green 1998; Thompson 1991: 155; Ring 1989: 15–17; 1980: 159–181).

Unlike Narsing's experience, for others the nature of the calling to become a *jhākri* is immediately evident. As Shukra Bahādur Tamang described his experience:

When my father died, the gods and spirits that were with him entered my body. My father's ghost came to me as well. I began to shiver. At first, the spirits only whispered in my ears, I couldn't understand what they were saying. Then they appeared in person and spoke in their own voices. They told me exactly what to do. I did all they asked. That is how I became a *jhākri*.

Dul Temba Sherpa had a similar experience:

I began shivering when I was 13 years old. My heart would beat very fast. I could see the gods and spirits who came to me. I was not afraid of them. When they entered inside me, I could not do anything, I couldn't talk or move. I just shook. My father's brother became my guru. When I was sixteen, the goddess told me I could perform as a *jhākri*.

Gau Bahādur Gurung reported:

My grandfather and his father were *jhākris*, but my father was not. It was the spirit of my great grandfather (*jiju-buwā*), who seized and made me shake. My guru was my grandfather (*hajur-buwā*). He taught me how to take a pinch of ash between my thumb and finger, read a patient's pulse, see and control the gods and goddesses, or *nāg-nāginis*, and other spirits.

It was the same with Rabindra Rāi:

My ancestors were highly experienced *jhākris*. The divine power entered my body from them. I accepted the calling and started my training.

This early period in the shaman's career is fraught with danger, even if the initial encounter with the spirits is not necessarily a volatile one, and the novice is liable to descend into permanent psychosis. The threat remains until the relationship between the intruding spirit and their candidate undergoes ritual transformation (cf. Nicoletti 2004: 33; Höfer 1994: 24; Laughlin et al. 1992: 232). However, it is impossible to eliminate the danger completely, for every time the *jhākri* is possessed, there is the risk of falling into uncontrolled possession and "shaking 24 hours per day" (Mastromattei 1989: 228).

As several of the accounts above indicate, an individual afflicted by spirits must ultimately seek the help of a practicing *jhākri* who will act as his guru. A spiritual guide or teacher does not have to be a relative. Any qualified individual can act as tutor and guide for the new disciple (*cēla*) in return for gifts and tokens of cash, irrespective of creed and for the most part of caste. *Jhākris* will accept disciples from any ethnic or occupational group or caste (cf. Peters 1981: 65–66; Skafte 1992: 48). Nepalese shamanism, therefore, overlaps caste and ethnic distinctions (Hitchcock 1967; Jones 1976: 55; Macdonald 1975: 113, 1976a).

There are, however, some exceptions to this general pattern. In some cases, the tutelary god or spirit teaches the initiate all the necessary mantras, songs, and rituals and these individuals acknowledge no other teachers (cf. Allen 1976a: 145; Michl 1976: 157; Nicoletti 2004: 19; Riboli 2000: 67, 70–71). Self-made *jhākri*s exist. However, they too acquire much of their knowledge from their peers by attending, whenever possible, the performances of other *jhākri*s (Holmberg 1989: 148; Jones 1976: 52; Michl 1976: 157).

As noted previously, being seized by spirits, or showing the symptoms of spirit possession, does not necessarily mean there is a *jhākri* in the making. As Dul Temba Sherpa pointed out:

> There are two kinds of shivering. If you shiver from gods and goddesses, or ancestral spirits who choose you . . . you can become a *jhākri*. If you shiver from other spirits, you are sick.

*Jhākri*s are unanimous on this point, as Nir Bahādur Jirel pointed out: "a god, goddess, or spirits must seize you; otherwise you cannot become a *jhākri*." Kami Singh Tamang observed that "the power comes from the gods. They will seize our bodies and shake us and give us power."

The guru must therefore first determine the nature of the problem afflicting the initiate who has approached him, that is, whether the condition is caused by a god or ancestral spirit wishing him to become a *jhākri*, or whether it is an assault by an offended divinity, or a malicious witch, ghost, or evil spirit. The latter condition is curable by sacrificial offerings and exorcisms, whereas the former can only be assuaged by taking up the vocation. In order to do this, the guru will ask the candidate various questions and he may use divination or appeal to his own tutelary spirit for advice. As Gau Bahādur Gurung explained:

> To find out what is the source of the possession we have to make a diagnosis (*jokhanā hernu*). There are different methods. Feeling the pulse (*nāri*) on the person's wrists is one way to do this. Alternatively, we use the rice to diagnose. On a clean brass or copper plate, we put rice, incense, coins or notes, and take some rice and touch the patient with it. We then throw the rice on the plate and look at the pattern.

Once the condition is determined to be shamanic in nature, it is necessary to establish the identity of the spirit involved. This is required because the transmission of tutelary spirits is not predetermined or straightforward. Any one of a vast array of spirits of famous ancestral shamans may turn out to be the agent afflicting the student. Through his association with the spirit of a famous shaman and ancestor, whose identity is established by the guru, the new shaman acquires a degree of respect and validation (cf. Peters 1982: 32).

I was present on an occasion when Narsing Jirel undertook this identification process for his young student, Ramkaji. It took place in Narsing's house after dark. Ramkaji sat cross-legged facing his guru. They were both wearing their everyday clothes. After uttering mantras, Narsing picked up his drum, began playing, and started to call the gods and spirits in succession to possess him. As he played, he began to shake and started bouncing up and down, a visible sign that the spirit he was calling had manifested itself. Each time Narsing embodied the spirit, he momentarily struggled to restrain it, twisting and pulling his drum handle toward his abdomen as if trying to rein it in like a horse. Then he transmitted the possessing spirit into his student's body by touching him with the point of his drum handle. In response, Ramkaji shuddered, an indication that the spirit was now inside him. This process went on for about twenty minutes, with first Narsing shaking and bouncing and then Ramkaji repeating the motion, as spirits were passed back and forth. Then Ramkaji began to shake intensely and started hissing and choking, a sign I found out later that the correct spirit was now inside him. At this point, the possessing spirit revealed its identity, speaking through Ramkaji.

Alternatively, the assailing spirit may reveal its identity directly to the candidate or his teacher in a dream or vision (cf. Höfer 1995: 24), although this was not the case for the *jhākris* with whom I have worked. Once identification is successful, the guru must ensure that the spirits desist assailing the candidate and assume the role of tutelary spirits (*guru-deutā*). The relationship between the candidate and the spirits must be ritually transformed by pledging that the candidate will thereafter honor and worship them (cf. Höfer 1995: 24). The candidate's spirit-encounter experience thus acquires a new definition and social purpose. The tutelary spirit will remain with the *jhākri* for life. According to Jhākri Dawa Sherpa, the initiate not only acquires a tutelary spirit, often the ghost of an ancestral shaman, but may also obtain the ancestral shaman's entourage of helping spirits.

Jhākri Nir Bahādur Jirel's tutelary spirit is the ghost of his grandfather, a famous and powerful shaman. He honors and worships his tutelary spirit (*guru-pujā*) at various times, at the start of his rituals, and several times during the proceedings. It is through the tutelary spirit that the neophyte will become acquainted with innumerable other deities and spirits in the course of his activities as a practitioner.

The guru-*cēla* relationship is now underway. The guru will interpret and reveal the meaning and significance of the neophyte's experiences according to the culture's shamanic cosmology and mythological system and impart the knowledge necessary to contend with the supernatural intrusion that throws lives in disarray and sets some along the path toward the *jhākri* vocation. As Laughlin et al. (1992: 280) have put it:

It is myth that instructs, stabilizes, and integrates the shaman's experiences and provides the context and meaning without which he might sink into psychosis . . . it is myth that tells the shaman what he's seen and how it fits into a coherent whole . . . to the extent that myths reflect the dreams and visions of previous shamans who have surpassed the empirical ego, it can assist and guide them to further transcendence.

Under such guidance, the initiate enters the next stage in the transformative process, which Eliade (1964: 14) described as "ecstatic and didactic." This entails attaining further transpersonal experiences through direct encounters with the paranormal world and its myriad inhabitants and the exploration of the structure of the multitiered universe or cosmos known to the initiate until now only through the culture's lore and mythology. Thus, what began initially as terrifying visions passively experienced becomes an active process of familiarization, accommodation, and assimilation of newly discovered worlds or realities (cf. Laughlin et al. 1992: 271, 272, 273). If successful, the process of training results in a dramatic transformation in which a reordering of the initiate's identity and relations with the social and spiritual worlds take place. It marks a transition and disengagement from conventional behavior (Maskarinec 1995: 203), a "psychological deconstruction" (Winkelman 2000: 81), and the creation of an entirely new identity and social place in the world.

Apprenticeship is long and arduous and can last from months to several years, sometimes under the tutelage of several different gurus from different ethnic groups or castes. During this time, the student will repeatedly embody spirits under the guidance of his teachers, in order to learn how to control the possession events. Sometimes as the master *jhākri* becomes possessed in the context of a ceremony, his student in the audience will also begin shaking. As a novice, he will be unable to restrain himself, having not yet mastered the spirits, and he thrashes about uncontrollably. Control comes in due time, with repetition of such experiences. This social conditioning once completed enables the initiate to induce at will the altered state of consciousness associated with spirit possession. Cognitive psychologists have noted the importance of social conditioning as a factor in triggering ASC (Beyerstein 1988: 255).

During training, the student incorporates in his repertoire not only esoteric knowledge, ritual techniques, and concepts and ideas taken from Hinduism and Buddhism, but also the tutelary spirits and pantheons of their gurus. Shukra Bahādur Tamang provided a short list of some of the deities that take part in his ceremonies: Lord of the Earth, Lord of the Sky, Lanka Guru, Hanumān Guru, Rām Lakṣman Guru, Lord Buddha, Gauri Pārbati, Ganga Mai, Samundra Mai, Lord Mahādev, Bhairava (fierce aspect of Śiva), Kālī, Guru Bhagawān, Dolakha Bhimsen, not including his tutelary spirit (*guru-deutā*) and clan deities (*kul-deutā*). Nir Bahādur Jirel's pantheon includes in addition to the Hindu deities such as Mahādev, Kali (Durgā), and many others Dolakha Bhimsen, gods of Tibet, and Grand-mother Spirit Baju, along with his clan gods Papu Cherenji and Chomu, and ancestral spirits. As Shukra Bahādur put it:

> the more gods one can summon the more power one has. Sometimes when *jhākris* meet during pilgrimages [*jātrā*], they challenge one another in calling gods. The one who calls the greatest number of gods to appear and manifest themselves wins the contest.

A *jhākri* who trained under gurus from different ethnic groups tends to recite the mantras in the language in which these were taught. Thus, Nir Bahādur Jirel recites mantras in the Nepāli, Jirel, and Sherpa languages. The invocation of pan-Nepalese gods is in Nepāli. Among some groups, even the nomenclature for the *jhākri's* ritual paraphernalia comes from other languages, such as Nepāli and Tibetan (cf. Fournier 1976: 109-110; Nicoletti 2004: 67).

All *jhākris*, irrespective of their ethnic background, are cognizant of the repertoires of other practitioners, and when and where permitted, attend one another's performances (Jones 1976: 52). Consequently there has been considerable diffusion of ideas, practices, and ritual paraphernalia among *jhākris* belonging to different ethnic groups (see Allen 1976a: 124; Desjarlais 1989: 304; Fournier 1976: 118; Hitchcock 1976: 171; Jones 1976: 52; Macdonald 1975: 113; Miller 1997: 20; Ortner 1995: 359; Paul 1976: 145; Peters 1981: 68; Townsend 1997: 44). This process of unconstrained borrowing, synthesis, and incorporation has contributed to the formation of a cosmological outlook and pragmatism that is flexible and "experimental," as Höfer (1994: 20) has put it in reference to the Tamang *bǫmbos*. This is why *jhākri* beliefs and practices are a truly pan-Nepalese phenomenon. Nepalese shamanism is, therefore, a dynamic, synthetic, and evolving tradition, rather than a static, ossified leftover relic from a bygone era, as shamanism is often depicted. What Höfer (1994: 20) says of the Tamang shamans, is to a large extent true of Nepalese shamanism in general:

> the open and private character of his institution enables the *bǫmbo* to react to cultural change by updating and "actualizing" the frame of reference of his own interpretations in such a way that what tends to assert itself "monologically" as an ethnic or local or even confessional context of tradition becomes interconnected with wider cultural contexts predominant at the regional or national level.

Training includes memorizing ritual texts of differing lengths, mantras, and songs that are the repository of a vast store of accumulated knowledge that has been passed on from generation to generation of practitioners, while they have engaged in their cosmic struggle against the forces of chaos and disorder. Long periods of study are devoted to the careful memorization of these narratives. This is done incrementally, during spare time, or when student and teacher are able to retreat to a secluded location where instruction takes place.

The power of the words that make up the texts rests in their precise recitation (cf. Jones 1976: 31). The secret of "mastering spirits" is encoded in and depends upon the mastery of these mantras and oral texts that are recited or chanted and sung. The texts go together with and bestow numinous power to each ritual action (Macfarlane 1981: 119). The memorization of songs along with the melodies is accomplished through recitation. Songs become supernaturally efficacious through performance and musical accompaniment by inducing appropriate altered states of consciousness (cf. Shirokogoroff 1935: 325). During interviews, I noted that *jhākris* access information regarding particular aspects of their practice by reciting or singing relevant passages of their oral texts and then elaborate upon the meaning of the passages, rather than offering a straightforward response to my questions.

These are standard texts, although infrequently variants appear through the revelatory inspirations of particularly creative *jhākris* (cf. Höfer 1994: 37; Riboli 2000: 119). These variant narratives become part of the repertoire of their innovator and are disseminated and passed on through his students. *Jhākri* texts structure and frame the performances and fix the parameters that limit the degree of permissible improvisation. In this respect, Nepalese shamanism differs from the Siberian variant if Soviet ethnographers (cf. Sokolova 1989: 161–162; Zornickaja 1978; Diószegi 1960: 169, 283–290) were correct regarding the highly improvisational nature of the Siberian shamans' performances.

Anthropologists who have collected and analyzed an extensive corpus of Nepalese shaman oral texts have observed that these texts are not merely prose, but are intended for recitals and have "poetic qualities" (see Maskarinec 1995, 1998; Höfer 1981, 1985, 1994). Moreover, these texts are not simply recited, but are performed. Audiences comprehend the texts in terms of their performative qualities, for they are things not for contemplation, but things that become self-effective once they are recited and acted out (Höfer 1985: 26; Hitchcock 1974a). The performance becomes the communicative context in which the texts are understood. Their effects to induce psychological changes and healing depend upon their comprehension in this manner by the target audiences (see chapters 10 and 11). As ethnologist András Höfer (1985: 26) has noted about this kind of "text-understanding" with respect to Tamang ritual texts, "there is evidence that this understanding works partly at a sub-rational (rather than unconscious) level and is thus related to the . . . effectiveness of symbols."

Although I have been unable to detect the degree of uniformity and coherence in *jhākri* recitals as Maskarinec's (1995) materials from western Nepal suggest, his observations regarding these texts are correct. There are several categories of texts. First, there are those that are recited publicly, while the *jhākri* beats his drum and dances. These texts are like instruction manuals that provide guidelines for shamanizing and structure the performances. Embedded in these texts is a comprehensive etiological model, involving theories of affliction and causality and delineation of causative agents. The texts also specify why certain categories of illness require the intervention of *jhākris* (Maskarinec 1998; 1995: 26–27, 28, 49; Höfer 1981; 1985; 1994). The texts relate the origins of witchcraft, curses, and demonic forces. To cure ailments attributed to these causes, the *jhākri* relates their origins (Maskarinec 1995: 123).

A second category of text consists of concise magical formulas called *mantras* (Maskarinec 1995: 58–93). Every *jhākri* tries to commit to memory a large number of mantras. The belief in the efficacy of these incantations is widely held in Nepal (Maskarinec 1989: 209). Some villagers know certain mantras for particular ailments as well. The only requisite for a mantra's efficacy is its correct utterance (Maskarinec 1989: 209).

Mantras are magically potent texts, phrases, sequences of words, and sounds that are infused with palpable dynamic power (*śakti*) that conjure up the forces to which they refer and manifest desired actions (see Alper 1989). The power of mantras stems from the belief that objective reality is manifested and shaped through intentionality. Directive, protective, and curative incantations, mantras are recited and then ritually blown (*phukphak garnu*) onto objects and substances, such as rice, ashes, holy water, or afflicted parts of a patient's anatomy (Maskarinec 1993). Mantric utterances are a central component of Vedic, Tantric, and Śaivite ritualism, as well as Tibetan Buddhism and Nepalese shamanism.

Jhākris recite mantras during the performance of particular ritual tasks, such as blessing his drum, outfit, and other paraphernalia at the start of the curing ceremonies, as well as when summoning helping spirits (see chapter 10). Some mantras counteract the harmful effects of witchcraft or a sorcerer's spells. Others work to cure particular ailments, such as headaches, toothaches, impotence, scorpion stings, and snakebites.

Jhākris also know mantras for raising the spirits of the dead. They call up these spirits to consult them (*masān jagāunu*) about their role in a patient's affliction or they may send them on errands or to perform certain tasks (cf. Sagant 1988: 12). Sometimes an initiate must raise the spirit of the dead as part of his training. Dawa Sherpa described how he did this during his discipleship:

My teacher and I went to the graveyard at midnight. We had to wait for a moonless night. We had with us a human thighbone trumpet [*rkaṅg-gliṅg*], and a tiger bone trumpet [*stag-gliṅg*]. My teacher also had his magic spear [*barsā*], a weapon that can be used to kill the *masān* [*bir masān*: spirit of the dead or graveyard demons]. These are the weapons of the fierce gods. The human thighbone trumpet is used to raise the *masān*. The tiger bone is the right hand of Kali and is used to kill the *masān* and also demons. We also brought a cock because raising the dead requires blood sacrifice. I had to get a cock and not a hen because I was to raise a male spirit. To do this ritual one must go naked. I took off my clothes and my teacher smeared my body with the ashes he collected from the cremation place [*masān-ghāṭ*] like *sādhus* [ascetics]. My teacher then thrust his spear into the ground and asked me to walk around it in a circle and blow the thighbone trumpet to call the *masān*. I then recited the ghost mantra repeatedly [*jap*: repetition of magical utterance] and sounded the bone trumpet again. My teacher recited protection mantras. At his command, I cut off the chicken's head and sprayed the ground with the blood. The ground began to move slightly and then more violently. I could feel the spirits of the place moving around. Then the *masān* appeared in front of us and could be seen, terrifying and terrible. I made the *masān* dance. I made him dance downside up and upside down with my mantras. Then after some time I sent him back to where he belonged with another mantra.

Some *jhākri*s call up the *masān* and unleash them against their enemies or rivals. By raising the dead for such purposes, the *jhākri* ventures into the dubious and antisocial realm of malevolent magic. If suspected of such an enterprise, he will lose his credibility and may even provoke communal retaliation. Very reluctantly, Dawa recited for me the mantras for "calling the ghosts," but not before warning of its dangers.

> Bishnumati ghāt, Bagmati ghāt [cremation grounds]
> Those who belong to the seven oceans
> Those who belong to the river Ganges
> *Karbir-masān*, wake up
> You who takes the *dhūp* [incense] of corpses, wake up
> Ten thousand, wake up!
> Corpse eaters, wake up!
> Bone chewers, wake up!
> Ash eaters, wake up!
> O *karbir-masān*, who can enter inside men
> Wake up dead souls, wake up!
> O my *karbir-masān*, who can wreak havoc
> Wake up!
> Go north, go south
> Go east, go west, my *karbir-masān*,
> O my guru, wake him up!

Dawa also noted that *jhākris* must learn the mantra for sending ghosts away:

> The oath made to my guru
> My sixteen gurus, Lord of the Earth, Lord of the Sky
> By the oath of my guru
> *Karbir-masān* return dancing upside down
> *Karbir-masān* return dancing downside up
> Let the Ganges return upside down
> Go *karbir-masān*
> The oath of my guru is testament
> No *bir masān* can cling to my body
> Henceforth everyone to their own place
> Blow mantar
> Offer coins
> Throw rice, throw dirt
> Go back to your own place!

Jhākri oral texts constitute the corpus of information or database of magical knowledge in Nepalese shamanism. Command of such knowledge is a requisite in order for a person to become a practicing *jhākri*. Practitioners take pride in their mastery of these sacred narratives and mantras. They sometimes challenge one another on this matter while on pilgrimages and public gatherings, called *melā* (cf. Miller 1997: 42–55). According to Jhākri Gau Bahādur Gurung:

> A *jhākri* with an evil mind will blow mantras on some rice and toss it in the direction of his rival. When they throw it, the grains of rice become fiery projectiles. It does not matter where or how far the target is, as long as he is performing as a *jhākri* [i.e., is in a trance] the projectiles will reach him. If the target is unable to see the danger and dodge, he will be struck. He may faint; sometimes victims die. If he is strong enough and has inner vision to see, he can deflect the attack [*lāgu pharkanu*]. He utters mantras and the projectiles turn back upon the one who launched them.

Jhākri Kami Singh Tamang noted that such competitions sometimes turn ugly and ruin festivals and pilgrimages. He related an incident in 1998 at the pilgrimage site of Narayanthan, north of Kathmandu, where a challenger allegedly died after succumbing to his rival's power.

Being victorious in such competitions has its benefits. Nir Bahādur Jirel related the following story about Chandule, one of his *jhākri* ancestors:

> The name of the ancestor of my clan is Chandule. He was a very powerful *jhākri*. In those days, Jungu village in Lower Shikri had many powerful and arrogant *jhākris*. Chandule got into a war of tantrism with those *jhākris*. The

rivals went on a *jātrā* to Jiri Shuri, where many people had gathered to worship. The rival *jhākris* came there and the strongest one challenged Chandule to show his powers. Such demonstrations of *jhākri* powers impress people and the *jhākri* who does the best acquires more followers. There was a large crowd of onlookers from the villages of both *jhākris*. The agreement was that whoever could make the other stop shivering with mantras [i.e., end their trance state] would be the winner and could take possession of one of the loser's clan god statues. The *jhākris* began drumming, called their gods, and started shivering. Chandule began shivering violently and he started reciting very powerful mantras and his rival not only stopped shivering, he became mute, and fell down unconscious. The victorious Chandule then went to Jungu village with all his supporters behind him and brought back the idol of the goddess Bajhu-Abhi to our village. It was a great victory. The only drawback was that this goddess does not like people eating buffalo meat, so the villagers had to give up eating buffalo meat. After losing, the other *jhākri* stopped performing.

Maskarinec (1995: 208) has stated that "texts create shamans," whereas Peters and Price-Williams (1980: 405) suggest that "mastery of the trance states" makes the shaman. Both points of view are correct with respect to Nepalese shamans. The words recited resonate with supernatural potency. The mere mentioning of the names of spirits invokes their presence and may trigger a possession episode (Maskarinec 1995: 207). This happened during one of my interviews with a *jhākri* living in the outskirts of Kathmandu. Too old to perform any longer, the old man agreed to discuss his practice and career. In the midst of a casual conversation, as he was reciting lines from a mantra, he began trembling and bouncing as if he were in the midst of a ceremony. It is for this reason that many *jhākris* are reluctant to discuss their mantras and songs for calling the gods or other paranormal beings in any detail. To recite is to activate the power of the words and that leads to the manifestation of the supernatural beings named.

Aside from learning texts, the student will accompany his teacher while conducting healing ceremonies and other rituals, thereby acquiring an understanding of different rites, how to construct altars, execute dance moves, perfecting different drumming techniques, mastering *mudnīs*, and learning a codified system of drawing divinities and symbols of power using powdered paints (cf. Riboli 1995: 85). On some occasions, after completing the main segments of a healing ceremony, the guru gives his drum to his student and bids him to call his tutelary spirits. Through such training, *jhākris* learn to manipulate the drum to achieve various tones and resonances by singing close to the skin (Höfer 1994: 68) as well as how to produce syncopated rhythms. *Jhākris* use such effects to dramatize or punctuate their dancing and singing (Maskarinec 1995: 210).The guru will carefully observe his student and correct his performance as necessary.

During such sessions the novice will undergo repeated spirit possessions, and will in due time generate internal strength (*śakti*) to exercise increasing command over the spirits. As Shukra Bahādur Tamang often stated, "the *jhākri*'s power comes from within and is the basis of his claim to superiority over the *lāmā*'s book learning and scriptural authority."

Thus, over time, a novice achieves the ability to control his shivering. He has now acquired a skill vital for the *jhākri* practice. The physical sensation of controlled trembling is similar to a paranormal sensory device and is an invaluable capacity. It not only physically reveals to onlookers the presence of supernatural beings, but it is how the *jhākri* knows that he has obtained a correct answer to his queries or questions put to him by clients. This is illustrated in Jhākri Dawa Sherpa's account of how he obtained the wood with which he constructed the frame and handle for his drum.

> My guru [tutelary spirit] appeared to me in a dream and took me to uncultivated grounds above the village and pointed to a tall tree next to a stream and said, "there is your drum." The next day, I set out with my brother, who is also a *jhākri*, to the place in my dream. There were several trees there, near the running water. I approached each one for a closer look, touched several trees, but could not say if it was the right one or not. Then I came upon one large tree that sent tremors through my body. My brother began to tremble as well. We knew we had found the right tree. After reciting mantras and thanking our gurus, we sacrificed a goat, and then cut the tree and brought the lumber to the village where I made my drum.

Dawa's tutelary spirit also revealed to him where to find a suitable animal, the sacred *ghoral*, a wild mountain goat, the skin of which he used to cover his drum. After hunting and killing the animal, its blood was offered to the spirits; while those who helped Dawa in procuring his equipment shared the meat during a ritual feast.

With enough practice, the disciple is able to control the possession events and embody spirits at will. A noteworthy transformation thus takes place. Unlike the initial episodes of possession, when the initiate was not in charge of his facilities, now the shaking and shivering do not overpower him. He remains seated, beats his drum, sings, and recites ritual texts (Hitchcock 1976a: 169). In addition, instead of grunting, hissing, or mumbling incomprehensibly, as he did at the beginning, the voices of the gods and spirits speaking through him are intelligible. At this stage, the *jhākri* is a master of "a group of spirits" able at will to call spiritual agencies into his body, restrain them, put their powers to use, and expel those agencies from his body upon the completion of his task (cf. Shirokogoroff 1935: 271). The spirits are now allies and they become a source of knowledge, imparting special mantras for healing and counteracting the effects of witchcraft.

The shaman emerges from the psychological chaos that first propelled him down the *jhākri* path with a new sense of control and psychological well-being as a fully functional member of society who will use his abilities for public good. In place of terrifying chaos and disorder, there is now a new heightened awareness of the meaningfulness and interconnection between all aspects of experience, a sense of apophenia. The ability to make connections between what ordinary individuals perceive as discrete categories underlies the *jhākri*'s creativity as interpreter of the world. As one who now controls the supernatural forces that nearly overwhelmed him, and which constantly intrude upon the lives of other human beings devastating them with sickness, anguish, and disorder, the *jhākri* is therefore in a position to provide assurance to people in his community. The assurance is that there are specialists among them who are able to "see" spirits and fight demons, sickness and death (cf. Eliade 1961: 184).

Embodying spirits or undergoing controlled possession events alone is not sufficient to make a shaman. He must complete the last stage of the transformative processes, which is acceptance by the community. As Peters and Price-Williams (1980: 406) have put it, "the practicing shaman must adapt himself to the role expectations of the community." This involves initiation into the vocation and convincing performances and cures. Only then is he entitled to own and use the *jhākri* drum and wear the ritual outfit.

Initiation rituals marking a student's full-fledged entry into the vocations vary. Some entail elaborate public ceremonies, such as the *suwī* pole-climbing rite of the Kam-Magars in western Nepal (Watters 1975). Others may involve a ritual in which the guru touches his student's head and shoulders with a *bumba* containing holy water, thereby officially bestowing the tutelary spirit, such as among the Tamang shamans studied by Höfer (1994: 24). Jhākri Shukra Bahādur Tamang described how he initiates a student into the vocation:

> After teaching him the necessary knowledge, I call the spirits and gods to enter into his body one by one. If he can control them, and if the spirit's voice speaking through him is comprehensible, then he is ready. I then touch his head and shoulders with the *bumba* containing holy water and throw consecrated rice (*achētā*) on his head.

Jhākri Narsing Jirel described his initiation as follows:

> After two years, my guru decided to find out if I was ready to practice as a *jhākri*. The ceremony was held in my house. My family and kinsmen were there as well. I put on my costume and hat [five-paneled *rigs lnga* crown] and started playing the drum and recited my mantras to call the gods. My guru began drumming as well and started to shiver. Then he asked me to hold a

bumba, which contained flowers and was filled with water, and have the gods and spirits enter into it. I continued chanting and calling them, and the *bumba* in my hand began to shake the same way the *jhākris* shake when spirits descend on their bodies. My guru continued beating the drum and the vessel continued to vibrate. Then he stopped drumming and asked me to balance the *bumba* on my head and dance. I danced with the *bumba* on my head and the power of the mantras prevented it from falling down. My guru was very happy and told me that my mantras were strong. He took the *bumba* and said, "This is power . . . drink it." I did so. Then he poured some holy water on my head, I began to shake very hard. I felt the power inside my body. Then using the flowers my guru sprinkled the spectators with the holy water. That is how I became a *jhākri.* I use the *bumba* in the same way when I treat some patients.

This initiation ritual is highly reminiscent of the initiation of Tibetan *dpa.'bo* described in chapter 3. Jhākri Rabindra Rāi, who trained for five years before becoming an independent practitioner, described his initiation as follows:

I memorized mantras and songs. I learned how to diagnose by reading the patient's pulse and how to cure ghost illnesses and fight witches. Before I became independent, my guru tested my power. I made a *torma* for my *guru-deutā* and called the gods and spirits, my protectors, by reciting and beating the drum. Then my guru gave me the fire . . . seven burning wicks [*saat watā diyo battī*], which I had to offer to the gods and then eat. I was unharmed because of the power of the spirits. The fire does not burn when the spirits are with us.

Nir Bahādur Jirel and Dawa Sherpa also ate burning wicks as part of their initiation, as a final test. The ability of Nepalese shamans to drink burning oil, lick red-hot iron, put their hands in boiling water, and walk on hot coals is well known (Nicoletti 2004: 43; Peters and Price-Williams 1980: 401; Watters 1975: 147). These acts represent practical demonstrations of the supernatural powers conferred upon the *jhākris* and such demonstrations of power were commonly expected of Siberian shamans as well (cf. Hutton 2001: 94; Znamenski 2003: 83).

The shaman who achieves professional status in the process obtains a new social identity and new possibilities of navigating his social world. Poverty, disease, and other hardships that make day-to-day survival a constant struggle characterize the *jhākri's* social reality. Exacerbating life's vicissitudes is a rigid caste-based social hierarchy and marked sociopolitical and economic inequalities and social injustice. This hierarchy sets forth inflexible parameters that circumscribe the social space within which individuals may operate as actors. *Jhākris* are able to operate outside these inflexible parameters that circumscribe the social space of the ordinary Nepalese, even though these practitioners are drawn from among the economically marginalized and powerless segments of society. Jones (1976: 8) made astute observations regarding this point that are as relevant today as they were three decades ago:

> Throughout Nepal the caste system and ethnic pluralism operates to deny many individuals self-respect and prestige in the village setting. This is especially the case with lower castes such as metalworkers, tailors or leather-workers. Frequently, these castes provide the village shaman or religious specialist who combats disease and misfortune through controlled spirit possession. In this way the avenue is open for such people to cross caste boundaries and gain self-respect and prestige.

This, more than monetary rewards, seems to be the motivating factor for pursuing the *jhākri* vocation. Ethnographers agree that *jhākris* are not economically better off than other members of their community (Allen 1976a: 126; Michl 1976: 155; Messerschmidt 1976: 202). Like their counterparts in Siberia, what income *jhākris* earn is insubstantial, in comparison to the length of time and amount of effort required to conduct their rituals (Miller 1997: 208; see chapter 10). None of the *jhākris* with whom I work is able to make a full-time living based solely upon their vocation.

Through long years of training and fortitude required to master the vocation, the individual not only transforms himself from a farmer or blacksmith into a *jhākri*, but upon taking up his new identity renegotiates his social relations with other members of the community, who are transformed into patients, students, admirers, and those who fear him. As Maskarinec (1995: 77) has noted with regard to *jhākris* in western Nepal, "One who becomes a shaman dislodges hegemonic constraint to connect social webs and personal relations in new, advantageous ways, that others are forced to acknowledge." It is for this reason that one seldom encounters assessments of a *jhākri* in terms of his caste or ethnic origins (cf. Macdonald 1976a: 318). What is crucial is how proficient he is as a professional, rather than his mundane earthly characteristics or associations. The *jhākri* therefore exercises a degree of freedom from social constraints that impinge upon his relatives and fellow villagers. Thus, while *jhākris* may originate from marginal and powerless strata of society, as practitioners they are far from marginal individuals.

The *jhākri* is also free of any professional organizations for the validation of his status. There is no formal institutional training or course of study. Unlike a priest, the *jhākri* is not part of a monastic order or larger religious hierarchy and does not occupy any formal offices that define his relationship to the supernatural world and from which he derives his authority as a practitioner. There is a master-disciple relation formed when an individual voluntarily places himself under the guidance of a master or guru. During this time, the disciple must follow his guru's teachings. However, as pointed out earlier, he is also free to choose another teacher and often a single practitioner, during the course of his training, will have a number of gurus (cf. Miller 1997: 21). Those who achieve mastery in their vocation are not compelled to acknowledge other practitioners as their superiors.

The *jhākri's* relationship with the supernatural world is a personal and direct one, involving controlled interaction with spirits or gods. Moreover, his concerns are with remedying problems of health and prosperity for his client in this life, rather than with an afterlife (Paul 1976: 149). Nepalese shamans never employ their privileged position as intermediaries between the world of humans and spirits to influence or take part in local politics (contra Vitebsky 1995: 119). The gods they shoulder or embody never issue political directives or advice like, for example, the Tibetan state oracle, Dorje Drak-den, or Nechung. The gods with whom the *jhākris* interact are content merely with food offerings and worship (cf. Miller 1997: 238–240).

Ultimately, the *jhākri's* authority and his reputation as a ritual intercessor receives endorsement almost entirely according to how convincing his performances are and how successful he is in harnessing supernatural forces for the benefit of his clients (Miller 1997: 22). The *jhākri's* reputation is a combination of rumors, public acknowledgment of his abilities, and the number of successful and spectacular cures he has been able to accomplish (Macdonald 1976a: 318). A reputation thus earned may give an individual practitioner the basis for claiming superiority over fellow *jhākris*.

The *jhākri* has a well-defined and unique social position. He has a "transcendental persona." However, his social position and status are also highly ambivalent (Hitchcock 1974: 153; Maskarinec 1995: 113; Riboli 2000: 65–66). This ambivalence stems principally from what the *jhākri* does. He traffics with and embodies evil or potentially evil paranormal beings. He can raise evil spirits and the ghosts of the dead and compel them into nefarious actions. There is something highly dubious and irregular about these abilities. The *jhākri* is a healer and intercessor on behalf of his community and yet by virtue of the very abilities that empower him he is simultaneously a potentially dangerous figure, an embodiment of evil, even a potential sorcerer or witch (Hitchcock 1974: 153). It is not infrequent for *jhākris* to be suspected of using their powers for malevolent purposes (cf. Sagant 1988; Riboli 2000: 66). The ambivalent nature of Nepalese shamans is not unique. Siberian shamans also had similar ambivalent personas (Hutton 2001: 142; for other contexts see Brown 1989). As Krader (1978: 181) noted in his description of the Buryat shaman: "he has . . . a dual social personality. He is at once hated and needed, reflecting the ambivalent relation in society of the 'wild,' 'bad' social type that is necessary for the orderly functioning of the traditional social group."

The materials in this chapter clearly demonstrate the remarkable unity of beliefs and practice among *jhākris* as a distinct group of practitioners. This lends considerable support to the idea that shamanism is a unitary pan-Nepalese phenomenon. Similarities in training procedures, a common vision of the world, and identical ritual techniques used by shamans throughout the country further confirm the unitary nature of Nepalese shamanism. Adopting the "shamanisms" approach would result in a distorted picture of Nepalese shamanism. Moreover, the Nepalese shaman's calling, training, and initiation parallel those of "classic" shamanism of Siberia. This brings into question typologies that differentiate between genuine shamans and shamanistic healers, as proposed by writers like Winkelman.

5

Ornaments and Instruments of the Gods: The *Jhãkri*'s Ritual Outfit and Paraphernalia

Once a candidate completes his training and is initiated into the vocation he must obtain a costume and ritual paraphernalia, the tools of the trade. Either a new *jhãkri* may receive these from his guru or, alternatively, he may inherit his gear, or have them made to his specifications. The *jhãkri*'s drum, equipment, and costume constitute his arsenal and protective armor against the forces of evil and disorder (cf. Oppitz 1992: 80).

Each element of the *jhãkri*'s outfit possesses cosmological and symbolic significance. As Nicoletti (2004: 43) has put it, "the costume is redundant with symbols. Burdened with these objects, the [*jhãkri*'s] body absorbs this medley of signs, thus transforming him—for the observer—into a dynamic code." For Eliade (1964: 145) the shaman's costume "discloses not only a sacred presence, but also cosmic symbols and metapsychic itineraries." By wearing the costume, the *jhãkri* "transcends profane space" and begins his entry into the realm of the sacred (cf. Eliade 1964: 147). What Shirokogoroff (1935: 287) wrote in reference to the Tungus shaman's costume applies to Nepalese shamans as well: "In fact, the costumes and other paraphernalia are needed by most shamans for the production of self-excitement, self-hypnosis and hypnotic influence over the audience."

The ritual paraphernalia that make up the *jhãkri*'s outfit, drum, costume, and gear are known collectively as the "ornaments and instruments of the gods" (*deutãka gahanã ra aujarharu*). The prototype for the paraphernalia of present-day practitioners is the equipment of the primordial shamans described in the *jhãkri* oral narratives (Maskarinec 1995: 102; Macdonald 1976a: 319–322; Watters 1975: 139–141). These narratives, which detail the origins, history and uses of the various implements, are chanted during healing ceremonies and when *jhākris* repair their gear (cf. Watters 1975: 140).

Nepalese shamans use two types of drums, the single sided drum, used by the Kham-Magar, Gurung, and Chepang in western and south-central Nepal, and the double-sided drum used in the eastern parts of the country (Oppitz 1991: 84; Riboli 1995: 82; 2000: 95–11). The latter is known as a *dhyāgro*, a term which, according to Macdonald (1976a: 328–329), is used exclusively in reference to the *jhākri's* instrument. With the exception of Jhākri Gau Bahādur Gurung, the practitioners with whom I work all used the *dhyāgro*. The drum is the *jhākri's* principal instrument of power through which he summons the spirits and enters into altered states of consciousness upon which depend his abilities to go into the spirit world and commune with divinities and other numinous beings and to combat evil (see Fournier 1976: 108–110; Höfer 1994: 65–69; Watters 1975: 141). Ownership of the drum signifies mastery over spirits (Walter 2001: 112) and a license to practice as a *jhākri*.

Oral narratives relate how Mahādev fashioned the *jhākri's* magical drum, which he used as a mount to fly into the sky like Tibetan Bönpo magicians and Siberian shamans (cf. Eliade 1964: 168–169; Macdonald 1976a: 337–338; Ellingson-Waugh 1974):

> Mahādeu sent the porcupine quill to the jungle to bring . . . wood from which to make the frame of the drum. Then he sent the porcupine quill . . . to the Himalayas in search of a deer. . . . Mahādeu waited for three days without doing anything else to the animal; then he skinned it without killing it. From the skin, he made the drumheads. Then he sent the [bell] to fetch [cane] from which he made the straps to brace the drumheads. Mahādeu had an assistant by the name of Sime [a term used by *jhākris* to denote *bhume deutā*, earth divinities]. He sent Sime to Modes (the plains of India) to look for *dubho* [a kind of grass, *Cynodon dactylon*, used in worship of the god Gaṇeś]. Sime brought back seven *dubho* branches. Upon the order of Mahādeu, he again set out to bring back *rudnācche* from Kailas. After having done this, he again left for Modes and brought back *riṭṭho* [the black seed of *Sapindus mukerossi*]. Mahādeu closed the drum by attaching the *murrā* (handle). Before closing it, he put seven blades of *dubho* and a *rudnācche* bead inside. (Macdonald 1976a: 319)

Höfer (1981: 32) has called attention to the general similarities between the *dhyāgro* and the drum used by Tibetan lamas (see Macdonald 1976a: 329). The *dhyāgro* is identical to the old Tibetan drum that is part of the Tibetan collection of the Rijksmuseum voor Volkenkunde (Leiden), reproduced in plate IX in Nebesky-Wojkowitz's work *Oracles and Demons of Tibet* (1956). If the Tibetan double-sided drum was the prototype of the shamanic drum used by groups in central and north Asia, as Shirokogoroff (1935: 299) and others believed (see Eliade 1964: 502; Watters 1975: 141), then it could also have also been the prototype for the *jhākri*'s drum. The *ḍhyāgro* is approximately seventeen inches in diameter and four inches deep, and consists of a circular wooden frame with a carved wooden handle about eleven inches in length. The handle is attached to the drum's frame and is secured with strips of cane that are connected to the drum's cane rims. The leather membranes covering both sides of the drum are from the skin of the ghoral, the wild Himalayan goat (*Nemorhae-dus ghoral*), a sacred animal associated with Paśupati (Śiva), "Lord of the Beasts" (Majupuria 1991: 135). The skin membranes are folded on each side over cane rims on the exterior circumference of the frame. Interlaced strips of cane secure the drumheads. *Jhākris* hold the drum in one hand and play it from the front or side with a curved cane drumstick (*gajo*).

The drum handle (*murnā*) resembles the *phurba* (*phur-pa*, the Tibetan ritual knife with a three-sided blade). Although the handle has intricate designs, consultants are unsure about the precise significance of the iconography (cf. Höfer 1994: 64). Typically, the handle consists of upper, middle and lower parts. The upper part is carved with three faces, identified as gods. The deities represented on the *phurba* handle include Hayagrīva, Mahakālā, and Vajrakīla (Meredith 1967: 237, 244), although my *jhākri*

Figure 5.1. A *jhākri* playing the double-sided *dhyāgro* (Photo by H. Sidky)

consultants have never mentioned these divinities in this connection. The middle part, which is round in cross-section, may contain Hindu and Buddhist symbols, such as the endless knot (*shrivatsa*), thunderbolt (*vajra*), and lotus leaves. The lower part, which is triangular in cross-section and ends in a sharp point, has images of intertwined snakes, the primordial serpent gods, or *nāg-nāginis*, associated with the underworld. *Garuḍas*, winged divinities, who counteract *nāgas* that produce illness, sometimes appear just above the blade. The imagery on the drum handle is suggestive of the shaman's multitiered cosmos, an upper world of the gods, a middle world of people, and an underworld, the dwelling place of snake-like beings and rulers of the netherworld.

Aside from its use as an instrument for beckoning the gods, the drum, with its *phurba*-shaped handle, is also used an offensive weapon. A *jhākri* uses the handle to point to the patient's body to neutralize evil influences. The drum also serves as a physical shield to ward off magical attacks (Watters 1975: 142; Skafte 1992: 48). *Jhākris* also use their drum for divination (see chapter 10).

During public festivals, flowers decorate the rim. Some *jhākris* may also tie ribbons from pieces of cloth offered to the gods to the handle of their drum. Like Siberian shamans, *jhākris* also make line drawings of sacred images on the skins of the drum using white clay and paint (cf. Eliade 1964: 172). In reference to artwork and shamanic trance, it may be noted that *jhākris* draw these images prior to ceremonies and never while they are in altered states of consciousness. The diagrams include circles, lines, sun, moon, drum motifs, sexual motifs, *triśūls*, as well as cosmograms. Anthropologist Michael Oppitz (1992) has analyzed the motifs on Nepalese shamanic drums in eastern and western Nepal, as well as compared them to the Siberian varieties. The *jhākri*'s "drum graffiti" regardless of the motif serve the same function, "they are a means of repulsion and act as deterrents of inimical spirits" (Oppitz 1992: 80). According to Oppitz (1992: 80):

> in this function the drawings can be associated with the shaman's paraphernalia in general. They become an additional dimension of his spirit-averting armor. In fact, the drawings complete the magical healer's weapons of defense against the forces of destruction.

When constructing the drum, *jhākris* follow Mahādev's example by placing a *rudnācche* and *riṭṭho* bead inside it. They may also include bits of crystal and a Nepalese copper coin bearing a propitious symbol, such as the trident of Śiva, which rattle when the instrument is played (cf. Höfer 1994: 68). The double-sided drum has violent (male) and peaceful (female) sides and *jhākris* use different techniques for beating the drum. When expelling spirits and demons the *jhākri* beats the violent side, when beckoning the gods, he strikes the peaceful side (cf. Höfer 1994: 68; Riboli 1995: 83). As in the case of the Siberian shamans, tutelary spirits disclose the location of the tree from which the *jhākri* constructs his drum, as illustrated by Dawa Sherpa's account discussed in chapter 4 (cf. Eliade 1964: 169–170; Nicoletti 2004: 82; Watters 1975: 141). Numinous energy saturates the drum. Its power in part emanates from the materials with which it is constructed: wood from the forest, the dwelling place of the primordial *ban-jhākri* and *ban-deutā*, and the skin of the sacred ghoral, which Jhākri Nir Bahādur Jirel calls a "*jhākri* animal." In contrast to the skin of domestic animals, which is polluting or impure (*jutho*), ghoral skin is pure (*cokho*) and nonpolluting. The drum, therefore, represents a physical and symbolic link between its owner and the forest divinities (Walter 2001: 112).

Jhākris consecrate their *ḍhyāgros* to their tutelary spirits. As Jhākri Dul Temba Sherpa puts it, "this is the instrument of the gods." Jhākri Bir Bahādur Tamang describes the drum in almost identical words. For this reason, *jhākris* safeguard the instrument from ritual impurity, such as the touch of a pregnant or menstruating female. The drum is a living thing that must periodically be fed blood during ceremonies honoring tutelary spirits (Riboli 1995: 83; Walter 2001: 112). Some *jhākris* assert that when they perform, supernatural beings and gods inhabit and partially control the instrument (cf. Höfer 1994: 68). The *jhākri* thus feels the mystical energy as he beats the drum during his performance.

Aside from the drum, another important ritual implement in the *jhākri*'s arsenal is the *phurba* (Tibetan *phur-pa*), which I briefly discussed while describing the design of the *jhākri*'s drum handle. The Sanskrit equivalent of the term *phurba* is *kilā* (Huntington 1975: 1), referring to the magic peg or nail used by exorcists to neutralize evil spirits after defeating them by nailing them to the ground (Meredith 1967: 237). The *phurba* also serves as a magical projectile that can be fired at enemies in remote locations. Art historian John Huntington (1975: vii) notes that the idea of dispatching enemies over long distances using magical nails, darts, or daggers and using such implements to eradicate negative forces both spiritual and human is widespread and probably of shamanistic origin. "The phur-pa, a three bladed dart or dagger," Huntington (1975: vii) adds, "is the implement of this action in Tibet and its use is quite common throughout the areas of Tibetan religious influence." Priests of the old Bön used *phurbas* for destructive magic (Nebesky-Wojkowitz 1956: 476, 486; Huntington 1975: 12, 56). Regarding the uses of the magic dagger, historian Georgette Meredith (1967: 248) observes that:

> phurbu of one kind or another is manipulated by lamas, monks, sorcerers, Bon priests, and deities against demons, specifically of the earth and sky, or

to produce or prevent illness or bad luck, to prevent hail, to bring on hail, and to consecrate the ground.

The *phurba*s used by *jhākri*s are usually made of wood and are about eight inches in length, similar in design to the handle of the drum described above. These implements sit upright inside wooden receptacles on the altar or they may be driven point first into the ground next to the altar. While manipulating the *phurba*, the *jhākri* recites special mantras. There are mantras that make the *phurba* fly like a magical dart or projectile, while other mantras activate its power to absorb and neutralize negative energy and impale evil spirits. Red and white ribbons attached to the *phurba* serve as whips against evil spirits and may be used in this manner to brush off harmful influences from a patient's body. The implement also functions as an offensive weapon when the *jhākri* is engaged in physical combat with a deity or evil spirit (see chapter 10). The use of *phurba*s in conjunction with *mudrā*s, or mystical hand gestures, is also a common feature of the *jhākri*s' repertoire. Höfer's (1994: 68) remark that the *phurba* is superfluous and that shamans never use it aside from keeping it on the altar is somewhat puzzling.

Another implement used by the *jhākri*s is the bone trumpet. One kind is made of a human thighbone (*rkaïg-gliïg*), and the other from a tiger bone (*stag-gliïg*). These instruments are similar to those used by *lāmā*s (cf. Höfer 1994: 63; 1981: 32). The sound of the thighbone trumpet frightens away evil spirits, while the tiger bone instrument is used to kill *masān* and also demons. Some consultants state that both these trumpets serve to summon evil spirits and ghosts.

*Jhākri*s construct the trumpets themselves (cf. Macdonald 1976a: 331; Skafte 1990: 54-57). Dul Temba Sherpa described how shamans acquire their human bone trumpet:

> We use the shinbone or thighbone of a man for this purpose. The bones of suicides are the best because their spirits stays in the bones and this gives the trumpet power. The bones of someone who has been executed by hanging also work well. We take vows to Gauri Pārbati and Lord Mahādev, purify our bodies, shave our heads, and protect ourselves with a spell . . . the mantra that causes blue flames to fly from our mouths. Only evil spirits and ghosts can see or feel this power. Then at midnight, we strip, cover our bodies with ash and excavate the corpse, reciting protective mantras so that *bir masān*s do not attack us. After cutting the bone, we bring it home, wash it, make a hole in it, and cover the end we blow on with silver. The sound of this trumpet makes the ghosts and evil spirits fly away, it terrifies them. We use it to fight *bir masān*s. The sound has power. Also, *jhākri*s can challenge each other by blowing on their trumpets. The weak one's trumpet bursts during such duels.

Figure 5.2.　A *jhākri* blowing a human bone trumpet (Photo by H. Sidky)

The human and tiger bone femur trumpets, as well as other items, such as quartz crystals, are kept in a pouch slung crosswise over the *jhākri*'s back, which hangs on the right side. They are also sometimes placed among the items on the altar during healing ceremonies.

Included in the *jhākri*'s arsenal of offensive weapons is a magical lance, called *barsā*. Shamans kill *bir masāns* with this weapon. It is manufactured from the metal of a *khukurī* knife (a male weapon) and a *ha˜siyā*, or sickle (a female implement), which are taken from graveyards or cremation grounds where the belongings of the deceased are buried.

The *jhākri*'s ritual outfit includes bells and necklaces. The *ghaṇṭa-mālā* are straps of small metal bells of different sizes attached to strips of goatskin leather or cloth that are worn crosswise like bandoliers, one extending from the left shoulder to the right hip, and one from the right shoulder to the left hip. Like the metal implements on the Siberian shaman's costume (Eliade 1964: 148–149), these sound off when the *jhākri* dances, they especially ring loudly during the powerful trembling when he embodies spirits. The bells invite the gods to come and frighten evil spirits away. Some *jhākris* tie horns of the sacred ghoral to these bandoliers as protective amulets.

Jhākris wear several types of bead necklaces. When Mahādev fashioned the prototype of the *jhākri*'s drum he also made five *riṭṭho-mālā*s and seven *rudrācche-mālā*s for protection against evil spirits. The black *riṭṭho-mālā* is used when reciting *jap* against *masān-desān* (evil spirit-epidemic/disease), and the *rudrācche-mālā* is used with Śrī Gorkhānath protective *jap*. *Rudrācche* beads symbolize Śiva, whose other name is Rudra.

Another type of necklace is the *nāg mālā*, made from the vertebrae of a snake, which is reminiscent of Śiva's protective cobra necklace. Bir Bahādur described the making of the *nāg mālā*:

> We recite mantras and ask our gurus for help in finding the snake. We learn where to look in dreams or when an image enters into our mind. After killing the snake, we stretch its body lengthwise and bury it in the ground saying prayers. We leave it in the ground for one maybe two months. Then, we come back, dig it up, wash and pick off the remaining flesh and string the bones together. It is important that all the pieces are there and that they are strung together according to their original order. We use the *nāg mālā* mainly to circle the altar to keep evil spirits away. When it is around our necks, it protects us from magical attacks by witches and other *jhākris*.

The snake vertebrae necklace is also used to diagnose a patient's condition. According to Bir Bahādur, they vibrate when brought close to a patient suffering from a supernatural attack (cf. Oppitz 1992: 74). The type of vibration gives clues as to the nature of the problem.

Like his ritual implements, the *jhākri*'s costume is also distinctive and distinguishes him from all other Nepalese ritual intercessors. The apparel consists of a long-sleeved white robe (*jamā*), which extends to the ankles and is tied at the waist with a cloth belt. A vest may go over the robe. However, some *jhākris* wear only an ankle-length white skirt that is fastened around the waist. Protective amulets attached to ribbons complete the outfit.

I have recorded three types of headgear. Some *jhākris* wear a headband with porcupine quills (*dumsi ko kāro/kānda*) over which they tie a long cotton band as a turban with two ends hanging down the back. *Jhākri* consultants noted that the porcupine quills are powerful objects in their arsenal, serving as magic darts against evil spirits. With mantras, they fly "like arrows from a bow." Their use in headbands is to repel magical attacks against the head, which is regarded as the body's "temple."

Another kind of headband is made of peacock feathers, sometimes interspersed with porcupine quills. For Eliade (1964: 156–158, 177) ornithological symbolism of the shaman's costume means one thing, flight to the other world. However, *jhākris* maintained that the peacock feathers are

Figure 5.3. The peacock feather headgear. For Nepalese shamans such ornithological symbolism is decorative rather than denoting "shamanic flight" (Photo by H. Sidky)

decorative, calling them "ornaments of the gods." One *jhākri* maintained that peacock feathers represent the Hindu deity Indra. Ornithological symbolism does not necessarily correspond to Eliade's vision of shamans and their ritual gear. This sheds light on the problematic nature of such interpretations; take, for example, the treatment of the *atlatl* with the bird decoration from Lascaux as signifying shamanic flight (see chapter 1).

Finally, there is also a headdress, or crown, consisting of five pointed panels painted with images of Buddhist deities, or the five archetypal Buddha forms, similar to the *rigslnga* worn by mediums in Ladakh (see Yamada 1999: 13). Mediums (*dpa'.bo*) in Tibet also wear this type of headgear (Berglie 1978: 43).

When the *jhākri* is in his full regalia, he is acting in the role of the original intercessors, the primordial shamans. The power of the *jhākri's* ritual garb is recounted in "the Song of the Nine Little Sisters" recorded among the Kham-Magars (Watters 1975: 139–141; Maskarinec 1995: 102–103). This song relates how the various components of the total outfit, such as headdress, beads and necklaces, brass bells, and so on, protect respective parts of the *jhākri's* body from witches trying to devour him. The outfit has magical properties. *Jhākris* maintain that their costume not only enhances the efficacy of their powers and capacities to commune with the supernatural world, but it also provides protection from evil spirits, an idea also found among Siberian shamans (Watters 1975: 137; Znamenski 2003: 147). Not all *jhākris* wear the full regalia at all times. They may wear the full outfit during pilgrimages and public festivals, but put on only elements of the total assemblage for special purposes, such as healing ceremonies (see chapter 10).

As shown in this chapter, there are notable similarities and minor differences in the costume, ritual paraphernalia, and associated techniques used by shamans throughout Nepal. The *jhākri's* tools of the trade therefore indicate a significant unity of belief and practice among Nepalese shamans. Noteworthy similarities also exist between the *jhākri's* equipment and the ritual gear of Siberian and north Asiatic shamans.

6

✛

Altered States of Consciousness, Hallucinogenic Drugs, Spirit Possession, and Shamanism

Spirit possession, as discussed in the previous chapters, is a central feature of Nepalese shamanism. What is spirit possession? What forms does spirit possession take? How is spirit possession related to altered states of consciousness? Anthropologists working in Nepal in the 1960s and 1970s attempted to address some of these questions. Jones (1976: 1) made the following observation:

> Spirit possession can be defined as an altered state of consciousness on the part of the individual as a result of what is perceived or believed to be the incorporation of an alien form with vital and spiritual attributes, e.g., the spirit of a superhuman form such as a witch, sorcerer, god, goddess, or other religious divinity.

Jones uses the phrase "altered state of consciousness" (ASC) instead of terms such a "trance" and "ecstasy" utilized widely in the earlier literature because of their misleading connotations (Jones 1976: 17, 20). Ecstasy implies "rapture" and "euphoria," conditions associated with loss of self-control, while "trance" alludes to "hypnotic" states, which can denote a wide range of mental states, none of which are necessarily applicable to all shamanistic experiences (Reinhard 1976: 17; Tart 1986: 70; Townsend 1997: 441–443; on the use of the terms "trance" and "ecstasy" by scholars in different fields, see Morris 2006: 19).

Before discussing spirit possession in the context of Nepalese shamanism, it may be useful to look briefly at the concept of ASC. The term "altered states of consciousness," was coined by psychologist Charles Tart (1969) to refer to any mental state that departs radically from ordinary waking consciousness. Put differently, ASC refers to perceptible changes in the awareness of self and the world (see Beyerstein 1996a; Ludwig 1990). In the altered state, psychological functions and potentials not available in the baseline state of consciousness are thought to become available.

In the anthropological literature, ASC is described as "nonordinary" states of consciousness, "experiences beyond ordinary rational ego identity and consciousness," or "transpersonal consciousness" (Townsend 1997: 442; Winkelman 2000: 6). Spirit possession is one of the nonordinary states subsumed under the label of ASC. Some writers wishing to distinguish shamanic experience from other forms of ASC have proposed the use of "shamanic states of consciousness" (SSC), as a distinct category of ASC, to specifically denote the shaman's "nonordinary psychic states" (Harner 1980: 20–30, 1999: 1–5; Townsend 1997: 442–443: Winkelman 2000: 124–126).

Tart (1975; 1980) proposed a hypothetical model for the stages involved in the alteration of consciousness (see Farthing 1992: 212–214; Laughlin et al. 1992: 149), which is useful in helping us think about the alteration of the *jhākri's* psychic states. Tart has hypothesized that alterations in consciousness occur in three stages: destabilization of the ordinary or baseline state of consciousness and breakdown of its organization under a destabilizing force; a transitional period; and reconstruction of a new self-stabilized state of consciousness under a special patterning force.

When a subject begins to enter a new state of consciousness certain props are needed, such as a supportive environment, in order to facilitate the transition to the altered state. Tart (1975) maintains that a supportive environment is necessary because the ordinary state of consciousness is geared toward maintaining its integrity in relation to changing environmental inputs and is extremely overlearned compared to nearly all other states of consciousness. There is therefore a tendency for repatterning to the ordinary state. However, the need for additional props diminishes with repetition of the experience. This suggests that the ability to access and maintain altered states of consciousness is learned and is enhanced with practice (Walsh 1990: 164). As we have seen in the case of Nepalese shamans, it is during the novice's apprenticeship under a practicing *jhākri* that he is able to undergo repeated possession events until he is able to access ASC at will.

Destabilization forces may include hallucinogenic or psychotropic drugs and rhythmic stimulation, such as drumming and dancing (on the psychological effects of drumming, see Harner and Tyron 1996; Lane et al. 1988; Maurer et al. 1997; Maxfield 1994; Neher 1962; Rouget 1985: 172–176). Shirokogoroff's (1935: 325) observations regarding the ASC-inducing methods of the Tungus shamans fit the Nepalese case perfectly:

In almost all forms of shamanic performances, when the ecstasy of the shaman and the excitation of the audience are needed . . . several technical methods for bringing up a necessary psychic condition of the shaman and audience are used. These are rhythmic effects, music of the performance, particularly rhythmic movements, dancing, drumming and production of various noises with the costume, also singing or reciting, and the contents of the texts of the performance, i.e., descriptions in words of the relations between the shaman and the spirits, the people and the spirits.

With respect to the influence of *jhākri's* drumming, Höfer (1994: 68–69) remarks that:

Informant did not fail to note the self-inducing effect the drumming can have on the drummer himself in that a powerful drumming is likely to enhance the drummer's (feeling of his own) power, or that a "mild" beating may influence the drummer's state of mind correspondingly.

As Bir Bahādur Tamang explained:

The *dhyāgro* is the instrument of the gods. We pound it—tak-tak!, tak-tak!, tak-tak!, tak-tak!—and call the gods and spirits. When the spirits appear their power enters the drum. When we beat the drum, their powers reverberate through our bodies. This gives us insight and strength. Our powers become one. When we grasp our drums and pound it loudly—dum!, dum!, dum!—power reverberates and with this we can overcome demons and evil spirits.

Nepalese shamans do not use hallucinogenic drugs to enter into altered states of consciousness (cf. Riboli 2000: 61). Indeed, most of the practitioners with whom I work do not use any kind of drugs either to attain altered states of consciousness or in connection with their therapies. *Kacur,* a dried wild root of a medicinal plant, possibly *Curcuma zedoaria* (Turner 1931: 67), is mentioned in connection with shamans in western Nepal, who wear a piece of the root on a string around their neck and bite into it when performing as a means of protection against evil spirits. Whether this plant has any psychotropic effects is unknown, besides, the shamans never ingest the *kacur* (Watters 1975: 139, 162).

The exception I encountered was Shukra Bahādur Tamang and his associates who, when possessed by Mahādev, inhale *gājī* (ganja: resinous marijuana) in the fashion of the god himself and his followers. A small quantity of the drug, about the size of a pea, is placed on the dirt floor on top of a burning piece of charcoal. The *jhākri* leans over, inhales some of the smoke in one or two breaths, and immediately resumes his drumming. He does this once or twice during a performance that lasts fifteen hours or more and often ingestion of the drug occurs many hours after the start of the ceremony and when the *jhākri* has already experienced numerous possession events.

Figure 6.1. A devotee of Mahādev inhaling gājā (resinous marijuana) in the fashion of the god himself (Photo by H. Sidky)

Given the limited number of times this is done during a performance and the small quantity of ganja involved, such usage may be viewed as symbolic in nature, or as a means of momentarily augmenting the ASC, and not as a means of inducing ASC (on the effects of marijuana on consciousness, see Hastings 1990). Moreover, as Nicoletti (2004: 44) has pointed out in connection with the use of marijuana by Kulunge Rāi *jhākris*, "the reciting of specific mantras before taking the drug has, always according to the shamans, the aim of 'killing' the gājā, thus stopping it from causing 'inebriation'. . . [which is] deemed aberrant and obfuscatory for the consciousness."

The widely held belief that hallucinogenic drugs—a.k.a. entheogens, i.e., psychoactive substances that induce spiritual experiences (Alper 2003; Nichols and Chemel 2006: 5; Ott 1993; Roberts 2006; Ruck et al. 1979)—play a central role in shamanism in general stems from the publications of American anthropologists working with models based upon societies in Central and South America (cf. Hutton 2001: 100). In those areas, indigenous healers labeled as "shamans" rely on hallucinogens such as Ayahuasca (*Banisteriopsis caapi*), *Psilocybe* mushrooms, and peyote (*Lophophora williamsii*), among others, to achieve altered states of consciousness (cf. Brown 1988; Furst 1976; 1990; Harner 1973; La Barre 1972; Myerhoff 1997; Ripinsky-Naxon 1992; 1993: 131–150; 1998; Schultes 1998; Schultes and Hofmann 1992; Wilbert 1987). Generalization from this material has contributed to the unfounded belief that shamans everywhere and in prehistoric times routinely use hallucinogenic drugs. As Morris (2006: 20) has noted, the use of drugs in shamanism "is by no means essential or widely practiced."

The idea that drugs were indispensable in Siberian shamanism is also somewhat problematic. This notion was forwarded by various European writers who overstressed the role of drugs, such as fly-agaric (*Amanita muscaria*), reasoning that since this drug was used socially then shamans must have used it as well, a position that is not supported by the ethnographic information (Hutton 2001: 100–101: Kehoe 2000: 64–65). Anthropologist Marjorie Balzer (1997: xviii) maintains that she found evidence for the use of *Amanita muscaria* in Ob-Ugrian Khanty shamanism. Ethnologist Vladimir Basilov (1997: 12), however, urges caution when evaluating information regarding the use of drugs by Siberian shamans. One must be equally cautious concerning assertions regarding the widespread use of hallucinogenic drugs in prehistory (Long and Tipping 2001: 53).

The use of alcohol and tobacco is another matter. *Jhākris* use substantial quantities of these substances during their nightlong ceremonies. In the ceremony described in chapter 10, three *jhākris* consumed nearly four liters of distilled alcohol (40%, 80 proof) and smoked two cartons of cigarettes. Remarkably, they did not get drunk, as they often did when drinking during social occasions. Ethnologist Holger Kalweit (2000: 74) suggests that the same mechanism that confers extraordinary powers, such as extreme physical strength or the ability to resist heat, also works to neutralize the inebriating effects of ethanol. Alcohol and tobacco serve to magnify the effects produced by the dynamics of the performance, as was also the case in the performances of Siberian shamans (cf. Balzer 1997: 47; Hutton 2001: 100–101; Shirokogoroff 1935: 364). Along with the consumption of these substances, *jhākris* depend upon continued drumming and chanting to maintain their mental orientation through a night's performance (see chapter 10).

Having described the means by which the *jhākris* access ASC, we may now proceed to a discussion of spirit possession, which is one way Nepalese shamans experience ASC. Spirit possession as an altered state of consciousness takes on different forms. It can be voluntary or involuntary, and may differ in terms of prevailing cultural perceptions of the possessing agencies as good or evil and pathological (Castillo 1994a: 15; 1994b: 142; Krippner 1997: 344; 1994; Sidky 1997: 155–166).

Jones (1976b) distinguishes four categories of spirit possession in Nepal: reincarnate possession, oracular possession, tutelary possession, and peripheral possession. In reincarnate possession, a person embodies the spirit of a known deceased individual from the time of birth (see Bourguignon 1976a: 13; Stevenson 1966: 340). Such a person, for example a reincarnated *lāmā*, is believed to possess the power of exorcism, healing, and divination by virtue of his reincarnation. Reincarnated *lāmās* are full-time religious practitioners affiliated with an institutionalized religious organization, such as a monastery. In this form of spirit embodiment, place or space is designated, but time is not, as the condition is lifelong.

Oracular possession involves the embodiment of a god, goddess, or spirits on specific occasions in designated places, such as a shrine or temple dedicated to the possessing entity. In this type of possession, both time and space are designated. An example of oracular possession is the spirit-human interaction of the *dhāmis* in western Nepal, discussed in chapter 2.

In tutelary possession, a person embodies a spirit at a time of his own choosing, but the space/place in which the possession event will occur varies. This is characteristic of the *jhākri*, who can call spirits at will when he wishes, but where he does this will vary, depending on the circumstances, such as a patient's house, in a clan *pujā* room, outdoors at a cemetery or cremation ground, or at a pilgrimage site. A central feature of this form of possession—one that Jones does not elaborate upon—is that there are no significant discontinuities in memory or recall of the possession event by the *jhākri*.

Peripheral possession, an idea Jones adopted from Lewis (1971: 32), is uncontrolled in that time and space are not designated. It happens spontaneously, when and where it will occur is unpredictable. It could happen only once or several times and may be referred to as "possession illness" (Winkelman 2000: 267). An example of this would be someone who is the victim of witchcraft or sorcery. The *jhākri*'s initiatory possession experiences fall in this category, as was also the case with the initiatory crises of the Tungus and other Siberian shamans (cf. Böckman and Hultkrantz 1978: 25).

Offering a somewhat different typology, Bourguignon (1974) describes three types of altered states of consciousness: trance, an ASC in which communication with spirits occurs, but without spirit possession; possession trance, an ASC involving takeover of behavior and speech by an embodying spirit in which afterward the possessed individual does not recall the event; and possession, which is simply spirit intrusion causing illness (cf. Firth 1967: 296). Bourguignon's categories of "possession trance" and "possession" overlap with Jones's categories of oracular and peripheral possession. In terms of its experiential dimensions, Bourguignon (1976a: 8) describes possession trance as a state involving "alterations or discontinuity in consciousness, awareness, or personality or other aspects of psychological functioning" attributed to the idea that a "person is changed in some way through the presence in him of a spirit entity or power, other than his own personality, soul, or self." Bourguignon and Evascu (1977: 198) characterize such possession events as conditions "in which the altered state is explained due to a takeover (possession) of the body by a spirit entity" (see also Baruš 1996: 158).

Some anthropologists define spirit possession in terms of how members of a culture view the phenomenon. For example, anthropologist Vincent Crapanzano (1977: 7) defines it as "any altered state of consciousness indigenously interpreted in terms of the influence of an alien spirit." However, although possession experiences are indeed culturally mediated, they have psycho-physiological foundations. Psychologist Etzel

Cardeña's (1996: 92) comparative study of hypnosis and shamanism suggests that possession experiences are characterized by a sense of "alteration in body image and a not infrequent experience of weight or pressure on the shoulders or neck, frequently explained as being 'mounted' by a spirit," an equestrian metaphor which is identical to descriptions of possession experiences by Nepalese shamans. Cardeña (1996: 94) attributes these and other similarities between shamanic experience and deep hypnosis "to innate biological/cognitive dispositions."

Cardeña's (1996: 92) study also suggests that subjects who are possessed (i.e., in a possession trance) lose self-awareness and cannot remember what transpires during the event. Le Quellec (2001: 148), who considers spirit possession and "true shamanism" as binary opposites, emphasizes this point, maintaining that the shaman "is capable of narrating his travels contrary to what occurs in the case of the possessed." Le Quellec (2001: 148) tries to emphasize his distinction between shamanism and possession with reference to the "equestrian metaphor" noted above:

> Shamanism and possession are located at the two extremes of a continuum whose poles differ through the inversion of the "equestrian metaphor": at the shamanic pole, the . . . spirits become the shaman's mounts, whereas at the other pole, that of possession, man is the spirit's mount.

Le Quellec's binary characterization does not fit the *jhākri*'s experience. The inability to recall possession events is true of certain ritual specialists such as, for example, Tibetan mediums in Nepal and the medium of the Tibetan state oracle, whose performances I have recorded in Dharamsala, India, but this is not the case with the Nepalese shamans (on the Tibetan state oracle see Peter 1978 and Arnott 1989). *Jhākris*, perhaps apart from their initial encounter with spirits, do not exhibit significant discontinuities in consciousness and personality. In other words, during possession events, the medium's personality is completely displaced by the embodying entity, while the *jhākri*'s personality and memory remain intact even as he is assimilating the identities of numinous agencies and speaks with their voices. This is in accord with ethnologist Philippe Mitrani's (1992: 154) observation that, "Even in those cases where ethnologists speak of the incorporation of the spirits by shamans . . . the spirits neither replace the shaman's will nor act in his place; rather they confer special powers that allow him, when necessary, to become a spirit himself." Thus, the shaman's mastery over spirits extends to mastery over the altered state of consciousness itself (cf. Baumer 2002: 49; Böckman and Hultkrantz 1978: 25: Riboli 2000: 61; Torrance 1994: 138). Perhaps "spirit adhesion" is a better description of what happens to *jhākris* than "spirit possession." The ethnographic data, therefore, are at marked variance with the conventional

Figure 6.2. The inability to recall possession events is true of certain ritual specialists, such as Tibetan mediums in Nepal and the medium of Nechung, the Tibetan state oracle shown here in a state of deity possession (Photo courtesy of Dr. Deborah Akers, Department of Anthropology, Miami University)

understanding of the shaman's interaction with spirits and his altered states of consciousness.

Spirit possession involving "a takeover," although not commonly found among the *jhākris*, does occur among ordinary Nepalese people. During my first field season in eastern Nepal, I observed a particular type of spirit possession associated with Jirel funerary rites involving such a takeover, a description of which is useful for comparative purposes and to highlight general aspects of spirit possession in Nepal.

The Jirels inhabit the Jiri-Sikri valleys, located in the Dolakha District, in eastern Nepal. They number around 3,500 to 4,000 people, the majority of whom inhabit villages located on the slopes of the Jiri and Sikri valleys. Several other ethnic groups live here as well, including Sherpa, Tamang, Sunwar, along with groups belonging to the Brahman and Chetri Hindu castes. The Jirels speak their own distinct language, called Jirel, which is part of the Tibeto-Burman language group. They practice what ethnographer Dor Bahādur Bista (1987: 71) describes as "Lamaistic Buddhism," that is, Tibetan Buddhism. However, they also observe various Hindu rituals, revere Hindu deities, and pray at Hindu shrines, as well as adhering to their own shamanistic beliefs.

Spirit possession plays a significant role in a rite called *Sensing*, which is an important component of Jirel last rites, called *Gewa*, observed forty days after a deceased person's cremation (see Sidky et al. 2002: 120–128). These rites are crucial in ensuring that the soul of the deceased person is placated and undertakes the journey to its final destination, eventually to be reborn. Like many other Nepalese peoples, the Jirels believe that a soul that is not placated, or whose funeral rites are performed improperly (as well as the soul of someone who has died unnaturally), will remain in the village and is transformed into a malignant and dangerous entity that will attack the living. In the past shamans conducted this ceremony, but now *lāmās* officiate over the rites. The Jirels, who claim to have adopted Buddhism only five generations ago (Sidky et al. 2002: 72), also embraced the shaman-*lāmā* division of ritual labor discussed in chapter 3.

The *Sensing* rite is usually conducted outside, in a field or open area, under a woodframe structure covered on three sides. The observances culminate in the summoning of the deceased's spirit who is asked to enter the body of a family member and convey its last wishes. The ceremony is conducted twice, once late at night and a second time around mid- to late afternoon the following day.

The *lāmās* sit in a row on mats placed on the ground. In front of them a long wooden plank serves as a table for their ritual objects, bells, human thighbone trumpets (*thung* in Jirel, *rkaïg-gliïg* in Tibetan), cymbals, vessels containing holy water, incense burners, and offering bowls of millet. *Tormas* representing the gods are placed next to the ranking *lāmā*.

A large double-sided drum is hung from the wooden frame and paint-ings (*thangkas*) depicting representations of Buddha and other religious images are placed behind the *lāmās*. A small wooden tripod, about ten inches high, which is placed on the ground in front of the table, holds a woodblock imprint of the *Sensing* mantras in Tibetan. Members of the deceased's family sit on a mat on the floor facing the *lāmās*. Distant kin-folk and villagers stand in a half circle behind the seated members of the deceased's family.

The ceremony I will briefly describe here began about 2:00 am. Close to fifty villagers of all ages were in attendance. After all the preparations were complete and prayers said, a *lāmā*'s apprentice began pounding the big drum in a slow, steady rhythm, while the *lāmās* rang their bells, blew the thighbone trumpets, and played their cymbals. The *lāmās* began recit-ing the mantras calling the soul of the departed to enter the body of one of the family members present at the ceremony. I was told that male or fe-male relatives may be possessed, although in the eight ceremonies I at-tended, it was always a female.

There was a sense of expectation and eager anticipation on the part of those assembled, as no one knows ahead of time who will be chosen by the spirit. After about twenty minutes, with the drum still pounding in the background, an old woman, the sister of the deceased, became agi-tated and started trembling. The spirit had arrived. This possession event was fairly subdued in comparison to the possession states of the *jhākris*. Instead of displaying the forceful shaking, the Jirel woman appeared slug-gish and on the brink of losing consciousness. Relatives quickly gathered around her, their faces showing signs of considerable anticipation and concern over what might happen next. They held her hands and spoke as if they were talking to the deceased. They asked if he was satisfied or dis-satisfied with the funeral and last rites. The spirit began to speak. One woman burst out in tears when she heard the departed speak for the last time in this life. For the participants this was a very somber event.

The messages conveyed by the spirits summoned during *Sensing* often express family tensions and dynamics, the survivors' feelings regarding the death, and their relationship with the deceased during his or her life-time. These are now aired publicly by the deceased's spirit in front of the entire village. For example, if the family had not taken care of the de-ceased properly in life, it is very likely that his spirit will voice displeas-ure during *Sensing*.

Sometimes the spirit will refuse to speak, despite entreaties from the family. Silence is also a form of communication that expresses social ten-sions among the survivors. When this happens, family members will gather and discuss the reasons for the spirit's refusal to speak. They will then attempt to communicate with it once again the following day.

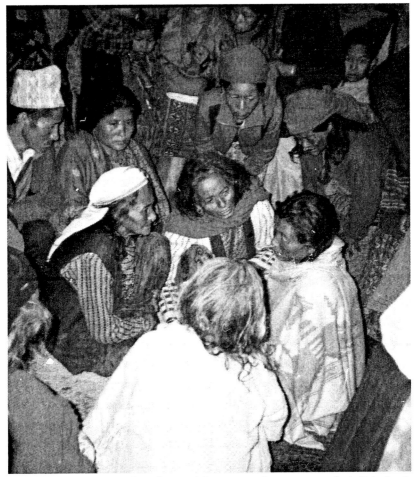

Figure 6.3.   Relatives gathered around the possessed woman attentively listening to the message from the deceased during the *Sensing* ritual (Photo by H. Sidky)

Other messages may convey instructions to grandchildren to work hard in their schoolwork, or for siblings to get along better, and so forth. In the event being described here, when the spirit finally concluded its messages, after about seven minutes, family members offered him (i.e., the possessed woman) water and milk to drink. The possessed woman was now showing signs of great fatigue. Relatives raised her off the ground and the *lāmā* uttered mantras and threw blessed rice at her, ending the possession and concluding the ritual.

In this context, we may view spirit possession as a normative form of communication centered upon issues and concerns of families, descent groups, and village communities. This example from Jirel ethnography illustrates clearly that spirit possession is not an idiosyncratic phenomenon but is linked in culturally patterned ways to a society's larger set of epistemological and ontological premises regarding supernatural beings. These included beliefs in the possibility of ghosts entering the body of living people, life after death, and beliefs about the spirit world and the relationship between that cosmological domain and the human world. There is nothing "intransigently exotic" or "unrecognizable" about what I have described among the Jirels, contra anthropologist Janice Boddy's (1994: 407) bombastic characterization of how anthropologists construe the phenomenon of spirit possession. Nor do I think any anthropologist with experience in actual field research has ever been unaware that other peoples' beliefs in spirits, gods, goddesses, and so on, rest on "epistemic principles" different from those of the outside observers' culture, contrary to Boddy's (1994: 407–414) assertion that "epistemic" difference is something only brought to light by "recent" postmodern, hermeneutic, humanistic "context replete accounts."

According to Höfer (1974a), the form of spirit possession I have described—that is, one that occurs among laity, is induced by a ritual specialist during an all-night ceremony, and involves the spirits of the dead possessing their relatives and speaking through them—is found primarily among Hindu populations of India and Nepal (cf. Höfer and Shrestha 1972). He contrasts this pattern with that found among the Tamang and other non-Hindu, or recently Hinduized, ethnic groups in the Himalayas, such as Gurung, Limbu, Rai, and others. Spirit possession among the Jirel clearly does not fit the pattern Höfer describes. Nor does it fit neatly into Jones's typology or anthropologist Peter Claus's (1979: 29) characterization of spirit possession in South Asia as either mediumistic or unsolicited and intrusive.

The possession event that occurs in the context of the Jirel *Sensing* ceremony represents a type of nonspontaneous spirit manifestation in which the time and place are designated by the *lāmās*, rather than through the volition of the spirits or the individual embodying those spirits. It sharply contrasts with the ability of shamans to induce such states voluntarily.

It is to this type of voluntarily induced states of possession among the *jhākris* that we shall turn next. A question that occupied researchers writing during the twentieth century was whether the shaman's "trance state" (i.e., ASC) was genuine or contrived. Some researchers maintained that the trances they observed were authentic, while others asserted the trances were faked and they characterized shamans as actors who were role-playing (Nadel 1965; Shirokogoroff 1935: 362). Part of the difficulty is that fieldworkers must rely on what they see and what practitioners report in order to make a determination as to whether or not a "trance state" has been achieved. In the context of Nepal, we might ask: what are the outward manifestations of ASC? Shaking? Dancing? Reciting texts? What do introspective reports by *jhākris* themselves reveal?

When the divine powers and spirits enter my body, I can't feel pain. I have power to use to fight witches and harmful spirits (Jhākri Gau Bahādur Gurung).

When the gods and spirits come, I feel pain in my heart, then I tremble a little, and then my whole body shakes. It is like a dream, I can see what is good and what is bad. The spirits cling to my back and some sit on my shoulders and I can feel their weight. Some also go inside, they enter my body and our minds are joined. (Jhākri Nir Bahādur Tamang)

My heart begins to beat faster like it is soaring. I can hear what the people [patients, spectators] are saying and understand their questions, but when I speak, the voice is that of the spirits and gods (*deutā baknu*) (Jhākri Dul Temba Sherpa).

I am able to understand things. I see things others cannot. My skin tingles; it feels like something on my head and back. Sometimes it is as if small insects are crawling over my body. My senses change . . . they feel like they are resonating, just like the skin of the *jhākri* drum when it is heated becomes taut and resonates when you tap it with the tip of the drumstick. I sometimes feel this way even when I am not performing. When spirits come this is how it feels. I get a sensation inside by stomach. (Jhākri Rabindra Rāi)

These statements suggest that perhaps through intense concentration the *jhākri* acquires a heightened awareness, a powerful sense of confidence, the ability to intuit, and clarity of vision that allows him to synthesize information in novel ways. Culture historian Morris Berman (2000: 30) recommends the use of the term "heightened awareness" rather than altered states of consciousness to describe the shaman's state of mind. The *jhākri* is after all "an interpreter of the world," as Macdonald put it long ago, for which he needs focus, clarity of vision, and creative engagement.

In reference to his Nepalese ethnographic findings, Hitchcock (1976: 168), emphasizing the difficulties of rendering judgments on the authenticity of a shaman's trance or lack thereof on the basis of field observations, made an honest and insightful comment: "I simply don't know 'what is going on' in their minds." Hamayon (1998: 177), writing 22 years later, raises the same issue with respect to the shaman's inner psychic states, arguing that shamans are merely acting out culturally defined roles, rather than undergoing psychic alterations. The "shaman," in other words, is a "showman" (Bahn 2001: 55). In agreement with this point of view, a number of writers maintain that shamanism has nothing to do with "trance" (Bahn 2001: 55; Francfort 2001a: 31; Le Quellec 2001: 150). Hamayon adds that it is impossible to know the shaman's inner psychic state and any such determinations are merely the observer's subjective judgments. Hamayon (1993b; 1998: 181–185) suggests that focusing on the shaman's trance impedes analysis and that shamanism is only meaningfully explained sociologically in terms of the shaman's behavior.

Part of the problem, as Peters and Price-Williams (1980: 400) have observed, has been the lack of consensus as to what constitutes an "authentic" ASC (see Shaara and Strathern 1992), coupled with a misunderstanding of the interactive nature of the shaman's performances, which involve communicative interaction not only with supernatural beings, but also with ritual participants, patients, and spectators (cf. Mastromattei 1989: 227). A review of my video footage of forty-seven all-night *jhākri* healing ceremonies taken between June 1999 and December 2006 confirms this.

The *jhākri's* altered states of consciousness vary considerably in intensity and duration at various points throughout any given performance. At times, the *jhākri* appears entirely absorbed in dealing with the spirits summoned, oblivious to everything around him, sweating profusely and shaking/ bouncing, as he struggles to bring the summoned invisible agencies under control. Alternatively, he may be transfixed and totally immobile for a period of time, as spirits appear to momentarily overwhelm him, or while he projects his soul into the supernatural world (see chapter 10). At times, he may beat himself with his drumstick, expressing the rage of the spirits because of some infraction on the *jhākri's* part. At other times, he fully engages with his surroundings, reciting mantras, singing songs, giving instructions to assistants, or reprimanding spectators for not being attentive in the presence of the gods and spirits. Running commentaries through long segments of the performance are common. At some stage, the *jhākri* may even take part in a three-way dialogue, talking to himself, the spirits, and the spectators.

The spectators, in turn, quiz the *jhākri* or ask for more information concerning his revelations. Abrupt stoppages occur periodically, when the *jhākri* takes a break to smoke a cigarette or have a swig of alcohol. During the breaks, he may adjust his costume or headdress, reposition items on the altar, ask a helper for incense or live coals, and talk to the people in the room. He will then pick up his drum and resume his recitation and drumming with great intensity and drama. Thus, during any given performance, the Nepalese shaman seems to enter, exit, and reenter altered states of consciousness, as prevailing circumstances dictate. However, as noted above, the *jhākri's* personality and memory remain intact even when he has embodied numinous agencies and speaks with their voices.

With respect to the contention that shamans are merely role-playing, Peters and Price-Williams (1980: 401) have observed that shamans during altered states of consciousness are able to undertake tasks that are outside the ordinary range of voluntary behavior. For example, the ability to lick red-hot iron, or eat burning wicks. In his rejoinder to Hamayon's (1993b: 14–15) assertion regarding shaman's ritual role-play, Hultkrantz (1998c: 189) emphasizes "physiological effects" as the indicator of altered states of consciousness. Lewis (2003: 23–24) has also taken issue with Hamayon's position, pointing out that "trance" represents "culturally conventionalized behavior recognized cross-culturally and readily observable to the anthropologist." In terms of my own field experiences, I have documented numerous instances of *jhākris* displaying extraordinary feats, such as putting their hands in cauldrons of boiling water, eating burning wicks, and dancing on hot coals with bare feet, exploits the *jhākris* themselves maintain they could not accomplish without embodying supernatural beings, that is, without being in ASC.

Another problem that preoccupied researchers during much of the twentieth century was the question of the psychological health of shamans and the nature of the "shamanic illness" (Atkinson 1992: 309; Peters and

Figure 6.4. A *jhākri* dancing on hot coals with bare feet, an exploit *jhākris* themselves maintain they could hot accomplish without being in an altered state of consciousness (Photo by H. Sidky)

Figure 6.5. A *jhākri* eating burning wicks as a demonstration of his power (Photo by H. Sidky)

Price-Williams 1980; Znamenski 2004: xxxvi–xxxviii; for an overview see Mitrani 1992). The debate was between those who maintained that shamanism was the consequence of a psychopathology, such as schizophrenia, psychotic disorder (Bogoras 1909; deMause 2002: 250–251; Devereux 1961; Howells 1962: 137; Kakar 1982; Kroeber 1940; LaBarre 1970: 319; Silverman 1967), or some other mental illness, such as *pibloktoq*, or "arctic hysteria" (Czaplicka 1914: 307–325), and those who maintained that shamans were individuals who may have been mentally ill at some point, but have been cured through the therapeutic characteristic of the shaman's initiation process (Acherknecht 1943: 46; Eliade 1964: 27; Grim 1983: 172–176; Halifax 1982: 5; Wallace 1966: 145–152; Walsh 1997: 112). Eliade was inspired into writing his tome on shamanism after reviewing a book that attributed the bizarre behavior of shamans to "arctic hysteria" (Kehoe 2000: 38).

More recently, the pathologized view of shamanism has given way to the perspective that the psychological states associated with shamanism are within the range of human norms (Atkinson 1992: 309; Krippner 2002; Van Ommeren et al. 2004). Winkelman (2000: 7) has pointed out that "shamanism and associated ASC constitute a normal alteration of the human consciousness, providing an integration of cognitive, emotional, and behavioral capacities through psychophysiological manipulations of the human brain." As anthropologist Stewart Guthrie (2004: 97), has observed regarding this shift, the shaman's image as a "neurotic and socially marginal charlatan who uses sleight of hand and ventriloquism to fool clients" has been rehabilitated to one depicting him as "a talented psychotherapist and dramaturge" doing service for the public good.

This change in perspective is based upon research that has shown, for example, that shamanism and schizophrenia constitute phenomenologically dissimilar experiences in terms of volition, thought contents, nature of perceptions, affect, sense of self, and relation to the external world (Noll 1983: 452–455; Mitrani 1992: 160–162; Walsh 2001: 34). For example, in considering the *jhākris* mentioned in chapter 4, it could be argued that their initiatory experiences, which involved perceptions of dying and seeing and hearing beings that are invisible and inaudible to others, are similar to those of a schizophrenic. However, as we have seen, the *jhākri* emerges from his experience reintegrated with a new positive social identity and sense of well-being and control (cf. Walsh 1993: 743; 1995: 42). Moreover, he emerges empowered with the ability to heal others. Indeed, Nepalese shamans with whom I worked are highly intelligent individuals who possess profound mystical knowledge and are masters of a large corpus of oral narratives. I found nothing pathological or abnormal about them. Another line of evidence in this connection comes from a psychiatric study of 42 Bhutanese shamans in Nepal by a team of researchers. Their conclusion was that "this first-ever, community-based, psychiatric epidemiological survey among shamans indicated no evidence that shamanism is an expression of psychopathology" (Van Ommeren et al. 2004).

Unlike the shaman, the schizophrenic remains disorganized and fragmented (Baruŝs 2003: 138). In addition, in contrast to the dysfunctional conditions of the schizophrenic, the shaman willfully enters into controlled ASC, he can distinguish between the ordinary and non-ordinary realities, engage in deliberate communication with others while in ASC, and the contents of his experiences are meaningful in terms of the cosmology of his society (cf. Walsh 1995: 42; Winkelman 2000: 79).

The changing view of shamans was facilitated by the growing interest in human consciousness, inspired partly by experimentation with psychedelic or hallucinogenic drugs during the 1960s (Atkinson 1992: 310; Bahn 2001: 55). Fieldworkers exposed to powerful hallucinogenic drugs used by indigenous magicoreligious practitioners in South America, for example, were convinced that they had gained direct access to the shaman's once exclusive and privileged universe (see Harner 1972; 1973; 1980; Furst 1990; Schultes and Hofmann 1992). The shaman's "non-ordinary reality" thus became a topic of considerable research interest for several years and shamanism itself was identified as a type of altered state of consciousness. In subsequent construals, hallucinogenic and psychotropic drug-use and shamanism became almost synonymous (e.g., Ripinsky-Naxon 1992; 1998), moving the topic far from the Siberian model or anything Eliade (1964: 401) had in mind. This vision of shamans as drug-tripping spiritual specialists operating in a "psychotropic universe" is at odds with ethnographic evidence from places such as Nepal.

Shamanism became a topic of particular interest to anthropologists interested in human consciousness. The anthropology of human consciousness entails cross-cultural investigations of shamanistic states of consciousness, the psychology of healing, and trance and meditation (Castillo 2004: 101). This field of study received a boost with the development of sophisticated neuro-imaging technologies that in laboratory settings can identify neurophysiological processes associated with particular states of consciousness (see d'Aquili and Newberg 1999; McNamara 2006). The approach to shamanism as an ASC represents a major departure from perspectives that view it primarily in terms of historical and sociocultural factors. This bypasses the long-standing quandary of how to find the defining assemblage of common attributes and techniques that could transcend particular cultural contexts (Hutton 2001: 51) by rooting shamanism in the universal neurophysiological and psychobiological functions of the human brain. This approach can certainly shed much light on the spirit possession states of shamans in Nepal and elsewhere. It also renders superfluous tedious diatribes regarding the place of "ecstasy" in shamanism (e.g., Hultkrantz 1998a, 1998b, 2001: 3–4; Hamayon 1998; 1993b).

Anthropologists who define their task as the "interpretation of culture" and the production of particularistic narrative ethnographies have disparagingly dismissed the neurophysiological approach as a deplorable attempt to "medicalize" and squeeze other peoples' experiences and beliefs into Western scientistic pigeonholes. These writers raise objections to the treatment of phenomenon such as spirit possession as an independent category of behavior, contending that altered states of consciousness are meaningful only because of their place in culturally constituted belief systems (Boddy 1994: 409). Atkinson (1992: 311), who espouses the "shamanisms" approach, points out along the same lines: "Understanding the neurophysiology of trance is valuable, but it does not explain the associated structures of ritual, knowledge, and society that have been the focus of so much research over the past decade." There is, of course, nothing remarkably original in these observations, originality not being a forte of these writers. Indeed, as Bourguignon (1973: 12) put it two decades earlier: "It must be stressed that although the capacity to experience ASC is a psychobiological capacity of the [human] species, and thus universal, its utilization, institutionalization, and patterning are, indeed, features of culture, and thus variable."

Bourguignon's astute observation was intended to stress the importance of a balanced perspective in the study of ASC. This is not the case with present-day writers who, in morally pretentious diatribes, categorically reject efforts at understanding the universal psychobiological dimensions of ASC and spirit possession. For example, Boddy (1994: 407), another subscriber of postmodern epistemological relativism (see chapter 1), declares that "recent studies . . . suggest that spirit possession rests on epistemic premises quite different from the infinitely differentiating, rationalizing, and reifying thrust of global materialism and its attendant scholarly traditions." For those who are schooled in these academic traditions, she adds, echoing Foucault (1973: 44–52), "spirit possession" appears exotic and incomprehensible, which accounts for their fixation to develop "objective frameworks for analysis" that "transcend folk epistemologies" so that it may be "understood" and "tamed" (Boddy 1994: 407). Boddy (1994: 410, 414) adds that such "reductive," "naturalizing," "rationalizing" approaches are misleading and "culturally solipsistic" because spirit possession phenomena "as imaginative productions evade all rational containment." Over these perspectives, Boddy (1994: 408–412) extols the virtues of "context replete accounts" that look at spirit possession "in its own terms in the societies where it is found."

This perspective has been reiterated more recently by Smith (2006: 37–53), who stresses the importance of context, calls for the prioritization of the emic, or insider's perspective (indigenous voices and interpretations), over that of the observer, and repudiates rational scientific categories and biomedical models, which he labels as ethnocentric and culturally insensitive. In rejecting scientific construals of spirit possession as intellectually and culturally biased, ethnocentric, and inappropriate, Smith (2006: 46–49, 50, 66) verges on admitting the ontological reality of paranormal beings and deity and spirit intrusion as things existing independently of the mind. It has become fashionable in some academic circles to proclaim the demise of objective scientific knowledge (with irrationalist philosophers such as Thomas Kuhn or scientifically illiterate writers like Foucault cited ad nauseam), extol the virtues of subjective approaches, and make disparaging remarks regarding "biomedical models" (e.g., Laughlin et al. 1992: 4–5, 155; for a critique see Sidky 2003a; 2006). However, although such perspectives may address some deep postmodern sensibilities and sensitivities on the part of the authors advocating them, they really amount to supernaturalism and the unwarranted mystification of the phenomenon under consideration. Mystification, as I have defined it elsewhere (Sidky 2004: 433), refers to ideological and discursive practices that obscure the concrete material causal relationships underlying a particular sociocultural or biopsychological phenomenon by attributing it to unfathomable, mysterious, and baffling forces and processes beyond human comprehension.

The writers mentioned above advocate ethnographic particularism or the idiographic approach, founded upon an epistemological relativist stance, a vacuous and failed early-twentieth-century theoretical perspective in American anthropology, as noted in chapter 1, which in its extreme forms is the ultimate expression of cultural solipsism, obfuscation, and mystification (Sidky 2006). Moreover, the inevitable outcome of hermeneutic research projects geared toward the close attention to words and tropes and cultural context is the banal conclusion that the explanation for the phenomenon under question is: "it's part of their culture." This perspective is inimical to the central task of the anthropological enterprise, which is to advance our understanding of humans, human behavior, and the operation of sociocultural systems.

The writers discussed above posit that all elements of anomalistic experiences, such as spirit possession, are the products of "imaginary subjective experiences shaped by tradition [i.e., culture]" (Hufford 1982: 14). This view is at odds with the evidence that suggests that such experiences have neurophysiological and neuropsychological bases. There are anomalistic experiences that occur with high frequency cross-culturally, for example, sleep paralysis and near-death experiences, that not only have universal features and are physiologically based, but they also shape cultural beliefs, and those beliefs are maintained in the face of mainstream cultural opposition (McClenon 2001: 63). Such physiologically based anomalous experiences that shape beliefs suggest that something more than "imaginative productions" is operative.

The epistemological relativist perspective is also at variance with the findings in evolutionary psychology regarding universal cognitive mechanisms, such as agency-detecting cognitive modules, that underlie cross-culturally recurrent beliefs in supernatural beings, such as spirits, demons, ghosts, deities, and other paranormal entities (see Atran 2002: 77, 84, 87, 165–169).

The neurophysiological approach is promising because it offers the possibility of determining the physiological bases of particular experiences, including the kinds of cognitive changes that occur in the patterns of neural activity and the brain's representational systems when the shaman is in an altered state of consciousness (i.e., possessed by spirits). This is obviously of considerable importance in helping us more fully comprehend the shamanic experience. Neurophysiological and psychobiological approaches can also potentially generate questions that could fruitfully inform ethnographic field research.

However, simply because this approach is potentially valuable in the study of shamanism does not mean that those writing from this perspective always attend to the basic requirement of scientific research. A good example is Winkelman (1997; 2000; 2002; 2006), whose laudable efforts to solve definitional problems through an empirical cross-cultural analysis of shamanism and to provide generalizations about the shaman's ASC are undermined by his uncritical adoption of Eliade's construal of shamanism as an ecstatic technique among ancient hunter-gatherers characterized by soul journeying that is not supported by historical or ethnographic evidence. Another problem is that, like Eliade, who was no fieldworker, Winkelman's familiarity with shamans is primarily secondhand. According to Winkelman, the universality of altered states of consciousness in human populations, or the drive to experience alternative phases of consciousness (see Bourguignon 1968; Laughlin et al. 1992: 227; Winkelman 1992), supports the hypothesis that this phenomenon is based upon underlying biological structures (Laughlin et al. 1992). ASC is universal, Winkelman (1997: 404) conjectures, because it has adaptive value:

> altering consciousness provides a variety of adaptive advantages through development of a more objective perception of the external world. Rather than being bound up in a habitualized subjectivity, altering consciousness is viewed as a means of recognizing the illusory and constructed nature of ordinary perception. This provides the basis for greater awareness. (Winkelman 2000: 116)

Winkelman (2000: 118) attempts to elucidate the nature of the biological structures underlying ASC by positing the existence of "multiple modes of consciousness," such as waking consciousness, deep sleep, REM sleep (rapid eye movement, dreaming), and a hypothesized "transpersonal consciousness." "Transpersonal consciousness" (a.k.a. mystical or transcendental consciousness), which Winkelman (2000: 101) associates with shamanism, is different from the other modes of consciousness because it entails integrative brain processes.

A brief discussion of how the brain is organized is necessary to clarify what Winkelman means by "integrative brain processes." Within the human brain, consciousness is fragmented or modulated, that is, it operates within separate brain modules. This modularity stems from the brain's multiple hierarchically organized functional systems, the triune (reptilian, paleomammalian, and neomammalian structures) and bilateral hemispheric organization (Beyerstein 1996a: 8; MacLean 1990; 1973; Mithen 1996; Pinker 1997; Winkelman 2006: 154–156). Modularity of brain function means that cognitive faculties are geared toward specific and exclusive or noninterchangeable operations, such as discriminating between living and nonliving things, comprehending human behavior, or being aware of other people's intentions (Guthrie 2004: 98). Shamanistic techniques for inducing ASC, such as drumming and chanting, override the modularity of human brain functions by synchronizing it through posited "integrative brain processes" (Winkelman 2000: 7). The "integrative mode of consciousness" unifies ordinarily discrete brain functions allowing cross-modal operations. This facilitates information processing by the brain in a way that is different from waking and the other modes of consciousness (Winkelman 2000: 7).

The "integrative mode of consciousness" allows the transmission of unconscious processes of limbic functions to the cortex, where they become conscious processes and are incorporated into other cortical processes, enabling cross-modular operations, such as comparing patterns and connecting experiences from different innate brain modules, for example, sound with color, or spatial patterns with temporal ones (Guthrie 2004: 97). This was the basis for the distinctive human cognitive capacity for metaphor, mimesis, and symbolism (Guthrie 2004: 97). Winkelman (2000: 45), who seems to have been influenced by the view of metaphor by postmodernist cultural anthropologists (e.g., Fernandez 1991), considers metaphor, mimesis, and symbolism central to how humans comprehend the world and asserts that these capacities, although essential to language, are prelinguistic facilities that developed earlier and independently of language (cf. Guthrie 2004: 97). The capacity for metaphor, mimesis, and symbolism were central elements in archaic shamanism.

Shamanism, according to Winkelman, therefore played a decisive role in the evolution of human cognition and the rapid rise of culture in modern *Homo sapiens* by overcoming the highly modular minds of premodern *Homo sapiens* (Winkelman 2000: 102). The modern human mind with all its intricacies, subtleties, and flexibility is still to a certain extent modular and hence shamanism, which can overcome this modularity, is still highly relevant (Guthrie 2004: 98). Thus, as Winkelman (2000: xiii) puts it:

> [Shamanism] represents adaptive potentials, an enhanced operation of consciousness derived from integrative brain functioning. Shamanism was the first human institution that systematized this integration, and its potentials and processes still have important implications for humans.

Integrative brain functioning, Winkelman (2000: xiii) adds, was the foundation for the development of "synthetic symbolic awareness" in early modern *Homo sapiens* and was the basis for the development of "mythological systems representing self, mind, other, and consciousness." For Winkelman, therefore, integrative consciousness contributed to the sense of "the other" that underlies the idea of animism and the experiences of guardian spirits, soul journeying, gods, and demons, "which constitute forms of self-objectification and role taking that expand human sociocognitive and intrapsychic dynamics" (Winkelman 2000: xiv).

> The integrative potentials of shamanism help explain the rapid rise of culture in modern Homo sapiens sapiens and the origin of shamanistic and religious features—animism, animatism, and totemism—from the cross-modal analogic and psychophysiological integration processes from different innate modules. (Winkelman 2000: 102)

In this view, ultimately integrative consciousness underlies the origin of religion (cf. Castillo 2004: 102). Shamanism therefore represents a "neurotheology" or a biological basis for spirituality and religiosity.

Shamanistic healing works because altered states of consciousness "enhance integration of information by eliciting cognitive capacities based in presentational symbolism, metaphor, analogy, and mimesis . . . representing preconscious and prelinguistic structures of the brain" (Winkelman 2002: 1874). In other words, the shaman in an altered state of consciousness is able to access levels of primary meaning at the "nonverbal and unconscious levels of the organism" (Winkelman 2000: 94). These primary meanings are "individual psychodynamics" expressed through the symbolism of the mythic world and conceptual framework of spirits (Winkelman 2000: 94). The shaman's manipulation of these symbols induces "a restructuring of self at levels below the conceptual and operational thought" and is a primordial level of communication (Winkelman 2000: 94, 102). Winkelman's treatise is almost entirely about the shaman's inner state and its potentials, and so on. Nowhere does he explicitly explain how that inner psychic state produces transformative changes in patients. Winkelman seems to have confused the experiences of the healer and those of the patient, a common mistake made by some investigators of systems of symbolic healing, as anthropologist James Dow (1986: 57) pointed out years ago.

While Winkelman's account may sound reasonable enough, a plausible narrative, there are two major flaws in his argument. First, he does not provide any evidence, other than Eliade's conjectures, that shamanism is indeed a Paleolithic phenomenon and that there were archaic shamans who were exploring the frontiers of human consciousness. The antiquity of shamanism is accepted as a given, simply because it has been iterated numerous times in the literature. Second, Winkelman's hypothetical "integrative mode of consciousness" has little empirical justification and his speculations are at odds with the latest neuroimaging studies that suggest dissociation as the mechanism for ASC (Castillo 2004: 101). Winkelman's work is also at variance with recent brain biology and chemistry studies (Krippner and Combs 2002: 81). What Winkelman fails to supply is compelling evidence that ancient humans practiced shamanism, as Eliade envisioned it, and that the ASC these hypothetical archaic shamans attained produced integrative modes of consciousness.

Another point to consider is that accessing ASC does not automatically lead to "adaptive" superior insights or "greater awareness." As Tart (1999) has cogently pointed out:

ASCs, like ordinary consciousness, are mixtures of pluses and minuses, insights and delusions, genuine creativity and misleading imagination, so the observations and insights from ASCs need to be subjected to empirical test, just as those of ordinary consciousness do. Kekule's dream ASC of a snake biting its tail, to use one well-known example, led him to discover the structure of benzene and so advanced chemistry considerably, but other ASC revelations have led people to begin holy wars and kill those who disagreed with their visions.

There is considerable evidence that ASCs do not involve integration, but occur when the ordinary meta-awareness that gives us our sense of personal identity and agency, and which operates atop the brain's cognitive hierarchy, is temporarily overtaken as a result of a dissociation, as brain imaging studies of hallucinatory experiences suggest (Beyerstein 1996a; Brugger 2001: 195; Castillo 2004: 102). Anomalous perceptions and subjective "psychic" experiences of the type that launches individuals along the *jhākri* path, experiences associated with what McClenon (1995: 113) calls "shamanic biography," correlate highly with dissociation experiences (Ganaway 1989; Joseph 2003b: 531–535; Putnam 1989; Richards 1991; Ross and Joshi 1992). The same is true of spirit possession, even though some researchers give it paranormal interpretations. For example, psychologist Imants Barušs (2003: 151) queries whether the cause of dissociative states may in fact be spirits or demons:

> Are the demons and dead relatives alter personalities or really demons and dead relatives? Is the mind open? Perhaps severe childhood trauma functions as an initiatic crisis, breaking down the boundaries of the psyche so that the intrusion of spirits becomes possible.

There is, of course, a more straightforward and mundane answer. Given the indisputable fact that "every paranormal belief in the world, whether labeled religious, magical, spiritual, metaphysical, occult, or parapsychological, is either nonfalsifiable or has been falsified" (Lett 1997b: 111), we are compelled to adopt the more mundane answer. States of spirit possession are explicable in terms of the compartmentalization of normal integrated mental processes, or dissociation, when parallel brain modules disengage from each other or from ordinary meta-awareness and operate independently, projecting thoughts onto awareness (Beyerstein 1996b: 544–552; Brugger 2001: 201–202; Oakley and Eames 1985). Thus, as psychologist Barry Beyerstein (1996b: 552) explains:

> what seems, introspectively, to be a unitary self is in reality a multiplicity of semi-autonomous subunits. Under various psychological and neurological conditions, these modules lose their normal cohesiveness and begin to act in an independent, even contradictory, fashion. At such times, behaviors regulated by unattended modules of the brain may begin to play out, minus the

normal sense of volition and self-direction, and may feel as though they are being dictated by powerful unseen external forces.

During dissociation, some aspect of experience is taken over by one of the parallel brain modules instead of self-aware consciousness (see Beyerstein 1996b: 549; Cardeña 1994; Farthing 1992: 126–151; Lynn and Rhue 1994). This results in "divided consciousness" or "separate streams of consciousness," generating perceptions that the resulting behavior is controlled by something or someone else, such as a possessing supernatural being (Castillo 1994b: 144; Kirmayer 1994). Thoughts and ideas generated also appear to come from some other entity (see Farthing 1992: 126–151), such as mantras attributed to spiritual gurus that enter the *jhākri's* mind, or the auditory and visual hallucinations during his initiatic possession states. If prolonged or repeated, as Castillo (1994a; 1994b: 144) has pointed out, this can result in the formation of separate "conscious entities with their own sense of identity, behavior, memories, and desires."

In the right cultural context, dissociation (splitting of consciousness) can be interpreted as involuntary spirit possession caused by an external entity, such as a ghost, demon, ancestral or tutelary spirit, god, or goddess, who has taken command of the helpless individual's body and volition (Beyerstein 1996b: 549), as in the case of Nepal. As medical and psychiatric anthropologist Richard Castillo (1994a: 15) has observed:

Various types of psychiatric phenomena such as hallucinations, delusions, psychogenic amnesia, blindness, seizures, anesthesia, paralysis, heightened affects, are possible in dissociative experience. However, these phenomena may or may not be considered mental illness depending on what is considered appropriate subjective experience and behavior in the prevailing culture.

The process of undergoing training as a *jhākri* appears to be a cultural mechanism for constructively dealing with dissociative states and providing them with an institutionalized framework for expression. As Laughlin et al. (1992: 270) have observed in this regard, shamans "live in times and in cultures that have an understanding of and a container for such experiences." As psychiatrist C. Jesse Groesbeck (1997: 33) has pointed out:

One of the most striking personality criteria of the shaman is his ability to dissociate. At the core of the shamanic experience is the dissociative quality that leads him into altered states of consciousness.

Dissociative states that underlie states of spirit possession can be triggered by various mechanisms that cause temporary compartmentalization of integrated mental processes. These include the manipulation of sensory inputs involving prolonged rhythmic auditory and motor activities, such as drumming and dancing, intense emotional states or psychological trauma, and social conditioning (Beyerstein 1988: 255; Castillo 1994a, 1994b; Neher 1990; Sargant 1957; 1973; Zusne and Jones 1989). These findings contradict Winkelman's construal of shamanic states of consciousness.

Winkelman's study is remarkable in that it restates Eliade's flawed suppositions about the antiquity of shamanism, archaic techniques of ecstasy, and the primacy of soul journey shamanism in the scientific jargon of cognitive neuroscience and transpersonal psychology. Winkelman (2002: 1873) provides a psycho-neuro-physiological rationale for Eliade's assertion that shamanism constitutes humanity's first "theological and spiritual system." The technical language and superfluity of neologisms make Winkelman's work appears impressive for those who are unable to decipher the highly technical passages, just as Eliade's piling of masses of bibliographic citations gave his tome an aura of immense erudition and scholarship. The relevance of shamanism to present-day life is emphasized and the shaman's altered state of consciousness is glamorized as "transpersonal consciousness," a milestone in the evolution of human cognition, a mode of consciousness with extraordinary potentials, Eliade's hierophany. All of this, of course, is pure speculation.

Winkelman's work in many ways reflects the romanticized vision of shamans and shamanism that characterizes the neoshamanism/core shamanism spiritual movements, whose adherents are in the pursuit of a timeless human religiosity, self-healing, and yearning to return to the eternal community of shamans. As I pointed out earlier, this literature is characterized by the assumption that shamanism entails something genuinely paranormal, miraculous, and extraordinary. No evidence that this is the case, other than anecdotal accounts and sheer speculation, has been provided anywhere.

For Winkelman, shamanism represents an ancient and timeless religiosity that is a reflection of the central place of religion in human life. He even takes the current popularity and adoption of shamanism in the West, fueled by a multimillion-dollar industry selling "shamanic journeys" (see Kehoe 2000: 81–89) cashing in on the disenchantment characteristic of late-twentieth and early-twenty-first century capitalist consumer societies, as evidence to support his argument that shamanism is an innate aspect of being human and proof that religious behavior is not ephemeral (Winkelman 2002: 1873; 2003: 398–397). Such a perspective does violence to ethnographic reality and caricaturizes the beliefs and practices of indigenous people. A relevant observation made by Hamayon (2001: 1) with respect to the influence of popular views of shamanism upon scholars is that "the scientific relevance of [their] works becomes thereby highly questionable insofar as basic epistemological principles are not respected."

7

The *Jhākri*'s Cosmos: The Nature of the Spirit World

In Nepal, shamanism constitutes a salient and collectively meaningful aspect of people's religious lives (Hitchcock 1976b: xiii). The *jhākri*'s cosmological beliefs are eclectic in nature having incorporated elements both from Hinduism and from Buddhism, yet they constitute a distinct and dynamic conceptual system. The eclectic and dynamic nature of Nepalese shamanism contributes to its continued relevance.

Jhākris do not possess a codified theology or books and treatises in which their beliefs might be articulated. The stories of the *lāmā-bombo* contest, discussed in chapter 3, specifically highlight the fact that the *jhākri* practices are based upon an oral rather than textual tradition. It is from what the *jhākri* says and does, from his oral narratives and his performances, that one is able to gain an understanding of the belief system that underlies his practice. We may begin with the following excerpts from Jhākri Dawa Sherpa's recitals about the creation of the universe:

> Omnipresent and eternal in nature, Mahādeu gave form to the formless and fashioned the heavens, earth, and the realms of the underworld. He then created all manner of beings and set them loose in the world. First, he made rākṣasas, voracious, unstoppable demons. Then he fashioned the race of man and all other creatures to populate the world. But when the Great God put breath into man and other creatures, the rākṣasas swarmed upon them from all sides and consumed them. There was chaos, there was disorder. Alarmed at the turn of events, Mahādeu created witches. He taught them incantations and told them to restrain the demons, but the demons were relentless, they were strong. All was in ruins. There was chaos and disorder. The more Mahādeu fashioned, the more the demons devoured. Outraged, Mahādeu

took his trident and drum and subdued the demons. Order was restored and humans began to flourish. Finally, Mahādeu created *jhākri*s to heal people. He equipped them with ritual implements, taught them *tantra-mantra* to heal people, and sent them to the four corners of the world, East, West, South, and North. This is how shamanism was established on earth.

To carry out their supernatural mandate to aid people against harmful forces, *jhākri*s are compelled to navigate the heavens, earth, and the realms of the underworld. This is a multitiered universe, which is analogous to the Siberian shaman's cosmos, consisting of an upper, middle, and lower worlds, with each level further subdivided into additional planes that extend spatially in four cardinal directions. These worlds and their sacred geographies may be seen as metaphors for the different realities or modalities of consciousness in which the shaman operates. This tripartite cosmogram, as Eliade (1964: 265) put it, serves as "the shaman's mystical itinerary."

The *jhākri*'s journeys and explorations are in the inner realms of human consciousness, the realm of Jungian archetypes, aspects of which are manifested symbolically in cognitive categories, such as sacred geographies or personifications of supernatural beings (cf. Gorf 1998: 19).

The *jhākri*'s universe is an animistic or "ensouled" (Gorf 1998: 17) one teeming with powerful spiritual entities, each with its own part in the overall scheme of things, some benevolent, some malevolent, and others indifferent, but all potentially dangerous. Many events that take place in the lives of human beings—be they auspicious or inauspicious—are attributed to the influence of the spirits that permeate and populate the *jhākri*'s cosmos. All beings and forces in this universe, while having different ontologies, are meaningfully interconnected with each other, including humans, whose relation with the environment and other entities is fluid and transactional (cf. Castillo 1994: 156). The sense of interconnectivity that is central to the *jhākri*'s vision of reality may be described as apophenia.

The upper level of the *jhākri*'s multitiered universe is the realm of Bhagavān and other major deities who, for the most part, are distant from human affairs. The middle world is the domain of humans, the *Bhume deutā* (gods of the land and water), elemental and earthbound divinities, and various classes of dangerous spirits. The lower world is the abode of primordial serpent gods and spirits of the underworld. The composition of the *jhākri*'s cosmology is similar to the "structure of the shaman's universe" specifically highlighted by Eliade (1964: 259–287).

Although the different levels of the *jhākri*'s cosmogram are distinct, there is no dichotomization between the realms of the sacred and profane in this model. A cosmic axis serves as a passageway between the worlds (Torrance 1994: 154). In Indian and Buddhist cosmology, Mount Meru (Semeru) represents this axis or center around which all of creation revolves (see Eliade 1964: 266–269). The cosmic mountain extends beyond the physical world, constitutes a link between the upper, middle, and lower worlds, and represents a variant of the *axis mundi*, or the cosmic tree (Laughlin et al., 1992: 224). In symbolic representations of the cosmos in the form of a mandala, Mount Meru is also the *axis mundi*. Jung (1967: 253) considered depictions of the shamanic cosmogram, whether in the form of a mandala or a tree, as representations of the self. Thus, the shaman's entranced ascent and descent into these levels, Jungians would say, represents "an interaction between human consciousness and the varied archetypal and transpersonal elements of the collective psyche" (TePaske 1997: 26). From the perspective of the *jhākri*, this internally generated symbolic field is experienced as "a world-out-there" (cf. Laughlin et al. 1992: 274).

The realm of humans, or the middle world in the cosmogram, is populated by supernatural beings of various classes. According to Jhākri Narsing Jirel, "spirits inhabit a parallel reality but the same geographical space people occupy." Although these beings are ordinarily invisible to most people most of the time, *jhākris* are able to see, interact, and communicate with them, and their intrusions into the lives and affairs of human beings are both visible and tangible to those afflicted. Spirits are therefore completely integrated into the natural human environment of the Nepalese *jhākri*, just as they were in the natural human environment of the Siberian shaman (cf. Hutton 2001: 67; Morris 2006: 19).

Some of these spirits are earthbound, some live in the atmosphere. All are willful and possess agency. The atmospheric and earthbound supernatural beings hover about unseen, materialize and disappear suddenly, and assault unsuspecting people at dawn, dusk, or at night, which are times of heightened paranormal activity, bringing sickness and disaster upon unfortunate humans. Other spirits remain tied to specific localities, causing harm to those who venture across their domain, streams, rivers, rocks, mountains, trees, and forests (cf. Greve 1981: 108). Because humans have a fluid and transactional relationship with their surroundings and its numinous denizens, they are susceptible to penetrations by various paranormal beings (cf. Castillo 1994: 156; Mumford 1989: 16). The human body is also susceptible to penetrations by supernatural objects, such as magical arrows (*ūn* or *bāṇ*) shot by numinous forest deities, or noxious substances magically hurled by sorcerers or witches.

Another feature of the *jhākri*'s animistic cosmology with analogues in Siberian shamanism involves the belief that humans and all living things possess more than one soul (cf. Krader 1978: 192–193; Hutton 2001: 61). According to Jhākri Kumar Thapa, these life forces affect health and vitality as well as illness and death. The number of souls varies, ranging from three to nine (Holmberg 1989: 191–192; Nicoletti 2004: 54; Pignède 1966: 375; Riboli 2000: 180; Steinmann 1987: 144–148; Watters 1975: 143), but the principle underlying the belief is the same. This is the idea that some of these souls remain connected to the human body or parts of the body, while others, or parts of others, can become detached and move about when a person is asleep. This capacity offers the possibility for some humans in the middle world to travel spiritually to the upper or lower worlds (Torrance 1994: 154).

However, souls can also be forcefully detached due to fright, a sudden fall, or through supernatural attack. Such disconnected souls stray and become lost. Some may lose their way while roaming free during sleep. A lost soul wanders aimlessly, unable to return, or else it can fall captive to one of numerous evil spirits and become enslaved, imprisoned, or conveyed to the realm of the dead. People whose souls are lost become weak and lethargic and suffer other debilitating conditions (cf. Desjarlais 1992: 13, 73–74). It falls upon the *jhākris* to undertake search-and-rescue missions to recover missing souls.

When people die, their souls must be properly dispatched to their place in the other side, otherwise they will linger behind, turn into evil spirits or shades, and cause havoc as revenants and haunters. The *lāmā-bombo* contest, discussed in chapter 3, was in part over the issue of which specialist was more qualified to escort the souls of the dead to their appropriate destination. This is why funerals involve elaborate processions designed to guide the soul physically and symbolically to where it must go. Among the Jirels, a man wielding a *khukuri* knife to ward off supernatural attacks leads the funeral procession, a *lāmā* dances and utters mantras alongside the people carrying the corpse, while other *lāmās* walk in front, playing *damarus* (double-sided hourglass-shaped drums), ringing bells, and blowing a *śaṅkha-cakra* (conch shell), creating a cacophony of sound. Some procession members bear flags. One person conveys the deceased's clothing and personal belongings (objects the dead person was attached to in life), which will be cremated along with the body. At crossroads, plates containing food serve to honor the dead person and mark the route for his spirit to follow (Sidky et al. 2002: 117).

Forty days after the deceased's cremation, relatives summon his spirit during the *Sensing* ritual described in chapter 6 to inquire about its circumstances and ensure that it is content and will stay where it belongs. After the *Sensing* ritual, a procession carrying food offerings tied to the end of a long scarf, which is held overhead, leads the spirit back toward the clan burial ground where a *chorten* to house the cremated remains is to be constructed (Sidky et al. 2002: 127).

The souls of suicides and those who die unnatural deaths are particularly troublesome and return to haunt the living. They must be ritually bound and eradicated and their ties with human society permanently severed. These activities fall within the exclusive domain of the *jhākri*.

Figure 7.1. Elaborate funeral rites are observed to physically and symbolically dispatch the souls of the dead to where they must go. Here a prossession carrying food offerings tied to the end of a long scarf, which is held overhead, leads the spirit back toward the clan burial ground (Photo by H. Sidky)

Figure 7.2. Construction of the *chorten* to house the deceased's cremated remains (Photo by H. Sidky)

The association between the dead and cremation grounds and grave-yards makes these locales supernaturally charged and especially danger-ous. This is not only because the ghosts of those who have not passed on linger there, but also because these places attract demons and evil spirits. They are epicenters of negative energy and evil influences. This is why in-cipient *jhākris* drawn to the spirit world gravitate toward such places dur-ing their "spiritual crisis," and why ordinary humans take great care to avoid such places, especially at night.

Given the ontological parameters of the *jhākri* universe, it is possible for some humans to enter into the spirit world and interact with, coerce, in-veigle, or compel its various denizens to comply with human demands. In this universe, words and ritual action are powerful vehicles for re-structuring reality to accord with human intentionality. This is a central operational premise upon which *jhākri* beliefs and practices are based.

When undertaking journeys to the spirit world, *jhākris* will first protect the location in which they are operating. After reining the spirits sum-moned, the *jhākris* dance around the altar and the hearth. They exit the room still dancing and drumming and leave the house. They dance in front of the house and circle the entire building in a clockwise fashion be-fore returning to the room where their patient is sitting quietly. This ac-tion creates a "barricade," as Dul Temba Sherpa explained, that is in-tended to protect the souls of all those inside the house from attacks by evil spirits when the *jhākris* embark on their journey.

Here I will describe the basic features of one form of spiritual travel, one in which the *jhākri* describes movement in geographical and mythical space as he dances and chants. The narrative of journey does not accom-pany another form of travel to the spirit world, which is covered in chap-ter 10. The words of the *jhākri* embarking on a spiritual journey transport his mind on a flight or excursion across space and into mythic time (Allen 1974; 1976a: 133; Nicoletti 2004: 51–53; Watters 1975: 146–147). This is a journey that brings the shaman into direct one-to-one contact with divini-ties and supernatural forces (cf. Höfer 1994: 29). According to Jhākri Ra-bindra Rāi, "the journey is fraught with dangers and obstacles and is un-dertaken in order to accomplish a specific objective, such as obtaining power, locating and retrieving a wandering or lost soul, or negotiating a reprieve for a gravely ill patient."

The anthropological literature suggests that the shaman accesses this al-ternate reality by inducing ASC (Noll 1985: 447; Laughlin et al. 1992: 273). The experience, as described by the *jhākris* themselves, is like a "waking dream" during which the shaman perceives vivid images. Peters and Price-Williams (1980: 405) have drawn comparisons between the shaman's visions or "imaginal processes" and psychological therapeutic techniques referred to as "directed daydreams" and "guided affective imagery" (see

Gallegos 1987). As Jhākri Kumar Thapa put it, "the *jhākri*, as if daydream-ing, is able to recollect his visions and narrates all that transpires to those present." In his chants he describes what he sees and in his movements he may mimic actions appropriate to the landscape being crossed at each stage of the journey. The tempo and rhythm of his drumbeat and his singing change accordingly. The patient and others who are present are thus drawn into the shamanic expedition and vicariously participate in the journey as described and acted out for them (Desjarlais 1989).

Starting from his altar, the *jhākri* moves along a clearly defined spiritual road map that takes him over a sacred landscape with distinct layers, re-spectively associated with specific divinities and supernatural beings. The shaman moves from the clan gods of the patient's household to village deities and to the familiar surrounding topographical features, such as cliffs, caves, and groves and forests that are the abodes of territorial deities and other spirits. Chanting and drumming, he moves past fields and forests, rivers, high mountain peaks, and alpine lakes. As the *jhākri* trav-erses each area, he names the sacred sites and requests the aid of the as-sociated divinities, as well as assimilating the mystical powers that exude from these holy places. Reference to topographical features is a symbolic means of creating order. As Maskarinec (1995: 126) has pointed out:

> The emergent pattern is not just an ideal topography of sanctified earth, but an active incorporation of geographic elements into the cure as prototypic or-der. The original patterns of the earth have a sacred order, the same order that every shaman must recreate in a patient's life.

Holy sites include mountain peaks, alpine lakes, pilgrimage places, sanctuaries, shrines, monasteries, and temples dedicated to various gods and goddesses belonging to the Hindu, Buddhist and shamanic pan-theons. He names the divinities encountered and invites them to descend on the altar. He then enters mythic time and space. He will visit locations associated with ancestral figures and important mythological origination events, such as the birthplace of the group's ancestors and the sanctuary of the primordial *jhākri*, whose actions and deeds constituted the prece-dents of the belief and practices of present-day practitioners. As Greve (1989: 220) has pointed out, "the mythical past must, therefore, be recalled and repeated through the present ritual, to ensure its future effectiveness and continuity."

The *jhākri* finally moves beyond the limits of the group's geographical comprehension, to the highest peaks in Nepal and Tibet that are bridges to the dwelling places of the major gods and goddesses. As Jhākri Nars-ing Jirel put it, "it is the sacred mountain, whether Ganesh Himal, Khum-bila, Everest, or Kailas, that connects the world of humans and that of the gods of the upper realms." The *jhākri's* journey across a vast spiritual landscape thus brings those present in direct contact with the deities residing in the distant summits. The latter simultaneously manifest themselves in the *jhākri's* altar.

Moving across the sacred geography containing supernaturally significant sites, the *jhākri* absorbs power and gleans the information necessary to deal with the crisis at hand. For example, he may identify the path that represents a patient's life force, which he will revitalize as he traverses it. Or once he reaches the highest point of the journey, according to Jhākri Gau Bahādur Gurung, "he will converse with the gods and inquire why his patient has been stricken with a life threatening illness and attempts to negotiate a reprieve."

"When seeking lost souls that have wandered away during sleep or have been dislodged because of supernatural attacks," Jhākri Shukra Bahādur Tamang observed, "the *jhākri* will rally his accompanying tutelary spirit and other supernatural helpers for the search-and-rescue missions." Together they conduct reconnaissance operations to locate a missing soul across the supernatural landscape. The *jhākri* will travel over the pathway that the souls of the dead traverse. He will descend into the land of the dead to retrieve souls snatched by the spirits of the underworld. The journey at every stage thus traces the sacred spatial geometry of the shamanic cosmos. When he has accomplished his task, the *jhākri* will retrace his steps along the same road map through the places he visited, back to the room where he is physically located. He will then attend to the procedures necessary to alleviate the patient's condition.

In many respects, the *jhākri's* supernatural travel is similar to the spirit-journeys of Siberian shamans who danced and beat their drums and provided a running commentary to the audience as they traveled in other worlds (Hutton 2001: 88). Nepalese shamans, therefore, not only embody spirits, they also undertake spirit-journeys and travel to other worlds to interact with divinities, and summon spirits and engage them in dialogue. These three methods of shamanizing can be combined in sequence or they can be utilized individually, as was also the case with Siberian shamans (Hutton 2001: 90; Riboli 2000: 63). This is further confirmation that the binarism of spirit possession and soul journey is simplistic and misleading.

The *jhākri's* conception of reality and how it operates, according to which he interprets the world, is private in the sense that ordinary people do not have firsthand access to it. However, the *jhākri's* cosmology, as articulated in his recitals and enacted in his ceremonies, is structured around elements of a commonly shared cultural and religious tradition. Thus, while ordinary people do not usually see spirits and are not privy to the *jhākri's* esoteric understanding of reality, they do share with him certain basic beliefs in the existence of powerful divinities, spirits, and demonic beings that bring chaos, misery, sickness, and death (Miller 1997: 4). This is why the *jhākri's* invocation of divinities, and his explanations for why witches attack people, or why the world needs shamans, makes sense to his fellow villagers and clients. This is also why, as psychologist Bradley TePaske (1997: 27) has put it, the shaman's experiences are recognized "as valid and collectively meaningful." The *jhākri's* activities, in other words, articulate with the wider system of beliefs and myths that justify his role as intercessor and provide the rationale for the legitimacy of his ritual practices.

The role of the shaman as intercessor is to ensure that the relationship between humans and the spirit world remains balanced and favorable and to ameliorate negative effects when they occur. His field of operations therefore extends well beyond the treatment of illnesses that debilitate his clients. As Jhākri Gau Bahādur Gurung noted, the basic job of the *jhākri* is to avert crises of all kinds.

For the Nepalese, the forces that affect the well-being and physical health of humans range from supernatural agencies to astrological influences based upon planetary misalignments, and the balance between of hot/cold associated with air and food in the human body (Pigg 1995; Stone 1976). These forces can influence a person individually or in various combinations with each other, producing complex sets of symptoms.

When people become ill they do not perfunctorily seek the aid of a *jhākri*. According to existing cultural conventions of interpreting illness, first a range of traditional or household cures may be employed. These could involve the application of herbal remedies, spells or mantras known to many, as well as dietary measures. People also have the option of consulting various specialists, such as the *jōtisi* (astrologer), *pujāri* (Brāhman priest), *lāmā, dhāmi, jānne mānche* (village wise man), *jhārphuke* (non-ecstatic healer who "blows" mantras and sweeps illnesses away), *baidya* (Ayurvedic doctor), or even biomedical healthcare provider. For local people, these differing therapeutic approaches are not mutually exclusive, nor are they viewed as part of a single system, but merely represent sets of available options (Pigg 1995: 22). Based on the perceived nature of the illness and availability of services, people may often use several of these therapies, either in succession or at the same time.

That Western medicine is not at the top of the list of sought-after therapies is not surprising in the context of rural Nepal. This is because effective delivery of biomedical care to rural populations is minimal and unevenly distributed (Niraula 1994; Shiba et al. 2001; Acharya 1994: 243–244). According to countrywide figures for the years 2001–2002, there was approximately one hospital bed for every 3,489 people, and one physician for every 18,000 individuals (WHO 2003). Corruption and inefficiency compound the problem of healthcare delivery (see Subedi et al.

Figure 7.3. A patient being taken to a bio-medical clinic for treatment. For the Nepalese, biomedicine and traditional systems of healing are not mutually exclusive (Photo by H. Sidky)

2000). Doctors assigned to rural areas seldom show up at their posts. Medical staff and medics are usually poorly trained. There is a lack of medication and often what is available is either of poor quality, has expired, is illegally sold at high prices, or is improperly administered (see Subedi et al. 2000). These factors contribute to the ineffectiveness of bio-medical treatment and the sometimes dismal success rates (Maskarinec 1995: 93). The long years of war between governmental forces and the Maoists have further hampered the delivery of modern healthcare to the countryside. Thus handicapped, the rural medic hardly does better than the *jhākri*. Spiritual intercessors, specially the *jhākris*, continue to provide the bulk of the healthcare services in the country.

Where Western medicine is effectively administered it commands great respect. Yet it is not necessarily seen as antagonistic to the treatments provided by the *jhākri* (cf. Okada 1976; Pigg 1995; 1996). Modern medicine is understood to be effective in curing symptoms. However, it is ineffective against the true causes of illnesses attributed to supernatural agencies. Dealing with such problems requires the services of the *jhākri* (cf. Maskarinec 1995: 28–29; Miller 1997: 5; Paul 1976: 142). In other words, it is the perceived actual cause of the problem, rather than outward manifestations or symptoms, which are the focus of the *jhākri's* rituals. In this connection, it may be pointed out that the widely held conception of the shaman as a type of doctor is inaccurate. Mastromattei (1989: 226) is correct in maintaining that the *jhākri* is not really a healer or a kind of "doctor." Rather, he adds, he is a ritual intercessor who while in an altered state of consciousness "fights the spirits who cause the disease, and does not heal or cure the disease as such." In other words, the *jhākri* addresses the "ontological conditions" that allow disease and social disorder (cf. Maskarinec 1995: 242).

Attempting to address a supernaturally caused malady by means of biomedicine alone is in many cases considered detrimental. This suggests that the *jhākri*'s sphere of practice is distinct from that of the medical doctor. As one consultant put it:

When you go to the forest and all of a sudden something hurts, or you feel as if something has entered your body, that is how you know that a spirit has attacked you. Modern doctors cannot cure these afflictions. In fact, the doctor's medicine will make your condition worse. In such cases, we go to the *jhākri*. He tells us the real reason for our troubles and what to do about it.

As various therapies are used and fail, and the repertoire of known cures is exhausted, suspicions will begin to develop that supernatural agencies are at work. "It is when the techniques or mantras of other healers fail," Jhākri Dawa Sherpa noted, "that people come to us, because we have greater powers than those others." The condition in question is now framed under a different etiological category. *Jhākris* use a compound term, *masān-desān* (evil spirit-epidemic/disease), to refer to ailments of supernatural origins. For the hill people of Nepal, the invisible spirits (i.e., *masān-desān*) that inhabit land and space are as real and potent as invisible "germs" and "microbes" are to people in the West (cf. Maquet 1981: 3).

In the cognized universe of the *jhākri* and his clients, spirits roam everywhere and they often strike humans. The question is, what motivates such supernatural assaults? The answer lies in the way humans are interrelated to their surroundings and the world and universe. Human actions are nestled within a wide web of overlapping interconnections, reciprocal relations, and obligations with respect to the natural and spirit worlds. These relations and obligations must be carefully attended to at the risk of dire consequences. Negligence, therefore, is the ultimate reason underlying supernatural assaults. As Jones (1976: 7) succinctly put it:

People frequently recognize that human neglect is usually the basis for supernatural discontent. For example, the failure to propitiate household or village gods and goddesses is frequently cited as the source of their anger, or . . . human envy and jealousy leaves the individual or family open to attacks by witches or evil spirits. Through human failure and neglect supernatural forces are unleashed and bring chaos, disorder, and disaster.

The *jhākri*, in his role as "the interpreter of the world," must decipher the field of human social actions, seek out recondite connections or relationships, and pinpoint the precise nature of the neglect of which perpetrators are often oblivious.

Afflictions may descend upon people from any number of sources. There are hearth gods, clan gods, and goddesses. There are divinities associated with mountain peaks, alpine lakes, and waterfalls. There are water spirits, or *jal-nāgs* and *nāg-debi*s (or *nāg-nāgini*s), and spirits of the wilderness, such as *ban-jhākri* (see chapter 9), *ban-deutā* (various gods of the forest), and *sikāri* (hunter spirits). Although not necessarily intrinsically evil, these beings are wrathful and will strike when there is human neglect, such as failure to attend to ritual obligations owed to them, sacrilegious acts such as defiling or encroaching upon their sacred space, or failure to maintain their shrines. The consequence of such failures is spiritual decline, sickness, and suffering by children or adults.

Ancestral spirits may also send illness if clan members neglect their collective obligations, if they fail to offer homage, or if they are negligent in conducting *pujā* to the ancestors. The attack is not malicious, but is intended to call attention to the breach of obligations. The harm is withdrawn once the offense is rectified. When dealing with gods and ancestral spirits, the *jhākri* employs propitiatory acts, such as sacrificing animals and making promises that the breach of obligation will not be repeated in the future. The *jhākri* also enjoins the patient and his or her family to follow his instructions to avoid a recurrence of the problem.

Threats also come from witchcraft, which, as Jhākri Rabindra Rāi pointed out, "is an ancient evil." Witches cause harm through innate powers of their own, by using mantras, or by harnessing evil spirits to attack people and livestock. According to one shaman's narrative, witches obtained their powers from Mahādev, but turned to evil. In another narrative, it is Pārbati, Mahādev's wife, the archetypal witch, who confers upon human witches the ability to cause harm. To counteract his wife's misdeed, Mahādev teaches the *jhākri* mantras to negate the power of witches. In either case, it is the gods who are the source of power both for witches and *for jhākris*. Thus, since ancient times, combating witches has been one of the *jhākri's* major functions. For this reason, I address the issue of witchcraft and witch beliefs in a separate chapter.

Other sources of danger are ravenous and predatory evil spirits, demons, ghosts, and phantoms that infest the terrain around villages, or dwell in crossroads, graveyards, and cremation grounds. Some demand to be fed and call attention to themselves by entering human bodies and making them shake. Others strike out of anger. They latch on to the backs of passersby, dog villagers as they move about, and hover near them out of a desire for company or because they are hungry. They may strike randomly of their own volition, or they may be mobilized by a shaman, sorcerer, or witch. In any case, the result is illness and suffering.

There is considerable ambiguity among consultants, including *jhākris*, when it comes to the characteristics of this class of supernatural beings. Often the same set of attributes is assigned to different types of spirits and demons, such as *bir masān, bāyu, piaīs, bhut, pret, rākṣas*, and others. This ambiguity is reflected in ethnographic accounts (Allen 1976b; Blustain 1976; Holmberg 1989: 142–179; Maskarinec 1995: 30–31, 42–46,174–75, 203–207;

Miller 1997: 21, 94–95, 128–129, 209–221; Peters 1979; 1982; Riboli 2000: 263–165; Stone 1976; Watters 1975). Rather than attempt to cross-reference all the sources, which would undoubtedly be an unproductive exercise, here I will present the information provided by my own consultants.

Among the supernatural entities in question are the spirits of dead people whose corpses were defiled, who were not properly dispatched to the place of the dead through funeral rites, or who died unnaturally. They bring sickness or cause harm by possessing their victims. These spirits include *bir masān*, *bāyu*, *picās*, *bhut*, and *pret*.

The *bir masān* comes from the graveyards and river banks, where cremations take place. Some *bir masān* roam outside the villages waiting for unwary victims. These entities are believed by some to be the spirits of dead people and are considered to be exceptionally malevolent. However, consultants disagree regarding the exact genesis of the *bir masān*. Some maintain that they are the spirits of suicides, those who did not live full lives, or individuals whose corpses were touched by members of other castes. Others affirm that *bir masān* are the spirits of evil people. A few consultants believed that *bir masān* are demons of nonhuman origin who are attracted to graveyards and cremation grounds, which are local hot spots of negative spiritual activities.

*Bir masān*s can attack on their own volition, or they may be sent by sorcerers or witches. According to Jhākri Rabindra Rāi, when a person encounters them directly, he will become sick, vomit blood, and will die if not treated by a *jhākri*. If the encounter is indirect, the person becomes ill,

Figure 7.4.   Places where cremations take place are considered local hot spots of negative spiritual activities (Photo by H. Sidky)

loses his appetite, and may eventually die if not treated. *Bir masān* can also possess their victims. Poltergeist activity is attributed to these spirits as well, who are said to come to houses late at night and make strange sounds and throw stones to disturb people. There are numerous other types of *bir*, white, black, green, red, or blue, although consultants could not agree as to the significance of the colors. Jhākri Shukra Bahādur Tamang explained that these spirits are hierarchically ranked:

> *Karbir masān* is the *rajā* [king] of these spirits, *bir masān* is the commander or general, and the rest are like foot soldiers. They are, altogether, an army of evil spirits.

Bāyu is the spirit of a person whose corpse was touched by a person of a different caste. It returns to attack his kinsmen with disease. It will continue vexing them until it is ritually recognized as an ancestral spirit and regularly honored. One form, the *masān-bāyu*, lingers in cremation grounds and takes the form of wind. *Picās* or *piśāc* (*pisacas* in Sanskrit) is the ghost of someone who died in an accident, such as a landslide. In Hindu mythology they are considered residues of human spirits or elementary spirits. *Picās* are said to be drawn to the homes of sick people, exacerbating the condition of the afflicted. These beings are not as powerful as the *bir masān* and mainly cause nausea, vomiting, and body pains. They are appeased by simple offerings consisting of consecrated rice mixed with black beans and turmeric.

Bhuts (*bhūta* in Sanskrit) are the restless spirits of people who have died of unnatural causes, such as suicide or execution. They linger either because the appropriate rituals were not performed during their funerals, or no rites were performed at all. *Bhuts* roam about nocturnally attacking people at crossroads and are drawn to polluted places. They linger in groves and abandoned houses, and infest the hearths and roofs of people's homes. *Pret* (*pretas* in Sanskrit) are the ghost of evil people. They are always hungry and can never be satisfied. They linger in their earthly homes out of greed and cause harm to their relatives. Various misfortunes are attributed to these spirits, including infertility in women, spontaneous abortions, death of children at birth, loss of property and cattle, and crop failure. The term is sometimes used together with *bhut*, in the compound form *bhut-pret*. Some consultants observed that rather than referring to a particular entity or entities, *bhut-pret* denotes the category "ghost-spirits" to which all of the above-mentioned supernatural beings belong.

In addition to supernatural beings of human origin, there are also various evil spirits and demons. Malicious, greedy, and always hungry, they too dwell in crossroads, graveyards, and cremation grounds, or hover in the atmosphere in great numbers. They are predatory and attack people and livestock by their own volition, sapping their life force and causing sickness and death. These beings come in a variety of forms, such as horses, pigs, buffaloes, and dogs. Some are humanoid but lack heads, some have heads that are backward, others have two heads. Some do not have faces. Many have long teeth or fangs. In size, they can be very small, but some are as large as an adult human.

Rākṣas (*raksasas* in Sanskrit) are demons that haunt graveyards. They indulge in wanton destruction, killing people and livestock. They come in various shapes, most commonly in the form of a horse and rider, but they may also take the shape of animals as well. *Murkaṭṭo* is another malevolent demonic entity. It resembles a man with no head and it also appears in the form of a human skeleton. Some consultants noted that *murkaṭṭo* is not a demon, but the spirit of a person who was beheaded and that this entity moves about carrying its severed cranium under its arm. It also frequents cremation grounds. Encounters with it are lethal.

What are we to make of the spirit world of the Nepalese shamans? Western writers have pondered the nature of the spirit beings that are central in the shaman's universe. Psychiatrist Roger Walsh (1990: 130), for example, asks, "what is the psychological and ontological status of spirits?" Shirokogoroff (1935: 366) suggested that spirits are the projections of the shaman's alter ego, or as restated by anthropologist Vitebsky (1995: 93), spirits are metaphors for something inside the shaman's mind (Hutton 2001: 67). As discussed in chapter 6, in the earlier literature, the shaman's visions and encounters with spirits were taken as indications or symptoms of psychopathological conditions, such as schizophrenia or psychosis. Subsequently, investigators writing from the perspective of anomalistic psychology attempted to provide plausible and naturalistic explanations of the shamanic encounter with spirits in terms of altered states of consciousness, viewed as atypical but, not necessarily pathological (cf. Beyerstein 2002: 20; Jones 1976b; Laughlin et al. 1992: 269; Reed 1988). Jungian psychologists treat the spirit world as part of the collective unconscious, a separate reality of numinous archetypical personages that is accessible to the human psyche (Sandner 1997: 5). The shamans have their own view. As Jhākri Kami Singh Tamang says:

> I see spirits and gods, they talk to me . . . I talk to them. I can also feel them. Other people cannot see or feel them, but they are there!

For the shaman, spirits are integral parts of an external reality that is hidden to most, but one that exerts considerable force upon the visible world. Thus, as Hutton (2001: 67) has noted in the context of his discussion of Siberian shamanism, what anthropologists or psychologists might characterize as matters internal to the human mind, the practitioners themselves construe as "relationships with an external world as objectively real as the physical one."

At issue is the clash of worldviews between the outside observer's treatment of shamanic experiences as manifestations of psychological processes inside people's heads, and the perspective of the shamans themselves, who view these experiences as interactions with an external reality as objectively real as the physical world (Hutton 2001: 67; Walsh 1990: 130). For some, this has brought into question the wisdom of extending Western clinical diagnostic categories to experiences that make sense to and are perfectly understood by members of the culture itself (Walsh 1997). Some writers are willing to admit the possibility that the shamanic conceptions of spirits and the spirit world may be completely valid in an objective sense. As Walsh (1990: 135) writes, "we must acknowledge that we have not disproved the possible existence of spirits (intelligent, non-material entities independent of the [shaman's] mind)." He adds that, "it is not at all clear that it is possible to disprove them." This argument is flawed. Walsh is committing the logical fallacy called "argument from ignorance" (Sidky 2004: 15). This is expressed in the following form: No one can prove that UFOs do not exist, therefore UFOs exist. The flaw in this argument is that it overlooks the important fact that in order to prove a proposition one must have evidence for it. No such evidence exists for UFOs or the paranormal phenomenon alluded to by Walsh.

The ex-anthropologist, now neoshaman guru, Michael Harner (1999) goes a step further. He points out that there are two realities: ordinary reality, which is perceived in an "ordinary state of consciousness" (OSC), and "nonordinary reality," which is accessed through the "shamanic state of consciousness" (SSC). According to Harner, "Each is recognized to have its own forms of knowledge and relevance to human existence." He adds that both "realities" are encountered through "direct perception with all the senses." The shaman uses his mind to enter into this other reality, but this other reality exists independently of the mind (Harner and Doore 1987: 4). The supernatural world of spirits, therefore, has the same ontological status as the ordinary world of everyday experience because both are accessed through the senses, or empirically. Using the term "empirical" in the way Harner does, one could argue that our dreams are as real as ordinary waking experiences because we clearly use our sensory perceptions, seeing, hearing, feeling, in dreams. If this were to be admitted, then it would follow that you could be arrested and convicted for murder simply because someone dreamed that you killed another human being (Lett 1997a: 100). As stated at the beginning of this chapter, the supernatural worlds shamans access are metaphors for the different modalities or inner realms of human consciousness, aspects of which manifest themselves symbolically in culturally meaningful cognitive categories. The inner world, however meaningful or spiritually significant, does not have the same ontological status as the ordinary world of everyday experience.

Harner (1999) goes on to point out that as long as science has not disproved "the theory of the existence of spirits," it cannot ignore the tangible reality of the spirit world. The dismissal of spirits by science, he asserts, is a "matter of faith." Harner thus also resorts to the logical fallacy of "argument from ignorance," mentioned above. Logical fallacies, as I noted earlier, abound in the shamanic studies literature.

There is no denying that people have "entity encounters" and related anomalous experiences. As McClenon (1995: 108) has pointed out:

> Apparitions, out-of-body experiences, near-death experiences, precognitions, night-paralysis, extrasensory perceptions (ESP), and contact with the dead contain universal features, allowing cross-culturally consistent classification. Such episodes occur frequently enough to have significant impact on all societies.

For folklorist David Hufford (1995: 28; 1982), such anomalous experiential events have physiological bases and exhibit universal features and are the sources of spiritual beliefs. McClenon (2001: 63, 80–81; 2006) even suggests that rudimentary anomalous experiences by Paleolithic peoples underlie the development of beliefs about ghosts, life after death, and even shamanism, "the first universal religious form."

However, one must be cautious not to equate frequency and cross-cultural occurrence of experiences with objective reality of spirit beings, that is, spirits as entities existing "independently of the mind." Neurologist Peter Brugger's (2001: 210) comments regarding one category of entity encounter experiences, "hauntings," are highly relevant here:

> The argument that the high frequency of individual reports of hauntings testifies to the reality of "outside forces" is obviously misleading. This consistency in fact only confirms something rather trivial, i.e., that the central nervous system of all humans exhibits some common functional properties.

Universality of experience or experiences with universal features are also insufficient as evidence for the ontological reality of spirit beings. Indeed, as Brugger (2001: 213) adds, "the fact that people universally see a red spot on a white wall after having stared at a green patch does not involve changes on the surface of the wall." Nor is the fact that more than one person may experience a ghostly manifestation at the same time sufficient to bolster the supernaturalist hypothesis (see Nickell 2001). As Brugger (2001: 210) points out with respect to simultaneous reports of poltergeist activities:

> The accounts that more than one person witnessed a poltergeist phenomenon likewise does not buttress the objectivity of a spooky event. Shared delusions

are commonplace in the records of psychiatry, and the mechanism of a perceptual contagion is reportedly quite powerful, even in places which are "thoroughly unhaunted."

Neuroscience is shedding considerable light upon how forces and activities initiated inside the brain are attributed to the actions of alien beings and numinous presences thought to originate outside (Brugger 2001: 195; Persinger 2003). To attribute ontological autonomy to these forces and activities is mystification.

According to the findings of evolutionary psychology, spirits or supernatural beings are products of innate "mental modules," evolutionarily programmed to seek out and identify agents, people/animals, as causes of complex and uncertain events or circumstances (Atran 2002: 49; 2006: 188–190). Agents are construed as having intentional causal psychic states, such as beliefs and desires, that is, they act purposefully toward some goal and operate at will as if propelled by some inner force. A cognitive schema or mental module that identifies animate beings as agents, with goals and internal motivations, would have allowed hominids to foresee the actions of predators in a manner that increased their chances of survival and reproductive success (Atran 2002: 61). However, the "agent-detection module" also processes other information not within its proper domain, such as creaking noises in a building, howling wind, patterns in the clouds that "readily trigger inferences to agency among people everywhere" (Atran 2002: 61). This generates experiences of entity encounters, feelings of the presence of shadowy or numinous beings, and sensations of fear or awe (Persinger 2003). As anthropologist Scott Atran (2002: 61) has pointed out,

> Cognitive schema for recognizing and interpreting inanimate agents may be a crucial part of our evolutionary heritage, which primes us to anticipate intention in the unseen causes of uncertain situations that carry risk and danger or the promise of opportunity, such as predators, protectors, and prey. If we, or our ancestors, were to find that the scratching at the door or the howling in the air was not the stalker that seems "automatically" to first come to mind but only the play of branches and leaves in the wind, we would suffer nothing. But if there were a stalker, we would be prepared and likely to suffer less than if we weren't. Natural selection may have prepared us to induce agency in potentially important but causally opaque situations.

Atran (2002: 78) adds,

> Natural selection designed the agency-detector system to deal rapidly and economically with stimulus situations involving people and animals as predators, protectors and prey. This resulted in the system's being trip-wired to respond to fragmentary information under conditions of uncertainty, inciting

perceptions of figures in the clouds, voices in the wind, lurking movements in the leaves, and emotions among interacting dots on a computer screen. This hair-triggering of agency detection mechanism readily lends itself to supernatural interpretation of uncertain or anxiety provoking events.

This evolutionary mechanism that allows the rapid detection and response to dangerous predators, snakes, tigers, or devious humans may account for the cross-cultural occurrence of beliefs in demons, devils, ghosts, ghouls, witches, vampires, and malevolent deities who in the counterintuitive, counterfactual worlds of religion can have dual roles as protectors (Atran 2002: 77–78, 79, 267).

Those who espouse paranormal perspectives adopt epistemological relativism and exalt subjectivity, intuition, and emotions over empirical evidence, scientific standards of proof and disproof, and rules of logic. Associated with the postmodern movement founded on the works of a few eccentric French philosophers during the 1980s, the antiscience anti-intellectualist perspective has become deeply entrenched in American academia because of the political benefits accrued by its proponents in terms of tenure and promotion (Sokal and Bricmont 1998; Gross and Levitt 1994). If there are no standards by which one can decide the veracity of any claims to knowledge, if we cannot distinguish between hallucinations and objective reality, then "anything goes" and irrationalism rules the day (Sidky 2003a; Sokal and Bricmont 1998; Gross and Levitt 1994). This intellectual trend has been a tremendous boom for the "snake oil" salesmen, neoshamans, and others touting bogus medical cures and alternate therapies over scientific medicine (Beyerstein 1999b; Alcock 1999).

Science dismisses the reality of the spirit or paranormal world not as a matter of faith, but because there is no tangible empirical evidence (empirical evidence here means publicly ascertainable evidence, not introspective reports of people in trances) for the existence of such a reality. Conjectures about spirits and the spirit world have not been disproven because such statements are unfalsifiable, that is, they are propositionally meaningless. As anthropologist James Lett (1997b: 111) has put it:

Religion [e.g., Harner's neoshamanism, or creationism, etc.] and science are not at odds because religion wants to be "supernatural," while science wants to be "empirical"; instead religion and science are at odds because religion wants to be irrational (relying ultimately upon beliefs that are either nonfalsifiable or falsified), while science wants to be rational (relying exclusively upon beliefs that are both falsifiable and unfalsified).

This is not to deny that the realms shamans access while in ASC are not real to them, or that the knowledge obtained from these experiences has no "relevance to human existence." As I have already stated, Nepalese shamans possess a vast body of mystical knowledge that is profoundly relevant to the lives of their clients. The problem with perspectives advocated by Walsh, Harner, and writers like them is that such analysis succumbs to "the will to believe" (Beyerstein 1997), which is a tendency highly characteristic of those attracted to neoshamanism and other New Age beliefs (cf. Basil 1988). If we extend our will to believe to shamanism, then we are obliged to do the same with respect to the closely related phenomenon of witchcraft and harmful magic and accept the validity of the reasons given for the persecution and murder of women accused of being witches (see chapter 8). To extend "the will to believe" in this way results in mystification and a kind of credulity that surpasses even the views of some people in societies with shamans. Take, for example, what two Nepalese consultants related:

> You get sick, you go to the *jhākri*. He tells you that a witch made you sick, or a ghost, or an evil spirit. This is what the *jhākri* tells us. We don't see these things. We have never seen a witch, or a ghost, or an evil spirit. How can we believe in them? (in Sidky et al. 2002: 158)

The will to believe also leads to the distortion of ethnographic descriptions, deters anthropological understanding, as well as undermines the credibility of the subject matter.

By adopting ethnographic particularism, cultural anthropologists have either allied themselves with the epistemological relativism and metaphysics of Harner and the like, or they have altogether removed themselves from such debates in the broader field of shamanistic studies. This is unfortunate because ethnographers are in a unique position to counterbalance through empirically grounded research many of the preposterous blanket statements and assertions that characterize the discourse on shamanism.

8

Implicated in Evil:
The Shaman and the Witch

The belief in witchcraft is prevalent among many groups throughout Nepal, including some members of the cosmopolitan urban elite (cf. Gellner 1994: 34). However, as in the case of beliefs regarding ghosts, demons, and spirits, there is little consensus among the public regarding witchcraft. People outside the cities are generally reluctant to discuss witches or witchcraft. This is either because they fear invoking the wrath of witches in their communities, or they are afraid of arousing suspicions against themselves should they reveal too much knowledge of the subject. A number of ethnographers have written on Nepalese witchcraft beliefs (Blustain 1976; Gellner 1994: 34–35; Glover 1972; Greve 1989; Hitchcock 1974b; Jones 1976: 45; Levine 1982; Macdonald 1976b; Maskarinec 1995: 78–83, 184–185; Miller 1997: 210–211, 229, 235, 245; Peters 1979; Stone 1976). However, to date no one has produced a systematic or comprehensive study of Nepalese witchcraft beliefs akin to, for example, Evans-Pritchard's (1937) study of witchcraft among the Azande, although the field of Nepalese witchcraft beliefs is as fertile as any in the world.

Witches are called *boksī*. Sometimes the terms *ḍakinī, ḍaini, ḍānkini* (witch spirit), and *kapṭi* are used as well. In the estimation of some Nepalese consultants, anyone who uses spells and magical techniques to harm another person may technically be called a witch. However, witches in Nepal are nearly always women. Although there is a masculine form of the word for witch, *bokso*, witchcraft in Nepal, as anthropologist Nancy Levine (1982: 259) has put it, is "inherently a female phenomenon." Witches are malevolent antisocial creatures who possess uncanny magical powers to cause harm (*boksī lāgnu*) to humans and livestock. They sow dissension, misfortune, penury, and economic disaster upon individuals or households. They can inflict upon their victims insomnia, nightmares, and nocturnal paralysis (*aīṭhan hunu*). Witches also enter people's homes at night and suck blood from the bodies of victims leaving mysterious marks called "*boksī* bites." Witches are greedy, cannibalistic, and sexually licentious. They attack members of their own family as readily as others, whether children, women, or men.

The *jhākri*s with whom I worked were unanimous in their belief that witches represent an evil from ancient times. The primordial or archetypal witch figures were female. Witches were created and endowed with lethal mystical powers at the beginning of time when the world was formed. Mesmerized by the magical abilities granted to them by the gods, witches turned to wanton evil and destruction (cf. Maskarinec 1995: 80). Witch evil has persisted over the eons and continues to manifest itself in the persons of present-day human witches (Hitchcock 1976a: 181).

Dealing with witchcraft is a major part of *jhākri* activities. Ethnographers who have focused on collecting *jhākri* oral texts have remarked about the surprisingly large number of antiwitch mantras that every practitioner possesses (Maskarinec 1995: 65). Witches, as Macdonald (1976b: 377) put it, "are the human adversaries of the *jhākri*." According to Jhākri Nir Bahādur Jirel:

> *Boksī*s despise *jhākri*s [*ghirnā garnu*]. When a *boksī* sees a *jhākri*, she will strike out and try to hurt him with *āṅkha* [the evil eye] or with *boksī* mantras. The *jhākri* must be on guard and deflect the attack with a stronger counter mantra. *Jhākri* and *boksī* are always at war with each other. It has always been this way.

Nir Bahādur recited his antiwitchcraft mantra:

> By the oath of Gauri Pārbati
> Malicious mantras
> Dim-witted *boksī*
> Casting evil spells
> Frog spirit
> Fox spirit
> Lizard spirit
> Snake spirit
> Fish spirit
> Blow mantra!
> Reverse your charm
> Nullify, I defeat!
> Repel
> Send away
> Malicious mantras

Dim-witted *boksī*
Casting evil spells
Water spirit
Land spirit
Spider spirit
Bee spirit
Wasp spirit
I reverse your charm
Nullify, I defeat!
Send away!
Blow mantra!
The oath of Gauri Pārbati

There are dangers involved when a *jhākri* attempts to cure a patient under the malevolent effects of a witch, as revealed in the following account related to me by a Jirel elder:

a *boksī* had attacked a small child, damaging its liver. The child's parents took the child to a famous *jhākri*. The *boksī* and the *jhākri* entered into a psychic battle using mantras. The *jhākri* failed and was killed. Then the boy's parents went to a second *jhākri*. He also failed and was killed. Finally, they took their child to Bikasim, a [*jhākri*] who could do amazing things. He felt the boy's pulse and immediately learned the *boksī*'s identity. He used *gaṅgā-jal* [holy water] and turmeric as part of his cure, and with his mantras killed the *boksī*. The boy was saved. (in Sidky et al. 2002: 152)

In Nepal, the witch exists alongside the shaman, as well as other intercessors, such as priests, mediums, and nonecstatic healers. This evidence contradicts evolutionary schemes inspired by Eliade in which the shaman is considered the original do-it-all ritual specialist whose functions are taken over by other types of practitioners as society develops greater complexity, with the priest inheriting the shaman's socially beneficial religious and magical functions and the witch and sorcerer his malevolent functions (e.g., Walsh 1990: 15–16; Winkelman 1992; 2004b).

The belief in witchcraft is a feature that sets Nepalese shamanism apart from Siberian shamanism. As Hutton (2001: 141) has pointed out, in Siberia unanticipated paranormal misfortunes were attributed to the spirits that were part of the natural order. If there were suspicions that such spiritual assaults were instigated by a human being, this was believed to be a shaman employed by enemies in other clans or people within the local community as part of a personal feud. What is absent, according to Hutton (2001: 141–142) is the stereotypical figure labeled as "witch" in other parts of the world. This witch figure is anonymous, operates surreptitiously, is inherently evil, and is entirely motivated by malice and envy, rather than mundane earthly interests such as material gain. The witch stereotype results in the identification of human scapegoats within the community who are blamed for mysterious calamities and illness, as in the case of the witch hunts in early modern Europe (see Sidky 1997). This, according to Hutton, did not exist in Siberia. While the so-called black shamans among peoples such as the Buryat resemble the stereotypical witch in certain respects, they are different because they have a formally recognized status and their powers are of material utility to some members of the community (Hutton 2001: 442). The prodigious female figures defeated by heroes in creation legends among the Buryat and some Turkic-speaking groups, at times identified as witches by Western translators, are fearsome female demigoddesses rather than witches. Hutton (2001: 142) adds:

> When Siberians felt themselves or their dependents to be the victims of uncanny bad luck or illness, they resorted to shamans to remove it by defeating or propitiating the spirits responsible. The shaman did not operate by detecting and accusing other human beings in the same community, who would be held directly responsible for the affliction concerned and forced to lift it, or else be removed themselves in order to break its power at its source. There is no structural reason why they should not have done so: the figure whom scholars called shamans in the Arctic zone of North America specialized in witch-finding, assisted by their spirit helpers in classic shamanic performances. This tradition has been found from the Tlingit of Alaska eastward across the whole continent to the Eskimo of eastern Greenland, but it did not obtain in Siberia.

In Nepal, one of the main functions of the shaman is to combat attacks by witches. According to these specialists:

> A *boksī* is an evil woman who tries to bring sickness to people by magic powers. I recognize them when I see them. I can see them even when I am not performing as a *jhākri*. I feel a sensation inside my stomach, like a tingling feeling, and I know that the woman in front of me is a *boksī* (Jhākri Dawa Sherpa).

According to Jhākri Nir Bahādur Jirel:

> *Boksī* are living women. The *boksī* is the opposite of the *jhākri* because, while the *jhākri* tries to help people suffering from evil spirits, the *boksī* uses her powers to make evil spirits even stronger and urges them to possess people. When such women are dissatisfied with anyone they send evil spirits into them. They also attack for no reason, but usually when they are angry, jealous, or envious, that is when their powers become operative. Sometimes the victims become dumb, some experience terrible headaches, others suffer from dizziness, anxiety, and weakness, others vomit blood and die.

Jhākri Kami Singh Tamang remarked on the number of witches in village communities:

In any village there are often more *boksīs* than *jhākris*; usually for every one *jhākri* there are at least four *boksīs*. When the *jhākri* is in a trance and trembling, his guru [tutelary spirit] will reveal the identity of the *boksī*.

According to Jhākri Gau Bahādur Gurung:

> The *boksī* are in some respects like the *jhākri*, but they do evil things. When she wants to do evil, she will prepare a powder and put it in the victim's food. The victim suffers and unless a *jhākri* cures him, the powder will change into lizards, frogs, scorpions and other poisonous creatures, and the victim's stomach becomes bloated and it bursts. Anyone in the village can be a *boksī*. Usually, we cannot say ahead of time who they are until they strike. Then, we can reveal the general location of their house, which direction the door faces, whether there are many household members in that place or not, and if the *boksī* is married, unmarried or a widow. But we never identify the *boksī* by name.

Jhākri Narsingh Jirel distinguished two types of witch:

> The first type is a woman who uses mantras and other magical skills, such as calling up and sending evil spirits to harm people. In the old days, witchcraft knowledge and mantras were passed on from mothers to daughters. Nowadays, this practice seems to have disappeared. The second type of witch is born with the power to harm others. These are females who are born on a bad day and under a bad planet sign. In these cases, witch evil comes through the birth with the child. Those who are born witches possess this quality, which is like an evil soul. The evil anchors itself inside the back of child's head and is active through her eyes. The *boksī*'s eyes are the source of power. They can poison your food or harm you with a glance. These days, almost all of the witches fall in this second category.

Although the powers of witchcraft are inherent, witches call upon divinities for help. As Jhākri Rabindra Rāi pointed out:

> Witches worship their own gods. At midnight, *boksī* carry burning candles on their heads and go naked to mother goddess temples to worship the wrathful female deities that give them power.

Among the goddesses of witchcraft in Kathmandu are Sobhā Bhagwati and Mhaipi Ajimā (Höfer 1994: 72). Witches also enter into relations with evil spirits. They are thought to worship and give regular offerings of food to *bir masān*. In return, the *bir masān* attacks people on the witch's command. As Jhākri Gau Bahādur Gurung put it:

> Late at night, *boksīs* meet just outside the village to offer sacrifice to *bir masān* [evil spirits]. Sometimes, you can see the blinking lights of their candles in the distance. *Boksī* have a special *pujā* for the *bir masān*. This requires that they

sacrifice an animal and thereafter they must make regular offerings to the *masān*. Some evil *jhākris* do this as well.

That *jhākris* may resort to this kind of sorcery highlights the similarities between witches and shamans. There are stories of *jhākris* tempted by a desire for wealth, or to augment their magical powers, taking up the worship of evil spirits (Miller 1997: 208). Individuals establish such a relationship by making regular offerings of food to the *bir masān*. A bond is thus established between the *jhākri* and the spirit. He can then unleash the spirit against his enemies or rivals. Public knowledge of a *jhākri* embarking down the path of evil would have dire repercussions, so the *pujā* to the evil spirit is always secret. Evil spirits are malicious, greedy, bloodthirsty, perpetually hungry, and their desire to be fed is insatiable. They demand food and blood sacrifice. One of the reasons they attack is to force people to feed them. To obtain relief, victims must make offerings to their supernatural assailants. Once a *jhākri* begins such a relationship with an evil spirit, he is obligated to continue making offerings for the rest of his life. Dreadful consequences follow if the offerings are stopped, as happens when the *jhākri* dies and the clandestine food offerings cease. The *bir masān* becomes angry and will attack the deceased's children and other relatives, inflicting them with sickness and misfortune (Miller 1997: 208). Therefore, dealing with evil spirits is not without dangers even for the shaman. The possibility that the *jhākris* can potentially enter into a compact with evil spirits, as witches are known to do, adds to the shaman's ambivalent social position.

Another feature of witchcraft is that it is a nocturnal enterprise. Witches undertake their most vicious activities at night under the cover of darkness. They seek out victims by shifting their shape into various animals and move about undetected:

> They can change themselves into the shape of cats, dogs, pigs, monkeys and other animals and enter people's houses to poison their food. (Jhākri Rabindra Rāi)

Witches are notorious for poisoning their victims' food:

> They use special poisons with magical qualities. Once they make this poison they must give it to the victim. But they are so evil that if they are unable to poison their enemies they will give it to their own children or husbands. They do this because if they throw their poisons outside, it will cause a landslide. (Jhākri Shukra Bahādur Tamang)

Witches can cause sickness by introducing various foreign objects into their victims' bodies or shooting them with life-draining magical arrows (*vān* or *bāṇ*). They also employ what is commonly known as sympathetic magic (on sympathetic and imitative magic see Rogers 1982: 46). This involves collecting articles connected to the victim, such as clothing, finger and toenail clippings, strands of hair, ashes from his hearth, and dirt upon which he has stepped barefoot, and subjecting these to violent acts and spells (cf. Peters 1979: 29; Gellner 1994: 34). Another way to achieve this is to draw a circle at a crossroad and bury items belonging to the victim in small holes inside the circle while reciting a harming mantra (Maskarinec 1995: 64). Techniques known as imitative magic involve making an effigy of the victim and subjecting it to harm, such as hanging it near a fire, which causes the victim to suffer from a fever, or piercing it with needles, which causes terrible pains. Sometimes the effigy may incorporate items belonging to the victim, such as a strand of hair or a piece of clothing, a combination of sympathetic and imitative magic.

The *jhākri* and the witch stand in a peculiar relationship with one another. As a Sherpa clan elder told me: "There is a saying: 'if there is no *boksī*, the *jhākri* cannot perform'" (*yadi tyahan boksī chaina bhane jhākrile karya gārna sakdaina*). This saying from the eastern hills of Nepal alludes to the narratives regarding the original witches and their confrontation with the first shaman collected in western Nepal (see Hitchcock 1974b; 1976; Maskarinec 1995: 79–84; Oppitz 1981: 8–10; Watters 1975). Called "Song of the Nine Witch Sisters," the story takes place in the First Age of time. Through the will of Mahādev a childless couple is granted the birth of nine daughters who are witches (cf. Maskarinec 1995: 79). The witch sisters grow up and go on a rampage of destruction (Hitchcock 1974b: 153; cf. Maskarinec 1995: 79).

The king summons the first shaman to combat the evil vexing humanity. The shaman in full costume approaches the witches, describing their beauty and charms at great length. He then asks them to accompany him on a journey across the world. The witches are weakened by the long trek and the shaman slays them one by one, until only the youngest, beautiful, and most sexually enticing of the sisters remains alive.

However, none of these witches are actually completely destroyed. Their physical form may be gone, but their evil lingers on in connection with the places they were killed. For example, the sister that is drowned becomes the witch spirit of watery places and the sister killed in the mountains becomes the witch spirit of upland pastures. Some linger on according to the manner in which they were killed. For example, the witch killed with cholera becomes the witch spirit of cholera, and so forth (Hitchcock 1976: 186). These beings personify the primal universal essence of witch evil that can cause havoc directly or it can manifest itself in localized forms through human witches (Hitchcock 1976a: 181).

After killing the eighth witch, the shaman turns to the youngest sister and is about to slay her, when she points out that if she is killed, evil will cease and he will no longer have a job. The shaman realizes the implications of his action and agrees to spare her life on the condition that she ceases vexing his clients whenever he conducts his antiwitchcraft ritual and offers her the appropriate food, blood mixed with rice and a ball of ash (Hitchcock 1976a: 183).

The story of the nine sisters highlights the seductive powers and erotic attractions of witches (Greve 1989: 220). Predictably, the shaman is attracted to the youngest witch and there are hints in some versions of the story of a sexual union between the two. The witch then begs the *jhākri* to allow her to come and live with him in his house with his faithful wife, who is patiently awaiting his return (Hitchcock 1974b: 153). The shaman is horrified at the idea when he contemplates the evils that the witch could inflict upon his house, lineage brothers, and the villagers. Refusing the witch shelter, he compels her to depart from the village and live at the crossroad, which represents the boundary between the secure domain of humans and the dangerous and wild territory of noxious spirits and demonic forces (Greve 1989: 219). All subsequent *jhākris* remind the witch of this pact every time they conduct healing rituals involving witchcraft.

According to one interpretation, the story brings to light aspects of gender relations in the context of bride-exchanging patrilineages. The contrast between the greedy sexually licentious witch and the shaman's faithful wife underscores female images that come into play in the ambivalent position of wives in present-day society (Greve 1989: 219). The wife holds an ambivalent position because upon marriage she is incorporated into the husband's household, but retains her relationship with members of her father's lineage. She represents divided loyalties and her position easily lends itself to a conflict of interest (Hitchcock 1974b: 154). Her incorporation into the husband's group is incomplete until she has children and her loyalties are unproven even though her sexuality is under control. These are the circumstances that give rise to suspicions of witchcraft. The story is a reminder that men must be wary of the dual nature of their wives and to ensure that the potential for witchcraft does not arise (Greve 1989: 220).

The story ends with the shaman reuniting with his faithful wife, but the fact of his alliance with the witch remains. This story, therefore, also highlights the ambiguous social status of the shaman. As Hitchcock (1974b: 154) concludes his analysis: "The shaman's power against evil comes from his knowledge of it and his implications in it." Evil remains. "He prevails. But just barely and only briefly, and he prevails at the cost of an alliance with evil, possibly even at the cost of 'knowing' the Witch, with the dual implication carried by the word" (Hitchcock 1974b: 154). The nine sisters continue to manifest their evil in the world by capriciously affecting female embryos, to cause new witches to be born (Hitchcock 1976a: 181).

Do women really practice witchcraft? No. Witches are not members of mysterious earth goddess cults, a shamanistic religion, or an indigenous female liberation movement in which magic serves to empower women in a rigid patriarchal society. Witches in fact do not exist. Witchcraft is a figure of belief. No one engages in the acts of which they are accused, whether it is conducting ghastly rites at the crossroads, attending nocturnal congregations at mother goddess temples, shifting shape, or mixing magic powders in people's food. In this respect, Nepalese witch-beliefs are similar to the witch-beliefs encountered by anthropologists in other ethnographic contexts (see Sidky 1997: 62–65).

It is not the witch herself, but rather the beliefs held by members of society about witches that provide clues about any witchcraft phenomenon. The term "witch" is a pejorative label denoting deviant antisocial behavior. Usually it is attached to individuals who are ill-tempered, quarrelsome, eccentric, or of questionable reputation (Macdonald 1976b: 377). As such, witchcraft beliefs may be seen in conventional anthropological terms as a mechanism that ensures that people conform to societal norms, lest they be suspected of witchcraft.

Moreover, witchcraft accusations are embedded in interpersonal relationships. The *jhākris* know very well the social dynamics of witchcraft beliefs and this is why they refuse to name specific individuals as witches. As Jhākri Shukra Bahādur Tamang pointed out:

> we know who the *boksīs* are, yes, but we do not reveal their names because this would cause much strife in the village. We do not want to bear the responsibility of causing such disturbances inside families and in our community.

Instead of pointing out specific individuals, the misfortune or illness at hand, which is often rooted in interpersonal conflicts, tensions, and ill feelings between family members, such as between daughter-in-law and mother-in-law, are restated in mystical terms. In this way, the misfortune is deflected by being projected outside and blamed upon a nebulous witch figure who purportedly lives somewhere nearby, in a house facing such and such direction, which has so many occupants, and so on.

When treating patients possessed by a witch, the *jhākri* asks the witch (i.e., the patient) directly why she has afflicted the patient and what must be done to appease her. The patient is in a sense providing a self-diagnosis (cf. Blustain 1976: 92), enabling the *jhākri* in his capacity as "interpreter of the world" to decipher his/her field of social relations. This is how he discovers social tensions within the family, and pinpoints the precise nature of the neglect of interpersonal or social obligations that had called forth the terrible supernatural force afflicting his client. Witchcraft beliefs also serve to provide an explanation for uncanny misfortunes that befall people, such as accidents, economic hardships, or the death of a child. The *jhākri* specifies why the calamity has befallen by attributing it to the machinations of anonymous witches and prescribes what people must do to restore order in their lives. Witchcraft beliefs, therefore, function as a theory the *jhākri* uses to explain misfortunes and a mechanism to defuse social tensions and anxieties.

This, however, does not mean that witchcraft beliefs always operate in these ways, that witchcraft accusations are a prelude to mending of social rifts, or that people do not reach their own conclusions about the precise identity of the witches in their communities, as the case I describe below indicates. In this context, it is the socially marginal, weak, and powerless members of a community who are targeted. The recurrent pattern here is that the unfortunate suspects are remarkably unlike the lethal, magically endowed figures discussed in the *jhākri's* narratives or as she exists in the public imagination. When harm befalls those who are privileged and powerful, and self-conscious of their privileges, they tend to demonize the impoverished and the weak by accusing them of thought crimes (envy projected as harm). Moreover, witchcraft accusations by those in positions of power to settle old scores are likely in some circumstances (cf. Sagant 1988).

It is often stated in the ethnographic literature on Nepal that witches may be suspected and gossip and rumors may circulate about these individuals, but no one is openly accused for fear of legal consequence. As it is nearly impossible to prove cases of witchcraft in court, accusers fear being sued for sullying the accused person's reputation (Miller 1997: 211–212). Ethnographers often state that Nepali law not only specifies harsh penalties (fines, confiscation of property, or imprisonment) for acts of witchcraft and sorcery, but also for those who fail to prove charges of witchcraft and sorcery against others (Peters 1981: 71; Hitchcock 1976a: 182; Maskarinec 1995: 22; Macdonald 1976b). Thus, the suspected witch is believed to remain in the community, her reputation besmirched, but otherwise unharmed.

Unfortunately, this is not the case. Open accusations are frequently reported. Violence against women is a corollary of witchcraft beliefs. An incident during one of my field seasons in the Jire area brought this particular issue tragically to light (Sidky et al. 2002: 148). Late one rainy afternoon in June 1999, a Sherpa man came walking up to the Jire police checkpoint on the road leading out of the valley. He was drenched and covered in blood. In one hand he carried a large blood-covered Nepalese *khukurī* knife. In the other hand he had the severed head of an old woman, which he grasped by the hair. He wanted to surrender to the police guard standing guard at the checkpoint. The guard who saw the horrific scene was frightened. Unsure of the knife-wielding man's intentions, he tried to put a cartridge into his rifle to stop him, but his hand shook so badly that he could not manage this. An officer alerted to what was happening at the guardpost rushed over, grabbed the rifle, loaded it, and captured the knife-wielding man. I followed the group of people rushing to the checkpoint and saw the man's apprehension.

In the investigation that ensued it was revealed that the man believed that the old woman was a witch who had destabilized his mind with her magic. A consultation with a *jhãkri* had confirmed his suspicion that he was bewitched, although the *jhãkri* had not identified the witch in question by name. His own suspicions led him to identify the victim as his tormentor. He then made up his mind to kill the witch and her daughter, whom he also suspected of being a witch, because it is widely believed that witchcraft runs in the family. Fortunately, the daughter was not home at the time of the attack. Unable to find the daughter after having dispatched the mother, in anger the knife-wielding man killed her goat that was tied outside the door.

Anthropologists conducting fieldwork in Nepal, concerned with theoretically innovative ways of producing erudite, dialogic ethnographic texts, seem to have overlooked what happens in the real world. Thus, discussions of Nepalese witch hunting and its horrible consequences are not to be found in the ethnographic literature. Gruesome and senseless acts of murder, such as the one described above, are not infrequent, but exact statistics are unknown. What we know, however, is that accused witches are often subjected to horrible cruelties. It is often the women and the elderly who are targets of abuse and humiliation.

During the nineteenth century there were various means used to deal with witchcraft, as indicated in the 1853 Jang Bahādur Rānā Code (Macdonald 1976b). For example, patients thought to be possessed by a witch were branded in the belief that the wound would be transferred to the witch wherever she was. Making the patient dance with the use of mantras was thought to also make the witch responsible for the affliction to dance, thereby revealing her identity. Ordeals were used as well. Suspected witches were asked to plunge their hands in containers of boiling water or hot oil or grasp red-hot irons with their bare hands. Guilt was determined based upon whether or not the suspect sustained an injury. The nineteenth-century legal code, although it did not deny the reality of witchcraft and sorcery, nevertheless stipulated strict provisions regarding the rules of evidence. For example, if a patient was branded, but such a wound did not appear on any suspected witches as it is supposed to, or if the patient was burned by the hot iron, the healer was subject to a fine. A suspect who was "neither branded nor made to dance" could not be subjected to the ordeal, driven out of the village, or brought before a judge regardless of verbal accusations.

At present, witch persecutions present a problem in Nepal and many of the restrictions specified in the Rānā legal code seem to have been forgotten. Accused witches are ostracized, driven from their homes, assaulted and violently beaten, tortured, whipped with stinging nettle, and their heads shaved or hair pulled out. These innocent victims are made to endure ghastly humiliating acts, such as being paraded around naked, and being forced to eat human feces in the belief that this renders witches powerless. Those who survive such treatment are often intimidated into silence with threats of further violence. Local officials, if not implicitly involved in encouraging the persecutions, often turn a blind eye to these matters. In cases I have heard of, murderers have gone unpunished. Such incidents are familiar to NGO workers and some even make the local newspapers (see Pyakurel 2006; Subedi 2004; Dhakal 2003; Amnesty International 2004).

Patients suspected of being possessed by witches are also subjected to cruel and inhuman procedures in the belief that the pain of the violence inflicted upon them is felt by the possessing witch. Branding with hot irons and caning in the pretext of punishing the witch are common procedures in such cures, even in places like Kathmandu (cf. Dietrich 1998: 190–191, 195).

These incidents belong to the dark side of shamanism because the witch and the shaman are inexorably connected. The presence of shamans implies the existence of witches and if witches are absent, shamans are out of business. As the saying goes, "if there is no *boksī*, the *jhākri* cannot perform." The shaman's implication in evil contributes to an implicit ambivalence people have toward shamanism.

9

+

Ban-Jhãkri:
Supernatural Abductions
and Shamanic Initiation

At the dawn of time, Mahādev projected his *ātmā* (soul) and created *ban-jhākri*, the first shaman. Mahādev trained him in the healing arts and enjoined him with two tasks: to help the sick, and to bring worthy candidates into the forest (*jaṅgal*) and train them as *jhākris* (Macdonald 1976a: 321). This event sets the precedent for the transmission of the shaman's sacred knowledge from master to disciple, from one generation to the next (cf. Miller 1997: 218). So it was and so it is down to the present.

The *ban-jhākri*, as Riboli (2000: 125, 134) observes, is responsible for initiating shamans throughout Nepal. Anthropologist Robert Paul (1976: 145) considers *ban-jhākri* to be an autochthonous Nepalese god and the tutelary deity of shamans. If correct, this would suggest that Nepalese shamanism developed in part from an indigenous tradition, centered upon this numinous being. Nepalese shamans refer to the *ban-jhākri* as the primordial *jhākri*, wielder of powerful magic and possessor of sacred knowledge passed down by the gods from a mythic past, a golden age when the universe was new. He is himself considered a divinity, the god of the forest, and the master of the wild beasts and the dangerous spirits of the wilderness. There are small shrines dedicated to *ban-jhākri*, where people offer blood sacrifice, and local people throughout the country point out particular caves as his abode (Miller 1997: 21; Peters 2005: 44).

To train new shamans, *ban-jhākri* kidnaps potential candidates and takes them into his lair deep in the forest. Cases of *ban-jhākri* abduction occur across the country. The only exception seems to be the far west, where *ban-jhākri* is associated with the spirit of dead shamans, rather than the forest god who initiates neophytes into the vocation (Maskarinec 1995: 196).

The *ban-jhākri* is therefore a nearly pan-Nepalese phenomenon. Not connected to any specific caste or ethnic group, this mystical being speaks all languages and converses with those he interacts in their own dialect (Nicoletti 2004: 22).

Macdonald provided the first scholarly treatment of the *ban-jhākri* and his role in Nepalese shamanism in an article published in 1962 (Macdonald 1976a: 311–312, 335–337; 1975: 123). References to the *ban-jhākri* abound in the subsequent ethnographic literature (Conton 2005; Desjarlais 1989: 295–296; Eigner 2001; Fournier 1976: 103–105; Hitchcock 1976a: 169–170; Maskarinec 1995: 196, 211; Miller 1997: 21, 216–223; Nicoletti 2004: 20–23; Paul 1976: 145; Peters 1981: 80, 2005; Riboli 2000: 80–90; Sagant 1976: 61, 68–69; Skafte 1992: 51–52; Sidky et al. 2002: 142–144; Winkler 1976: 250; Walter 2001: 112). Some writers have associated *ban-jhākri* with Yaksha, a Hindu and Buddhist demigod who was initially the tutelary god of the forest in Hindu mythology (Peters 2005: 41). Others have suggested a linkage between *ban-jhākri* and Hanumān, the monkey god of Hindu mythology, as well as the Yeti (Müller-Ebeling et al. 2002: 105). However, the *jhākris* with whom I work have categorically rejected such associations.

Known as *bash-puimbo* among the Sunwars (Fournier 1976: 103), *riphombo* among the Jirels (Sidky et al. 2002: 142) and Sherpas (Desjarlais 1992: 82), and *tampugma* among the Limbus (Sagant 1976: 69), *ban-jhākri* roams deep in the forests, away from human habitations, pounding his drum. As Jhākri Shukra Bahādur Tamang noted, "*ban-jhākri* is active in the evenings, midday, and midnight. You can hear him beating his drum, tak! tak! tak!" This is how the numinous being calls to, or invites, potential candidates into the wilderness where he will train them. Those beckoned may sometimes refuse to come back. They remain in the wilderness in solitude and succumb into possession states. The separation from the domain of humans is so complete that such individuals may be unable to recognize family members or relatives seeking them out. This "introversion and restructuring" dissociates the incipient shaman both from mundane ego consciousness and from people and society (cf. Laughlin et al. 1992: 272). The story of a Limbu man named Dhan Rup, collected by Sagant (1976: 68–70), exemplifies the theme of "flight to the forest:"

> At the age of 10 or 12, he was sick for a long time. . . .When he heard the sounds of the *ban-jhākri* . . . drums coming from the forest, he would go off alone at night into the forest to follow the sounds. . . . He would leave for the entire night. When he returned, he would beat a brass plate and dance in a trance. Or else he would remain prostrate in a stupor. . . . It was later, towards [the age of] 17, that he fled for good to the forest. . . . As soon as he had entered the forest he had thrown away his clothes. He lived there completely naked.

Figure 9.1.   Hanumān, the theriantropic monkey god of Hindu mythology
(Chamundi Temple, Himachel Pradesh, photo by H. Sidky)

. . . It was difficult to find him. Later he himself told how he was frightened by the men who approached him. He saw them with enormous heads, enormous eyes, making hellish noises. He ran to hide. He burrowed in the most impenetrable thickets. He followed his master, the *ban-jhākri*, who led him farther and farther into the jungle to hide. . . . The *ban-jhākri* had a human appearance. They [*ban-jhākri* and his wife] took good care of him. Better than a father or mother. They taught him to dance, to recite. They gave him cooked [food] on the backs of their hands. . . He was finally found lying prostrate. But when they tried to seize him, he struggled furiously. He bit them, he tried to flee. They grabbed him by the wrists and took him by force. (Sagant 1976: 68–69)

I experienced a *ban-jhākri* event during my fieldwork in the Kabhre Palanchok District, in eastern Nepal in 2000. I had spent the day with my students collecting data on local farming practices and decided to spend the night in a village in Kabhre. Around midnight when the small community was engulfed in darkness, I heard the sound of a beating drum in the distance. I thought that there was a *jhākri* performance and that I should go and watch. I asked one of my students and my field assistant Probin to find out where the *jhākri* was performing and to ask if we could attend. The two promptly departed. About ten minutes later, they returned with odd looks on their faces and said that there was no *jhākri* performing in the village that night. When I asked who was drumming, they replied that the villagers said it was not a *jhākri*, but *ban-jhākri* trying to entice disciples to join him in the forest. In disbelief, I ran outside, but the drumming had stopped. The villagers reported that they often heard *ban-jhākri* pounding his drum late at night. My consultants noted that ordinary people can hear *ban-jhākri* drumming, but they can only see him if he wishes it. He strikes others down with illness should they approach him, enter his domain uninvited, or anger him in some way.

Some say that the term *ban-jhākri* refers to a class of numinous entities (cf. Riboli 2000: 84), while others suggest that there is only one immortal being. Several of the *jhākris* with whom I worked showed me bones belonging to *ban-jhākri*. They distinguished these from "yeti bones," which were also included among their medicines. They noted that the bones of the *ban-jhākri* possess potent curative and protective magical powers (Sidky et al. 2002: 144), suggesting that perhaps there are many *ban-jhākris* and that these beings do die (cf. Conton 2005: 27; Skafte 1992: 52).

Nepalese shamans refer to *ban-jhākri* as the originator of their vocation and relate remarkably similar accounts:

Ban-jhākri is the god of the jungle (forest); he is the original *jhākri*. We make offerings to him. We make clay statues of him, decorate them with garlands of marigold flowers, and put them in a clean place. *Ban-jhākri* is small in stature and his feet point backwards. He goes around with his golden drum near the river, in the forest, and on steep slopes. I have seen him. He can instantly appear and disappear (Jhākri Dul Temba Sherpa).

Ban-jhākri is a special being. He did not issue through the union of man or woman, but came into being from the gods. He is the god of the forest. He can be benevolent or malevolent. Ordinary people cannot see him, only the powerful *jhākris* can see him. If a man walking in the jungle encounters *ban-jhākri*, he will succumb to illness. The symptoms include sudden violent shivering, random speech, rolling eyes, and dementia. This is a sickness that only a powerful *jhākri* can cure and then only if the patient is promptly brought for treatment. *Ban-jhākri* is very small, about the size of a nine or ten year old child. He has a mixture of human and monkey features. He has long matted hair, his feet point backwards, and he moves about naked. He wears *rudrācche mālā* and *riṭṭho mālā* and beats a *ḍhyāgro* made of gold. He steals children and trains them to become *jhākris*. He lives with his wife, the *ban-jhākrini*, in the jungles and remote parts of mountains and in caves. (Jhākri Shukra Bahādur Tamang)

Ban-jhākri is a real god. He stays deep in the jungle or the wilderness and people rarely see him. *Ban-jhākris* is from the time before . . . from ancient times. He kidnaps prepubescent boys and takes them into his cave in the jungles where he teaches them to become *jhākris*. We do *pujā* to *ban-jhākri* on occasions when he has made a patient ill. (Jhākri Rabindra Rāi)

Ban-jhākri is an ancient god. Mahādeu created him. He is small in size, is covered with hair like a monkey, and his feet are in the opposite direction of people's feet. I have seen him many times. He lives in the forest near rivers and cliffs. *Ban-jhākri* helps us, but sometimes he strikes people with illness and we have to exorcise him. If he overpowers us, we have to hold a *pujā* for him and worship him until our patient is cured. He sometimes steals children and trains them as *jhākris*. Those who survive become very strong *jhākris*. (Jhākri Nir Bahādur Jirel)

The *ban-jhākri* is clearly a therianthrope. Here one might recall that therianthropic beings in Paleolithic art have been interpreted either to be shamans in animal disguise, or the master of animals, a divine being and owner of animals who decides the success or failure of the hunt (Dickson 1990: 130–131; Hayden 2003: 135; Lommel 1967: 128). Nepalese ethnography offers an interesting insight into this issue. The therianthropic *ban-jhākri* is the god of the forest, master of animals and nature spirits, and the tutelary god of shamans, a clue that therianthropic beings do figure in shamanistic thought. However, while the *ban-jhākri* is of central importance to Nepalese shamanism, he does not figure in shamanic art.

As the accounts above suggest, *ban-jhākri* abducts potential candidates, usually adolescent males between the ages of eight and thirteen, and transports them by supernatural means to a cave or grotto deep in the forest where he trains them as *jhākris*. Those abducted really disappear from the village, corroborating the theme of "flight to the forest." Numerous abduction narratives have been recorded throughout Nepal (see Conton 2005; Eigner 2001; Riboli 2000: 80–90). The story Jhākri Narsing Jirel related about his grandfather's initiation as a shaman is a typical abduction narrative:

My grandfather told us this story: One day when I was eleven years old, I was sleeping by a rock near Khimti Khola [river/stream] when suddenly everything began to tremble. I looked up and saw a small figure appear in front of me, he was about my size, wore no clothes, and had long hair that went all the way past his knees. What was strange was his feet, they pointed backwards. He said in an eerie and thundering voice: "I am your guru, I am *ban-jhākri*." When I heard this I fainted. When I regained some sense, I felt like I was floating, my body was carried away, to the upland forests. I was very frightened, I tried to scream and resist but my body was paralyzed.

I don't know how long I was unconscious. When I awoke I was inside a large cave. It was bright, everything was radiating light, including my face and body; it seemed that the walls and everything else was made of pure gold. There were many strange and beautiful things there. I was very afraid and did not know what was happening. I thought I was dreaming or that maybe I was dead. I saw *ban-jhākri* and his wife, the *ban-jhākrini*, she was big, ugly, and naked, with large sagging breasts. She had sharp yellow teeth, fiery eyes, and a long red tongue, like that of a wild animal. She also had long hair. I was scared of her. *Ban-jhākrini* said she was hungry and wanted to kill me and cook my flesh for a meal. But *ban-jhākri* said that I was his student and warned her to stay away. They were speaking in a strange tongue, but somehow I was able to understand everything.

Ban-jhākri removed my clothes and examined my body for scars or deformities. Finding none, he was pleased and told me not to worry. He said that I had exceptional spiritual qualities and that he brought me there to teach me how to heal people. He said he would give me great powers and the ability to see evil spirits that roam in the world and cause terrible sickness. I was no longer afraid.

We did not eat or sleep much. When he gave me food, I had to eat it from the back of my hand as he did. Everyday, he taught me mantras against evil spirits and witches as well as how to do *pujā* and play the *nga* [*ḍhyāgro*, the *jhākri*'s drum]. I felt safe with the guru. I would recite the mantras and play the drum when the guru went outside the cave to make *pujā* to the gods. When he returned, the teaching resumed.

Then one day, I woke up and found myself in the same spot by the river from where the guru took me away. I was covered in dirt, my clothes were ripped, and my feet were bleeding. Everyone was shocked when I returned home. They told me that I was gone for over 8 days, but I did not know that. I did not know how long I had been gone, days, weeks, months. They thought that I had been killed by wild animals or drowned in the river. For many days, I could not utter a sound and I shook. This was taken as sign that I was to be a *jhākri*. *Ban-jhākri* took me to his cave three more times, when I was about thirteen years old. He taught me more mantras and all the skills I would need to conduct rituals. I did not visit him personally after that, but he still appears in my dreams and teaches me mantras.

Kumar Thapa, a Chetri *jhākri*, related his encounter with the *ban-jhākri* as follows:

My parents are from Okhaldhunga [part of Sagarmatha zone, eastern Nepal]. My father went to West Bengal, India [on the India-Bhutan border] in search of work and I was born there. We had a herd of cattle and though I was very young [five years old], it was my duty to look after the cattle as they grazed in the jungle. One day when I was in the jungle looking after the livestock I started to take a nap. The next thing I remember is seeing dust swirling in the wind, going round and round, and coming toward me. The whirlwind finally reached me and I had the feeling I was in its center and began to spin rapidly, round and round. I rose in the air and I heard sounds of ringing bells and beating drums. Then, there was complete darkness, like going through a tunnel, and I lost consciousness.

When I opened my eyes, I found myself inside a cave full of light. Later I found that the cave was inside a huge black stone between two waterfalls deep in the jungle. Light bathed the cave—it is a huge palace with many rooms, all of them filled with golden objects. Then I saw something that looked like a monkey or ape-like creature, about three to four feet tall, staring at me. He had a hairy body, the hair on his head was long, and his feet pointed toward his back. At first, I was terrified to see him, but he was looking at me affectionately and said, "Child, are you hungry? Do you want to eat something?" His tone reassured me. I was not frightened anymore and I was hungry. I said to him, I would like to eat rice. Upon my reply, he said that he was the *ban-jhākri* and he had brought me to his home to teach me *jhākri* lessons. He gave me two bananas and said that I should eat no other fruits, wild roots, or tubers during his teachings. He also said that *jhākris* who are trained by him must never drink alcohol.

Ban-jhākri whose appearance is ugly is actually very beautiful. When he shows his divine appearance, his face radiates in a halo. His wife is very ugly. She is twice as big as he is and has sharp teeth and a horrible face. She eats human flesh. *Ban-jhākri* told her not to come near me or try to devour me. She left me alone.

The day *ban-jhākri* took me was Tuesday and he said my lesson would start as of Thursday. *Ban-jhākris* teach three kinds of lessons to their students. These include *Herne* [looking], *Dekhne* [seeing/attention], and *Garne* [doing]. *Herne* is a kind of lesson in which he teaches his students to look at the present situation and how to determine people's problems. In *Dekhne*, he teaches how to see the future of the people, and in *Garne*, he teaches how to solve problems. But he may not teach all three to a single student. If the lessons start on Thursday, the student learns only *Herne* and *Garne*. Nevertheless, he gets some lesson of *Dekhne* also, just like an eye doctor also has to learn about other parts of the human body. If the lessons begin on Saturday, the student will learn all three lessons. As my lessons began on Thursday, I learned only *Herne* and *Garne*. He also taught me how to play the drum and dance. I learned many mantras, which he whispered in my ears.

I was in a trance or dreamlike state during the entire time I was there, except at the time of the teachings. I remained there for seven months. After seven months, when my lessons were completed, I found myself at the place from where *ban-jhākri* had taken me. It was like waking from a long dream. Although I received training as a *jhākri* at the age of five, I was too young to start practicing as a professional. I began curing people when I was 9 years old. I have no other teachers. *Ban-jhākri* continues to teach me in dreams.

Ban-jhākri is one of the seven brothers, the others are: *suna-jhākri* [golden], *ritthe-jhākri* [black], *latte-jhākri* [matted hair], *gore-jhākri* [fair-skinned], *rittai-jhākri* [unadorned], and *sete-jhākri* [white]. I do not know what the other brothers teach, but the ultimate Guru of all *jhākris* is Lord Śiva. One is named after the teacher, so one who has been taught by *ban-jhākri* is called *ban-jhākri*, one taught by *suna-jhākri* is called *suna-jhākri*, and so on. I am called *ban-jhākri*.

These spirit abductions occur frequently in Nepal and occasionally such incidents even make the local newspapers (Conton 2005: 27–28).

The stories are remarkably similar and are examples of a larger category of phenomena with similar dynamics known as "entity encounter experiences" (see Houran 2000; Houran and Thalbourne 2001). The abduction is sudden and unexpected. In some cases, the chosen individuals are taken as they wake up from sleep, in other cases dreams and hallucinations compel them to run into the forest where they are captured. All accounts have dreamlike characteristics. There is the sensation of floating or levitation. Passing through long dark passageways, the place where the abductees arrive is brightly lit and covered with gold. All accounts agree that *ban-jhākri* is a therianthropic being, with human and animal features. He is small in size, with a hairy body, a humanoid face with deep-set penetrating eyes, backward feet, and is the quintessential shaman who possesses mysterious superhuman powers and sacred knowledge rooted in nature. To obtain this knowledge, ordinary humans must exit the profane world of people and go deep into the heart of nature itself. *Ban-jhākri* goes about naked, but here nakedness is indicative of purity and holiness rather than sexuality.

Ban-jhākri lives in the forest with his wife, a huge ferocious cannibalistic monster with large pendulous breasts who tries to devour her husband's disciples. The Chepang of southern and central Nepal refer to *ban-jhākri*'s wife as *ban-boksini*, or "the witch of the forest" (Riboli 2000: 84). However, *ban-boksini*'s malice is seldom directed at people in the villages, unlike the human *boksis*, as she remains confined to her forest abode.

Candidates undergo inspection for signs of physical scars or deformities, which are indicative of spiritual imperfections. Sometimes, the *ban-jhākri* removes the candidate's entrails surgically and cleans his body of impurities (cf. Riboli 2000: 86–87), which represents a form of dismemberment, a well-known shamanistic initiatory motif. Failing the test results in the candidate's eviction from the cave. Sometimes, *ban-jhākrini* devours these unfortunate individuals. Villagers who periodically discover scattered human remains in the forest attribute them to the voraciousness of *ban-jhākrini* (cf. Nicoletti 2004: 22).

Those who pass the test remain with *ban-jhākri* anywhere from several days to several years, learning the sacred knowledge. Initiates often report feelings of trust in the *ban-jhākri* as their benevolent guru, who assumes the role of their teacher and protector from the *ban-jhākrini* and other dangers. At the completion of their training, the abductees are enjoined with the mission to use their new knowledge to help others. Thereafter the abductees abruptly find themselves back in their villages or homes. Often they do not know how long they were away, that is, they report temporal distortion or "missing time." They are in a state of shock, act confused, and display signs of physiological stress. Some have nightmares or experience hallucinations and may be unable to speak for a length of time, symptoms similar to the initiatory crisis of ordinary *jhākris*.

Eventually, certain abductees overcome the ontological crisis represented by the abduction, experience a psychological transformation, and reconstitute their identity by becoming *jhākris*. The abduction is therefore a conversion experience. These individuals may either take up the *jhākri* vocation immediately or, as is more common, do so after further training under the tutelage of human gurus. Exceptional candidates become self-generated *jhākris*, who claim to have learned all of their mantras and healing techniques directly from *ban-jhākri*. Such practitioners acknowledge no human gurus at all. The abduction experience is in some cases repeated and some candidates maintain lifelong psychic connections with their supernatural guru in dreams.

Abduction by *ban-jhākri* represents an alternate and culturally accepted trajectory toward the *jhākri*'s vocation. It is a more prestigious calling than the usual initiatory spirit possession described in chapter 4. Spirit abduction as a form of shamanic initiation also occurs elsewhere (cf. Eliade 1964: 87; Shirokogoroff 1935: 346; Hitchcock 1976a:169–170). Nebesky-Wojkowitz (1956: 550), for example, mentions stories of spirit abduction in the Tibetan Bön tradition:

Among the Siberian peoples circulate stories about shamans who were initiated at a juvenile age by spirits. Such a tradition is also found in one of the Bon works: it tells of a young Tibetan who was abducted by spirits and who roamed with them for thirteen years. During this time he acquired supernatural powers, which enabled him to communicate with spirits after his return among men. (Nebesky-Wojkowitz 1956: 550)

At the age of twenty-six, this young Tibetan abductee

came to himself with the power to see such and such a place inhabited by such and such demons for the benefit or harm of the people. He propagated the idea and methods of propitiation and subjugation of the demons. Thus originated the primitive practices of Bon to deal with demons in the under world, to worship deities in heaven, and to work for the welfare of people in between (An-Che 1948: 33).

While there are parallels here, supernatural abduction as a form of shamanic initiation by a forest divinity seems to be a distinctive and recurrent feature of Nepalese shamanism. Other elements of the experience, such as the phenomena of bright lights and halos, which often symbolize encounters with divinities, levitation or floating, and spiritual bodily examination and dismemberment are typical features of the shamanic initiation experience (Eliade 1964: 60–61).

One source of insight into *ban-jhākri* encounters is to look at what the imagery of the forest (*jaṅgal*) signifies for the Nepalese people. As Anthropologist Alan Fournier (1976: 105) put it, the forest represents

the evil world of wild beasts and hostile spirits. In this region, where adults are reluctant to enter, there are numerous stories of people being injured, deformed or lost in the jungle. Children go there to live for several days without food in the company of elves and malevolent spirits.

Relevant to this discussion are anthropologist Damian Walter's (2001: 112) observation regarding the association between the *ban-jhākri* and the forest:

This association is necessarily both physical and symbolic. In this sense, the forest is represented as being spatially distant from the social domain of house and village, and at the same time to be representative of all that is contrary to the principles that underlie this same social domain. That the [*jhākri*] shares many of these attributes with his tutelary deity is evident in the tales that are told by many [*jhākris*] describing their initial "capture" by the *ban-jhākri*, and the days or weeks they subsequently spend in the *ban-jhākri*'s lair deep in the heart of the forest. The forest is often described as the domain of wild animals, ghosts and bandits. It is a dangerous threatening zone, free from the constraints that normally impose order on the social world. From the *jhākri*'s perspective it is also a domain rife with symbolic associations and transformative potential.

The forest is an alien world, the quintessential realm of the nonhuman, numinous "Other." Expressing this otherness are traits such as nakedness, hairiness, supernatural powers, eating on the back of the hand, the *ban-jhākri*'s rearward and animal-like anatomical features, and the *ban-jhākrini's* monstrous desire for human flesh. As Desjarlais (1989: 295) has put it, the forest is an "experiential domain" for the Nepalese, a wild and dangerous place, where rationality and culture are absent, and goblins and the "wild side of human action runs rampant." The forest, he adds, is identical to an equally metaphorical image, what Westerners call "the unconscious." Venturing into the mysterious realm of the nonhuman Other, or "total otherness," as Nicoletti (2004: 22) puts it, is the requisite step toward acquiring shamanic powers. Meeting the *ban-jhākri* is also an encounter with "the psychically overpowering Other," which as Carl Jung (1978: 21) noted, has been a central characteristic of transformative religious experiences through time. The *ban-jhākri* abduction experience may thus be considered a metaphor for the plunge into the inner depths of the human psyche, or levels of primary meaning, unconscious depths—the level of archetypes.

In the conceptual framework of the mythic world of Nepalese shamanism, the *ban-jhākri* symbolizes the source of knowledge from nature, while his monstrous wife the dangers of the shamanic initiation, which requires an excursion into an alien world, the wilderness, wherein dwell wild and dangerous spirits (cf. Peters 2005: 47). Alternatively, Riboli (2000: 84) suggests that *ban-jhākri* and his wife symbolize the two fundamental and inseparable aspects of shamanism, its positive healing (white) and negative destructive (black) sides.

Anthropologist Leslie Conton (2005: 30) identifies three stages in the *ban-jhākri* abduction experience: the neophyte's removal from the human world and immersion into the nonordinary reality of the *ban-jhākri*; the period of bonding with the *ban-jhākri* and tutelage and absorption of shamanic knowledge; and return to the ordinary world of humans. She compares these to the archetypal rites of passage delineated by Arnold Van Gennep and elaborated upon by Victor Turner, with its stages of segregation, liminality, and reincorporation (Sidky 2004: 313–316).

In line with the current orientation within the general field of shamanic studies, Conton (2005: 33) prefers not to squeeze the Nepalese experiences and beliefs into Western rational framework, and is content to treat the *ban-jhākri* abduction phenomenon as an aspect of a "consensus consciousness" firmly anchored in a spiritual or cognitive reality valid in its own terms and context. This is a cultural determinist perspective that posits that all elements of anomalistic phenomena emanate entirely from imaginary subjective experiences shaped by culture (Hufford 1982: 14).

Ban-jhākri abductions are anomalous experiences that, in fact, bear a striking resemblance to an anomalous phenomenon in the West (primarily America), the so-called alien abductions, around which a cult has developed (cf. Appelle et al. 2000; Carroll 1999: 79; Fox 2000; Whitmore 1995: 81). As a number of writers have noted, there are also similarities between the experience of encountering alien beings and shamanic initiation in general (Bullard 2000: xix; Ring 1989: 15, 17; Whitmore 1995: 71). These cases may possibly involve what Hufford (1995: 28, 37; 2001: 19) calls "core supernatural experiences," these are anomalous experiences with recurrent universal features that give rise to folk supernatural beliefs in all who have them, regardless of prior beliefs. Such beliefs are widely held and are often at variance with official mainstream cultural tradition (McClenon 2001: 63). In America and Nepal, people have imputed narrative meaning and spiritual significance to these analogous anomalous experiences. By exploring this topic, I hope to make an important theoretical point regarding a particular problematic feature of the concept of shamanism in its current understanding and usage.

I first noted the parallels between the two types of experiences while discussing *ban-jhākri* abductions with Jhākri Kumar Thapa. During one conversation he asked me, "What happens in America? Don't people get snatched away by spirits?" I facetiously replied, "No, they are abducted by UFOs." On thinking about it, I realized that the parallels are remarkable. Although on the surface the topic of UFOs seems far removed from the domain of religious experience, however, as the psychologist Kenneth Ring has noted, they are similar in terms of their phenomenology and aftereffect. Hufford (1995: 37) has also commented on the similarities between beliefs regarding UFOs and beliefs about spirits or the spirit world in various religious traditions. Moreover, as author John Whitmore (1975: 74) adds, UFO beliefs represent the imposition of traditional religious themes on "a technological/science fiction framework." Thus, the comparison here seems appropriate.

Both experiences under discussion represent confrontations with the "superhuman Other" (cf. Whitmore 1995: 70) and are articulated through similar narrative structures. Like the *ban-jhākri* kidnappings, extraterrestrial abductions happen unexpectedly, have dreamlike qualities, and involve paralysis, paranormal transportation, disorientation, terror over the circumstances, fear of dying, imprisonment in brightly lit rooms, encounters with diminutive beings with nonhuman anatomical features, halos, and penetrating eyes (Baruss 2003: 152–159; Whitmore 1995: 70). UFO abductees report spiritual examinations for flaws and dismemberment (Whitmore 1995: 70). Medical procedures performed on the abductees are thematically parallel to shamanic dismemberment (Thompson 1991: 189).There are also reports of feelings of danger from some of the extraterrestrials and trust in the alien leader, who appears benevolent and the possessor of mysterious superhuman powers and advanced knowledge. There is also the parallel theme of "being chosen."

UFO abductees receive spiritual lessons and obtain psychic healing powers, as in the case of *ban-jhākri's* disciples. Finally, as in *ban-jhākri* abductions, the UFO encounter represents an ontological crisis and conversion experience (cf. Thompson 1991: 190). The experience ends with the abductees returning to the place from where they were taken, often feeling physically fatigued and unaware of the actual duration of the encounter. The feeling of "missing time" is a central component of UFO abductions (Baruš 2003: 152–153; Whitmore 1995: 71, 74) as it is with *ban-jhākri* events. The only notable differences are the elements of suppressed memories and overt sexual themes in the UFO encounters, which are absent among *ban-jhākri* abductees. As Whitmore (1995: 71) has summarized it:

> Shamanic initiations begin with the individual being pulled into the world of the Other, experiencing isolation from society. They involve brutal physical and mental ordeals, often centering on dismemberment and torture. After being judged worthy by his tormentors, the shaman's nature and mystical ancestry are revealed to him, much as the abductee is given knowledge of her descent. The shaman is often given eschatological knowledge and returns to society as a healer and religious authority chose by the spiritual realm. Inexplicable healings and feelings of having been chosen are also reported by UFO abductees. Both types of experience are extremely frightening, personality altering encounters with the Other, perceived at least at first as the Jungian Shadow [unconscious representation of negative aspects of the personality], mysterious and threatening to the conscious self. Both leave definite, permanent imprints on the psyche of the percipient.

What are we to make of these narratives? The abduction experiences are explicable in terms of the same neuropsychological processes and brain activities that underlie the phenomenon of spirit possession (Beyerstein 1999a; Blackmore 1994), as discussed in chapter 6. By stimulating certain parts of the brain with electrodes, neurophysiologist Michael Persinger (2003; 1989; 1987; 1983) has been able to create feelings analogous to those reported by paranormal abductees, such as hallucinations, disorientation, floating, experiencing the presence of spirits, and heightened sense of meaning. Such experiences center on electrical activity occurring in the temporal lobes (Mandel 1980; McClenon 2001: 63; Saver and Rabin 1997).

There is also a possible linkage between such experiences and sleep paralysis during the transition between sleeping and waking, when visual and auditory hallucinations similar to those of abductees are reported (Bower 2005; McNally and Clancy 2005; Cheyne 2001; Hinton et al.

2005; Hufford 2005; 1982). Many *ban-jhākri* abduction accounts involve individuals, such as Narsingh's grandfather and Kumar Thapa, who are
asleep, dreaming, are in the process of waking up from sleep, or who are
undergoing sleep disturbances at the time of their abduction (see Macdonald 1975: 122; Conton 2005: 28, 29, 30; Eigner 2001: 25–27; Peters 2005:
49; Skafte 1992: 50).

What does this say about the ontological status of the *ban-jhākri* kid-
napping and UFO abductions? One might speculate that perhaps we are
looking at an anomalous experience comparable to sleep paralysis with
recurrent universal features that generate similar independent subjective
accounts. In other words, what we are dealing with are historically/
ethnographically unrelated magicoreligious beliefs/behaviors with similarities due to the propensity of the human central nervous system to display common functional attributes in ASC. These types of similarities
have led to the classification of numerous historically/ethnographically
unrelated magicoreligious beliefs/behaviors under the label of shamanism. Are UFO abductees shamans? Are they connected to the histori-
cal/ethnographic shamanistic complex in Siberia? Are there associations
with the UFO phenomenon and Paleolithic hunting cultures? The answer
to these questions is obviously no. However, such lumping together of
similar but unrelated beliefs/behaviors is in part the reason for the intractability of the concept of shamanism, a topic to which I shall return in
the final chapter of this book.

Beyond these speculations, what we can say for certain with respect to
ban-jhākri is that many Nepalese, like Narsingh Jirel, Kumar Thapa, and
the other shamans, have no doubts about the authenticity and objective reality of the *ban-jhākri* encounters. As a figure of belief, *ban-jhākri* evinces
considerable awe, fear, and respect among many. An incident that took
place during my fieldwork in Nagarkot, in 2006, illustrates the pervasive-
ness of beliefs regarding the *ban-jhākri*. A local man who had stopped at a
roadside hotel to use the toilet facilities was found unconscious by the hotel staff. When revived, he reported that while he was walking down the
stairs leading to the toilet he noticed from the corner of his eyes a short
strange-looking man with long hair following him. When he turned
around and looked at the stranger he passed out. It seems that he had been
unconscious for about fifteen to twenty minutes before discovery. Although the man himself did not identify his alleged assailant, aside from
giving the description, local people and the hotel staff concluded that it
was *ban-jhākri*. The reason for the attack, people reported, was the man's
negligence to complete training as a *jhākri*, which he had initiated some
time before. This failure angered the *ban-jhākri*, provoking the attack.

I attended a healing ceremony in Nagarkot in 1999 involving a patient
whose affliction was attributed to the *ban-jhākri*. She had been ill for sev-

eral months. Medical treatment at the health post had not helped her. It was stated that her condition was "critical." The patient looked very weak and had to be assisted by family members during the curing rites. The remarkable aspect of this case was the high degree of anxiety and apprehension on the part of the shamans assembled for the healing ceremony. At the time, they refused to discuss what they were doing and it was only afterward that I learned the details of the case and the involvement of the *ban-jhākri*. As the senior officiating *jhākri* Man Bahādur Tamang put it, "*jhākris* encounter a dilemma when they have to treat patients afflicted by the *ban-jhākri*, as this brings them into confrontation with a powerful tutelary deity. This is not without risks."

Unlike any of the other healing ceremonies I have attended, seven senior students and five professional *jhākris* assisted the main *jhākri* in this case. Rather than taking on the task alone, the officiating *jhākri* called upon the assistance of his colleagues and former students. The proceedings began, not inside the patient's house as is customary, but outside in a nearby clearing. The *jhākris* began drumming and chanting. Together, they paid respect to the gods, offering incense and flowers, and danced as a group, "to call and make the gods happy." What was also extraordinary was that the healing rites were preceded by animal sacrifice, whereas ordinarily this takes place during or after the completion of a healing session (see chapter 10). A large altar was constructed outdoors, decorated with leaves and *sindūr* (red powder paint). Food offerings included rice, fruit, eggs, and alcohol. A goat was blessed, anointed with red powder and holy water. An assistant then sliced its throat with a knife and collected the blood in a receptacle. The animal's head was placed on the altar and the entire structure was doused with the blood. A cock was sacrificed and its blood sprinkled over the altar as well. The senior *jhākri* looked at its innards to determine the outcome of the ritual. The *jhākris* later explained that because they were undertaking a dangerous task, they first had to summon all the gods by making animal sacrifice and asking for their help and protection. They needed assurance of divine help before proceeding. After the sacrifice, the attending *jhākris* and onlookers ate the consecrated food (*parsād*). Only then did the *jhākris* feel confident enough to undertake their task.

The actual curing rites began after midnight. The senior *jhākri* and one of his most experienced colleagues began calling the gods and proceeded to shake and convulse. Working as a pair, they treated the patient by beating their drums, uttering mantras, and waving incense. Then something remarkable happened that startled many of those in attendance. The senior *jhākri* began to slap himself violently in the face, repeatedly, saying, "Why are you interfering?" Clearly, *ban-jhākri* was displeased and wished to punish the *jhākri* attempting to heal the patient. Only after receiving a

sound thrashing from the numinous entity he was embodying was the
shaman able to proceed. The ceremony lasted for several hours, and eventually the *jhākri*s were able to clarify the problem. As Man Bahādur
Tamang put it:

> the woman had neglected to attend a family obligation to the forest deity.
> Her grandfather was a great worshiper of *ban-jhākri* and then her father did
> the same. After his death, the obligation fell upon the daughter. She did the
> *pujā* for a few years, but stopped the worship once she became old. That is
> why the god made her sick.

The *ban-jhākri*, as I have attempted to point out in this chapter, represents a distinctive element of Nepalese shamanism. *Ban-jhākri* is an autochthonous mystical being whose role suggests that Nepalese shamanism may in part derive from an indigenous tradition that is distinct from
Hinduism or Buddhism. I have also tried to demonstrate how the
Nepalese ethnographic materials can provide insights into the problematic nature of the concept of shamanism as it is currently understood and
used. The *ban-jhākri* abductions have certain parallels with the anomalous
experiences reported by UFO abductees in America. Although the similarities are remarkable, we are dealing with two historically/ethnograph-
ically unrelated cultural phenomena. The tendency in the shamanism writ
large literature to lump together such analogous but unrelated phenomena is one reason for the intractability of the concept of shamanism.

10

Jhākri Basnu: Shamanizing and Ritual Drama

Many anthropologists agree that ritual drama can be a powerful means of evoking transformative states. One way of viewing ritual performances is as contextualized and dynamic social actions that are heightened modes of communication and interaction with theatrical attributes involving symbolism, metaphor, speech, gestures, costumes, staging, dance, and use of space (Claus 1997: 192–197; Morris 2006: 42). Rituals represent a deliberate display of "ideas and intentions" (Claus 1997: 200) based upon the culture's cosmology. Some anthropologists have focused upon rituals as communicative behavior from a linguistic or semiotic perspective, while some have approached it in terms of theater, as psychologically transformative performances of supernatural events by theatrical means (Claus 1997: 192–193). Others have focused on the effects of ritual performances upon the psychophysiology of participants and observers, a perspective that is of interest in relation to the *jhākri*'s practices and shamanistic healing

The Nepāli word for the *jhākri*'s all-night healing ceremony is *cintā*. This ceremony is a dynamic and dramatic event, sometimes inappropriately referred to as a séance (from the French *séance*, "sitting") a term which denotes immobility or stillness. *Jhākri basnu*, or shamanizing, involves elaborate and dynamic performances employing intense theatrical devices. The *jhākri* beckons spirits and divinities from all quarters by drumming, singing songs, dancing, and reciting mantras. He dramatically embodies these supernatural beings in order to remedy problems. A number of anthropologists working in Nepal have remarked about the theatrical qualities of *jhākri* performances, which often consist of several acts in which the

163

jhākri, the patient, and supernatural beings hold center stage, with minor walk-in parts given to the spectators (Fournier 1976: 118; Allen 1976a: 134–135). The ceremonies do indeed have theatrical qualities and *jhākris* are performing artists of sorts, some with exceptional skill, who employ modulations of sound, gestures, expressions, words, manipulation of objects, and varying drum accompaniments for maximum effect. The *cintā* is a ritual drama in every sense of the word, comparable in all respects to the dramatic performances of Siberian and north Asian shamans.

Laughlin et al. (1992: 212) construe ritual as "theatre of mind" that serves as a means of inducing particular states of consciousness in participants and audiences. The mechanism they suggest is "symbolic penetration," by which they mean "the effects exercised by the neural system mediating a symbolic precept . . . upon other neural, endocrine, and physiological systems within the being" (Laughlin et al. 1992: 190). By manipulating symbols, Laughlin et al. (1992: 195) add, "shamans are able to heal, evoke alternative phases of consciousness, stimulate inquiry and exploration, engender metaphorical-metonymic understanding, and transform ego identity." Ritual action establishes metaphorical reality, communicates messages, and draws and holds the attention of those present, thereby operating to amplify symbolic penetration and effect transformative changes (cf. Laughlin et al. 1992: 196). Power emanates from the ritual's communicative, experiential, and emotionally charged theatricality. The effectiveness of rituals, as Claus (1997: 196) has observed:

> is rooted in the emotions that precede the performance: anxiety, anger, tensions, and hope that the performance will resolve these. People enter the séance with a few general assumptions—reconfirmed with each successful performance—that there are spirits, that spirits can help discover the source of illness, and that séances can bring spirits to the people.

It is the drama and spectacle of the performance that must operate as a heightened mode of communication to hold attention, reconfirm, and bolster assumptions regarding the supernatural.

Jhākri healing ceremonies vary considerably depending upon the etiological picture and other factors, such as the *jhākri's* level of skill and showmanship, which add distinctive characteristics to every single performance. Maskarinec (1995: 118) is correct in pointing out that each performance constitutes an event that is unique and nonreplicable. Nevertheless, each performance represents an enactment of a broader cosmology and system of meanings shared by the *jhākri* and the members of his community (cf. Peters 1995). Here I shall provide an overview of some of the general features of the *jhākri* healing rituals based on ceremonies that I have attended and videotaped.

Cintā events are demarcated from ordinary experiences by the steps building up to the ritual performance, which includes solicitation of divinatory information, decisions regarding the type of ceremony to be performed, location and time, the organization of materials, sacrificial animals, and ritual paraphernalia necessary for the undertaking. Family members, kinsmen, and villagers take part in such preparations. These activities, which begin days or occasionally even weeks ahead of time, are not only meaningful, they also have evocative functions that serve to heighten emotions and expectations necessary to the ultimate outcome (cf. Claus 1997: 199).

Divination (*jokhānā hernu*) conducted during preliminary visits often precedes the *jhākri*'s decision to conduct a healing ceremony. Through divination, he is able to diagnose the cause of the problem and determine what type of ritual action is necessary. As Jhākri Kami Singh Tamang put it:

We diagnose by feeling the patient's pulse (*nāri*). We can tell whether there is a spirit inside his body, if a witch has attacked or has possessed the patient, or if a god or goddess is causing the problems. We *jhākris* do not ask our patient any questions we just feel their pulse and can find out the cause of the trouble. Feeling the pulse sets off sensations, like electricity, inside our bodies that tell us the nature of the problem. Another method of diagnosis is to drop rice on a plate and read the number and position of the rice grains. This can also reveal the source of the problem. We use one approach and if it is not effective, we use the other. This lets us know if it is a witch, a ghost, or an angry god. Then we know how to proceed.

Sometimes the *jhākri* will use the internal organs of sacrificial animals, such as the spleen of a goat or a chicken's liver, in order to divine the nature of the patient's maladies. Placing grains of rice on the membrane of a drum held horizontally, and striking it lightly from below to make the grains of rice align in patterns, is another form of divination.

Successful diagnosis depends upon the *jhākri*'s skills as "interpreter of the world" to associate a particular etiological condition with a socially meaningful supernatural cause, that is, meaningful to the patients, their kinfolk, and community. Divination is the first step in a larger process in which the *jhākri* redefines the problem in terms of the culture's symbols of the mythic world. He thus activates what medical anthropologist Arthur Kleinman (1988a: 108–141) refers to as a "symbolic bridge" that links experience, social relations, and cultural meanings and cosmology.

Once there is a determination through such preliminary diagnostic procedures, the *jhākri* sets the date of the ceremony and place, which is usually the patient's house. However, divinations are not always conclusive and the *jhākri* will make additional inquiries during the ceremony itself. The *jhākri* may also undergo *jokhānā* (divinatory) possession while in the midst of a nightlong healing ceremony, when he will sit in front of the patient and interrogate the spirits he is embodying to clarify the problem (see below).

The *jhākri* performs different rituals in a variety of contexts during the day and night, such as consecrating houses, propitiating local gods, making and dispensing charms (*buṭi*), conducting ancestral spirit rites, uttering protective mantras over children and pregnant women, performing divinations, and making amulets to protect taxi drivers from accidents or to cure sick cows. However, healing ceremonies always take place after dark. This is because "spirits are most active at night," Jhākri Kami Singh Tamang explained, "night is for them like day is for us [people]." These ceremonies usually last well past sunrise the next day.

The ceremony I will describe here involves a 43-year-old man suffering from stomach and chest pains and tingling sensations throughout his body. Doctors at the hospital in Kathmandu diagnosed his condition as asthma and heart problems. Having already spent 110,000 rupees (approximately $1,560 U.S. dollars in 2006) for these treatments without satisfactory results, he resorted to the services of the *jhākri*. By comparison, his total expenditure for the *cintā* is six thousand rupees (approximately $85 U.S. dollars), one thousand rupees as cash offerings, two thousand for the alcohol and cigarettes, and three thousand for rice and a chicken and goat for sacrifice.

After conducting divination, the *jhākri* informs his client that his planets are in an inauspicious alignment (*daśā garah*, or evil fortune from planets), in other words, that destructive cosmic forces are at work, and that he has become the target of several dangerous spells cast by a "known person who lives east of the patient's house." He names the spells causing the patient's symptom: *arīgal bheda* (hornet witchcraft); *mauri bheda* (bee witchcraft), *bhyāgutō bheda* (toad witchcraft); *sarpa bheda* (snake witchcraft). It is purely out of malice or envy that witches and sorcerers strike when someone is in a vulnerable condition. The purpose of the ritual I will describe is to avert ill fate or danger (*khargo kaṭāunu*, literally to cut or sever ill fate) due to *daśā garah*. Shukra Bahādur Tamang and his associates perform this ritual. Peters (1995: 53) who refers to this ritual as the *karga puja*, has noted that Tamang shamans perform it only for extremely critical cases.

To accomplish the task of *khargo kaṭāunu*, the *jhākris* will have to summon and negotiate with Yamarāja, "the God of Death," and his minions, the Yamadūta, who steal and consume people's souls. Yamarāja is the god who determines the fate of humans and exercises influence over planetary alignments that cause illness and death (cf. Höfer 1994: 193; Riboli 1995: 79). Therefore the shaman must negotiate with the divinity because he poses a serious danger to the patient's life (cf. Riboli 1995: 83). By deciding to conduct this ritual, the *jhākri* is in effect saying that the patient is dying. As the officiating *jhākri* put it, "we call Yamarāja, who is the king of all evils, to please him with our invocations or defeat him if the invocations do not work, so that he takes away the *daśā garah* affecting the patient who will otherwise die."

The patient and his immediate family, relatives, friends, and neighbors assemble in the dimly lit main room of the house. Some come because they have questions they wish to pose to the *jhākri*, some to break up the tedium of the evening, others to gossip with friends. The atmosphere during these occasions is informal and people drift in and out of the room at various times throughout the proceedings. This constant flow of people does not cease until well past midnight, when household children have fallen asleep and most onlookers have returned home (cf. Höfer 1994: 41).

In shamanistic healing, illness is a "public affair" in which more than just the patient and healer participate (cf. Riboli 2000: 159). It is the effect of the group as a whole and the sense of connection and understanding among them (i.e., intersubjectively constituted and negotiated social reality) that seems to be of some importance to the outcome (cf. Shirokogoroff 1935: 325). The audience gives the *cintā* its public dimension and this collective aspect is an important aspect of the healing process (Bulbulia 2006: 101; Sagant 1988). Onlookers are not passive observers, but as members of the patient's family, kin group, and community they forward their opinions regarding the diagnosis and curative procedures based upon their collective memories of past cases of illness and cures performed by other shamans. Their interactions with the officiating *jhākri*, inquiries about points of procedure, questions about technical details, and his responses concerning his performance, the divination, and prognosis of the patient's condition, constitute what Höfer (1994: 41) refers to as "a subtext" to the recitations. As Samuel (1995: 255) correctly points out, shamanic healing encompasses "mind, body, individual and social context."

The *jhākri* arrives in the evening. An assistant who carries the basket containing the shaman's drum and ritual paraphernalia accompanies him. The assistant's job is to pack and unpack the gear and help with other necessary preparations, such as setting up the altar (*thān*), replenish incense, supply wicks, fill the oil lamp, and serve alcohol and cigarettes to the shamans. However, some members of the audience also help in these tasks throughout the night. Accompanying the *jhākri* are two junior *jhākris* and disciples who will participate in the ceremony by singing and taking over drumming at times during the night.

The *jhākris* pay respects to the household deities by praying and asking for their help during the upcoming ritual. They then proceed to the main room where the patient and others are waiting. Now begins a lengthy process of preparation with considerable attention to minute details during each procedure. Attention to detail is essential in order to create the appropriate ambiance to facilitate the necessary mind-set for the *jhākris*, patient, and audience (cf. Walsh 1990: 165; Tart 1975). Through elaborate procedures, the *jhākris* first establish a magical barrier against the itinerant nocturnal spirits around the house where the *cintā* is being held and then construct a sacred "ritual space" in which the world and universe temporarily operate according to the ontological parameters of their cosmology and are subject to their enactments, exhortations, and entreaties. The limitations under which ordinary people live in everyday life temporarily cease, as the *jhākris* ritually mediate and reorder time and space. Within this dynamic sphere, the *jhākris* begin a process of protection, purification, exaltation, exploration, and negotiation. The metaphorical reality thus created, if successful, captivates the attention of all those present. This is how *jhākris* reconfigure and restore the imbalances in relationships and obligations that underlie the crisis at hand.

The senior *jhākri* begins by uttering mantras (*jap*) as he purifies his equipment with burning incense. He then begins counting the black beads on his *riṭṭho-mālā* and reciting the first of numerous protective mantras (*mālā japnu*). Meanwhile, the junior *jhākris* light a fire in the hearth to heat the drum, while the assistant starts unpacking the equipment. Next, the junior *jhākris* and assistant begin constructing the altar. The altar represents the focal point of the numinous energy in the ritual. It is a cosmogram infused with sacred symbols and divine power. The manipulation and placement of objects on the altar begins the process whereby the shaman "transcends profane space" and "enters into contact with the spiritual world" (Eliade 1964: 147). The altar is a kind of portal through which gods and spirits manifest themselves. Altars vary considerably in their construction and complexity according to the purpose at hand (see Allen 1976a: 132; Höfer 1994: 59–64; Jones 1976: 37–38; Holmberg 1989: 158–159; Riboli 1995: 84).

For the ceremony in question, the *jhākris* make 12 rice-dough images (*torma*) representing the gods who will give them power and protection if other *jhākris* or witches (*boksī*) attack while they are performing. The dough images will serve as temporary vessels for the deities. The divinities include Guru Rinpoche, Gurula Yum, God of the Earth, God of the East, God of the Twelve Horoscope Signs, God of the West, God of the North, and five bodyguard deities. A coin is inserted in each of the named *torma*s as an offering ("oblation to the gurus") and the images are placed on a rectangular bed of unhusked wheat, as a food offering or *prasād*, laid directly on the clay floor.

A wooden container holding two ritual daggers, or *phurba*s, a pot filled with millet beer, and an egg are placed alongside the images. On the right and left sides of the *torma*s, respectively, the *jhākris* put an oil lamp and a clay incense burner. A *khukuri* knife, a weapon with which the *jhākri* will combat supernatural beings, is stuck in the ground point first next to the oil lamp. A low wooden platform behind the bed of rice holds a metal plate covered with rice on which sit the *jhākri*'s sacred *mālās* and bandolier of bells. A *bumba*, a brass ritual vase, containing holy water and a stalk of *tite-pāti* (*Artemisia vulgaris*) used for purification, is placed on the wooden platform. Once the altar is completed, the *jhākris* purify and activate it. They do this by offering incense to the gods and their tutelary spirits (*duphālnu*) and sprinkling holy water over the assemblage of sacred items and images. The altar resonates with sacred power and is an object of veneration.

The sacred symbols and objects in the *jhākri*'s altar bring the participants into contact with the realm of the supernatural. Symbols store and transmit culturally significant information and rituals as "aggregation of symbols" serve as storehouses of and communication mechanisms for such information (Turner 1968: 1–8). Turner's (1967: 54) remarks regarding ritual symbols are appropriate in this context:

> ritual symbols are not merely signs representing known things; they are felt to possess ritual efficacy, to be charged with power from unknown sources,

Figure 10.1.   The altar for the ritual to negate the patient's *daśā garah* (Photo by H. Sidky)

and to be capable of acting on persons and groups coming into contact with them in such a way as to change them for the better or in a desired direction. . . . [Symbols] elicit emotion and express and mobilize desire.

The *jhākri* seems to be working with the understanding that cultural representations of supernatural beings and powers, or "the sacred other," as constituted and dramatized in the domain of ritual, provide coherence or integration for the cultural representations of human identity, or "the symbolic self" (cf. Pandian 1991: 3, 87). Coherence and integration, or reintegration, are the objectives of shamanistic healing.

When preparations are complete, the patient presents cigarettes and alcohol that he has brought as an offering to the *jhākri*s and withdraws. The senior *jhākri* sits behind the altar, flanked on both sides by his two colleagues, who will accompany him while he chants, and periodically take over drumming. The assistant sits behind them, while the patient quietly takes a seat behind him. The patient's family and friends take positions to one side of the room.

Throughout most of the proceedings, the patient does not appear to be the focus of the *jhākri*'s activities. There appears to be no empathy toward him in the course of the enactments. The *jhākri*'s recitals address the gods, ghosts, and spirits, never the patient, who remains directly uninvolved in the psychodrama. He does not undergo spirit possession, does not act out the role of symbolic beings, and does not engage in public acts of confession, reconciliation, or abreaction (cf. Höfer 1994: 40). As a rule, the patient in a *cintā*, if not incapacitated, sits quietly in an unobtrusive space observing the proceedings, often without showing any signs of emotion. Thus, once he enters inside the "ritual space," the patient acquires a "liminal persona" for he is between two fixed points, not well and not healed, and his status is for the moment ambiguous (cf. Turner 1974: 274). Liminality, as Turner (1969: 96) has pointed out, is "a moment in and out of time" and "in and out of secular social structure."

Most *jhākri*s wear their full ritual costume and accoutrements while conducting a *cintā*. Some practitioners, like those described here, do not, pointing out that the full regalia is for use only when *jhākri*s are performing communal rites or are on pilgrimage. The proceedings begin around 7:00 pm. The senior *jhākri* begins by taking a pinch of ash (*kharāni*) brought from the hearth and utters the following protection mantra:

> Red cloth, white cloth, black cloth,
> *Jhākri* colors
> Bells, beads, and charms
> We worship our guru

We call our guru
Jhākri spirit you live in heaven
Protect us
Ghosts may come
Demons may come
Witches may come
Stay around us
Protect us!

The *jhākri* then applies ash with a fingertip to his right and left shoulders, stomach, and knees. This protects or binds his body (*jiu bandhnu*) against attack by evil spirits while he performs. Protection spells are necessary because during the *cintā* the boundaries separating the natural and supernatural worlds become temporarily porous and permeable. The ritual space the *jhākri* creates is spiritually charged and dangerous because as long as it remains active, it serves as a conduit through which all varieties of supernatural beings can intrude upon the world of humans. Moreover, countless malicious spirits dwelling outside the village gravitate to the *jhākri*'s performance. The *jhākris* and everyone present are in danger. Numerous protective rites must therefore be performed prior to, during, and at the conclusion of their ceremonies. These procedures serve to underscore the contrast between the "heightened reality" of the sacred space of the ritual and the mundane reality of daily life (cf. Claus 1997: 199).

The performance is long and oscillates between moments of intense drama, when the onlookers are thoroughly captivated and in awe, to long and fairly mundane sequences of activities. The proceedings cease periodically throughout the night with numerous breaks, when the *jhākris* drink alcohol and smoke cigarettes. However, it is during the moments of high drama that the performance becomes what Eliade (1964: 51) described as a "spectacle unequalled in the world of daily experience . . . [during which] the 'laws of nature' are abolished." If anything, it would be moments such as these that "stimulate inquiry and exploration, engender metaphorical-metonymic understanding, and transform ego identity" (Laughlin et al. 1992: 195).

Maskarinec (1995: 118) has pointed to several sequences of high drama in *jhākri* performances, moments when he captivates and holds the attention of the audience: the beginning, when the *jhākri* strikes his drum and starts reciting; the period when the spirits manifest themselves and are absorbed into the *jhākri*'s body; and the climactic ending. These moments of high drama are sometimes creatively intensified even further by unanticipated theatricality, such as physical battles and cosmic struggles with spirits, or the use of fire and other media for sensational effects, as will be discussed below. In between, there are routine sequences of activities, when the spectators become distracted and revert to casual conversation and gossip, contributing to the informal atmosphere of these events. As the evening wears on, some people will even fall asleep.

Around 7:10 pm, the senior *jhākri* picks up his drum, marks it with ash, and throws a few grains of rice on it. He then extends the point of the handle toward the altar, bows, picks up the drumstick, and starts playing and chanting. The drum has a central place in *jhākri* rituals. As Walter (2001: 117) has put it:

> The drum, in more than one sense of the term, resonates with meaning. . . . It is first and foremost and instrument that sounds. The drum rhythms that are beaten out on its surface support and structure much of the ritual activity that takes place during the *cintā*. The percussive rhythm captures the attention of deities and spirits from elsewhere, and summons them to attend. Control of rhythm indicates mastery over the ritual space and, by implication, mastery of encounters with gods and ghosts alike.

The assisting *jhākris* seated on both sides of their teacher chant with him. Still playing the drum, the *jhākri* touches the center of the altar and four cardinal points on the ground around his body with the drum handle and starts his recital praising the gods and tutelary spirits. The recitation depicts the spirits, their attributes, and their relationship to the human world within the overall cosmological scheme, creating sequences of images in the minds of the listeners. The chant informs the gods of the offerings made to them and all the items on the altar and their sacred nature and power are individually described, reminding the participants that they are in direct contact with the realm of the supernatural.

Another song begins around 7:30 pm, addressed to all the household deities, hearth deities, local gods and goddesses, ancestral spirits, and *masān-desān*. The *jhākri* begins pounding the drum harder and the sound resonates throughout the room. He then proceeds to summon the gods (*deutā bolāunu*). This is the beginning of a moment of high drama in the performance. He has the full attention of the patient and those present in the crowded smoke-filled room.

> Come my guru, come
> Gauri Pārbati, Lord Mahādev!
> Śrī Gorkhānath, teacher
> Change into fire and flames
> Come
> *Jhākri* spirit
> Come
> Come and sit on my head
> Sit on my shoulders
> Sit on my chest

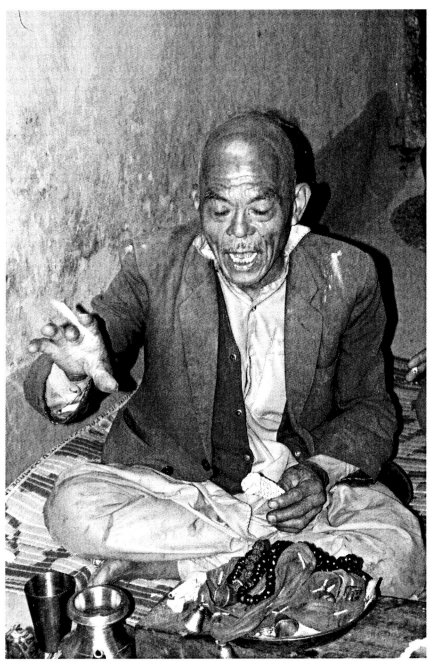

Figure 10.2.   Chanting to inform the gods of the offerings made to them and describing all of the items on the altar and their sacred nature and power (Photo by H. Sidky)

> Sit in front of me
> Sit behind me
> The oath of my guru
> Like arrows of fire
> *Om ma hūm*
> Śrī Gorkhānath,
> Gauri Pārbati, Lord Mahādev!

Gods, temples dedicated to gods, the primordial *jhākri*, and tutelary spirits are mentioned. This illustrates a point made by Höfer (1994: 72) regarding *jhākri* texts such as this, which abound in "enumerations of divine beings, sanctuaries, and . . . numinous entities," adding that this "'luxury of nomenclature' is afforded to achieve completeness or exhaustiveness."

Calling the divinities, or naming them, in effect manifests them. The spirits summoned not only include major divinities, such as Mahādev and Pārbati, who are addressed at the start and end of the performance, but also the *jhākri*'s own tutelary spirits (*guru-deutā*) and ancestral spirits, who are beckoned to actively assist him in his efforts.

> Come!
> Come with my guru
> Lanka guru, Hanumān guru,
> Rām Lakṣman guru,
> Bhairavkali, Gorkhākali,
> Dashinkali, Bhadrakali,
> Gods and goddesses
> Offerings I will make
> Service and honor I will give
> Come with my guru
> Come!

Also summoned are many other spirits, minor gods, and clan deities who are compelled to perform particular errands and tasks. The *jhākri* incorporates some of these spirits into his body, some he carries on his back and shoulders, and others he summons merely to interrogate. At various points later in the ceremony, the shaman's own spirit travels to the supernatural world. The *jhākri* is therefore simultaneously engaged in different types of interactions with spirits, which raises questions regarding schemes that define the shaman's relation with the supernatural world in terms of type of communication, either embodiment or soul journey.

The arrival of the spirits represents a sequence of high drama in the performance. All eyes are on the senior *jhākri* as he begins to violently shake and tremble (*kāmnu*), announcing that the spirits and gods have come (*deutā aayo*). A spectacular possession event ensues as the spirits are absorbed and restrained. The assisting *jhākri*s begin shaking as well. The pounding of the drum and the contorted look on the *jhākri*'s face make this quite a stirring episode. The *jhākri* continues to shake, eyes half closed, face distorted, forcefully bouncing up and down, until his body is several inches off the floor where he is sitting in a cross-legged position. He struggles with the spirits, whistles and trembles, as he swings the handle of his drum in a circular motion to the front and, grasping it with both hands twists the drum, bringing the point of the handle toward his abdomen, shouting "sshhhh – hhat!" as if reining some invisible beast. Repeating these motions, the *jhākri* shouts "sshhhh – hhat!" as the spirits embodied are reined in and brought under control. The trembling subsides and the *jhākri* resumes chanting. It is a moment in the ritual when the realm of the ordinary converges in a tangible way before people's eyes with the realm of the extraordinary. The *jhākri*'s physical being that becomes the temporary abode of powerful and dangerous supernatural entities, gods, and ancestral spirits evidences this convergence.

To the spectators the *jhākri* has demonstrated his mastery over spirits and his control of the forces that afflict humans with illness and calamities. It is a reenactment of the initial spirit intrusion that sent him down the shaman career path and his attainment of mastery over that initial uncontrollable and chaotic state (cf. Hitchcock 1976a: 169; Mastromattei 1989: 231). It represents the *jhākri*'s credentials as a full-fledged practitioner. More than that, the possession event has a greater significance. The shaman who has embodied spirits not only symbolizes the merger of the self with the sacred other, but he also puts his patients in touch with the sacred other, a process that has transformative or reconstitutive force. As Pandian (1991: 89) has observed, "to be in contact with or merged with the sacred other is the ultimate source of integration or coherence for the symbolic self."

Once the first possession event takes place, members of the audience put questions regarding their own affairs to the *jhākri*, addressing the divinities he embodies by placing a plate containing rice as a food offering (*prasād*) and money next to the altar. The spirits answer the questions speaking through the *jhākri*.

Possession events occur throughout the course of the ritual, as innumerable ghostly beings of sundry classes that are beckoned appear, and penetrate the *jhākri*'s body, causing it to tremble and shake, before they are dramatically restrained. Mastromattei (1989: 228) has aptly referred to this as "polymorphous possession." The *jhākri* chants:

> Come!
> Black Bhairav, Blue Bhairav,
> Red Bhairav, Green Bhairav
> Mountain *piaīs*
> Earth *piaīs*
> Water *piaīs*

Land *picās*
Kāco [unripe/unidentified] *picās*
Black *bir*, blue *bir*
Red *bir*, yellow *bir*
White *bir*, green *bir*
Water *masān*, Earth *masān*
Black *masān*, Red *masān*
Yellow *masān*, Green *masān*
Masān-desān
Come with my guru
Come!

Every time a possession event occurs, the patient and onlookers, whose attentions may have strayed, are once again captivated by the proceedings. The patient's reaction throughout, however, is to sit quietly in the background watching events unfold.

A break follows around 8:45 pm. The assistants scurry about adding fresh charcoal to the incense burner and replenishing wicks and incense sticks on the altar. Members of the household move about, talking and laughing, creating a scene repeated a number of times during the course of the next fifteen hours or so. The *jhākri*s drink more alcohol and smoke cigarettes. The senior *jhākri* wipes off the sweat from his face, instructs his assistants in minor tasks, such as supplying more incense for the altar, and engages in further conversation with the spectators. He clarifies the answers they received from the divinities as well as responds to questions regarding the ritual and his performance. These interchanges generate "a subtext" to the recitations, as noted before, and are a significant aspect of the proceedings. These interchanges confirm that the *jhākri* is able to recall fully the words of the deities he embodies as well as everything else that transpires during the possession event. It is for this reason that I have suggested that a better description of his interaction with supernatural beings is spirit adhesion rather than spirit possession.

While the *jhākri*s are talking to the onlookers, an assistant makes a "*daśā garah* plate" out of leaves with nine sections, each marked with a small colored cloth flag representing each of the nine planets (*nau garah*): *Budh* (Mercury), *Śukra* (Venus), *Prithivī* (Earth), *Maṅgal* (Mars), *Biryaspati* (Jupiter), *Śani* (Saturn), *Arun* (Uranus), *Varun* (Neptune), and *Yam* (Pluto). Once the plate is made he places it near the altar for use later in the ritual.

After several more drinks and cigarettes, the senior *jhākri* picks up his drum and the ritual resumes around 9:15 pm. He begins a protection chant asking the gods of the earth and sky to safeguard the house and the drum. After about 15 minutes, a new song begins, devoted to *Bhūme deutā*, or the earth gods. At the end of the chant, one of the junior *jhākri*s takes the drum and begins playing for the next song, which lasts from 9:45 to

10:20 pm. During this song, the ritual instruments are revered. The *jhākri*s relate the origins, history, and uses of the magical equipment on display, gesturing toward each implement to which the song refers.

A short break follows until around 10:45 pm. The senior *jhākri* resumes playing the drum and another song begins. The discursive focus now shifts to the patient. It starts with the imagery of the patient's house, its location, surroundings, the walls, number of rooms, windows, and doors and parallels are noted between the monumental task of building a house and the efforts to cure a patient. The patient is thus drawn into the imagery of the narrative even though he is not an active participant in the proceedings. The song then addresses the gods, asking if the offerings presented are appropriate and if the procedure the *jhākri*s intend to use for dealing with the patient's problems is the correct one. They query the gods as to the cause of the troubles:

> By the oath of Gorkhānath and Pārbati
> *Om ma hu˜m*!
> By the oath of my guru
> What witch has struck?
> What god has struck?
> Mountain gods or goddesses?
> Water spirits?
> Earth Spirit?
> Water *masān*?
> *Masān-desān*?
> *Boksī* or *ḍāini*?
> *Boksī* spirit?
> *Ḍāini* spirit?
> *Dhāmi* spirit?
> *Masān-desān*?
> *Om ma hu˜m*
> By the oath of my guru
> Reveal!

The chanting continues until 11:30 pm. Suddenly, another moment of high drama ensues, as the *jhākri* and his colleagues begin shaking intensely and the senior *jhākri* in a fit of frenzy begins beating himself on the head with his drumstick. He yells, "hheyy, hutt, kha-kha kha-kha," whistles, and then resumes pounding the drum. His associates take pinches of rice, touch it to their foreheads, and throw it over the altar feeding the gods, while the senior *jhākri* moves toward the patient at the rear of the room. The *jhākri* is now in a state of *jokhānā* possession, which involves inquiring about the patient's condition while embodying spirits. Violently pounding the drum, he asks the spirits to clarify the patient's condition. The patient sits in a meditative posture with eyes closed.

The eyes of those present are fixed upon the *jhākri*, who then resumes violently striking his head with the drumstick. The reason the spirits are angry and resort to violence, the *jhākri* reveals afterward, is the presence of the *jhākri*'s ceremonial outfit and feather headdress in the room. After this incident, the assistant promptly removes the costume. The *jhākri* then returns to his position in front of the altar and pounds the drum with great force. His students recite mantras under their breath and throw rice on the altar. Such theatricality, which occurs throughout the performance, draws and holds the attention of those present, facilitating the communicative aspect of the ritual.

The *jhākri* continues singing and forcefully pounding the drum. Then, in another dramatic moment, he abruptly throws his head back slightly, stops drumming, and remains motionless with eyes closed as he projects his spirit into the land of the gods. The *jhākri* later described this as "looking telescopically at the *daśā garah* of the patient in Yama Lok, the abode of Yamarāja." He announces what he encounters to the audience, "I see on the mighty hill near Yamarāja's palace, the patient's death flag." His body quivering lightly, bells jingling, he remains in this state for approximately five minutes. Suddenly, eyes wide open, he shouts, "hheyy," and resumes vigorous drumming. He bows to the altar as he continues to drum and chant. His junior colleagues join in the chanting.

Then the *jhākri* begins singing alone, elaborating on the patient's condition, when he became ill, and his symptoms, how he has suffered, and inquires once more about the causes of the affliction.

> Saturn, Jupiter, Venus, Cancer
> All those planets
> This victim has pains with fever burning
> This victim is continuously aching
> Pure incense and rice in my hand
> Look at the birth date, sacred day
> Ear, nose, and chest aching
> Left hand aching
> Right hand aching
> Left shoulder aching
> Right shoulder aching
> Ribs aching, body tingling
> The pain of the front and back,
> Pain from head to toe
> Pure incense and rice in my hand
> *Jhākri* spirit I consult

He reconfirms the initial diagnosis with more conviction and greater detail, stating that, "a person of known identity has cast spells," because of *daśī garah* (evil fortune from planets). There is considerable redundancy in the *jhākri*'s utterances and procedures throughout the ritual. Redundancy in

Figure 10.3. Spirit travel: the *jhākri* projects his spirit into Yama Lok, the realm of Ya-marāja, the Lord of Death (Photo by H. Sidky)

shamanic healing functions to emphasize the key ritual symbols (cf. Brown 1988: 112). The patient listens intently, but remains seated in the background without any changes in expression. As the *jhākri* sings, his junior colleagues begin violently shaking and bouncing in unison as numinous beings descend upon them. This segment of the ritual ends at around 1:00 am when the senior *jhākri* touches the altar with the point of his drum handle and his associates throw rice. A break follows around 1:15 am, as assistants scurry about once more to replenish items on the altar, bring more charcoal, and supply incense. The *jhākris* drink more alcohol and smoke cigarettes.

When the proceedings resume, it is one of the students who takes up drumming, while all three chant, calling the gods, Guru Rinpoche, and Paśupati, or Lord Śiva. The senior *jhākri* throws rice on the altar, as the *jhākri* drumming begins to shake violently, whistling, and shouting "hheyy." A break follows around 2:00 am. The *jhākris* drink more alcohol and smoke cigarettes.

The next phase of the ritual is important. It is during this stage of the proceedings, when most members of the audience have returned home or are sleeping, and when children are in bed, that the sleep-deprived patient experiences the full force of the ritual. He now has the opportunity to think about his circumstances and may even undergo alterations of consciousness or, as Höfer (1994: 41) has put it, "some psychosensory experience in the shape of a hallucinatory appearance that may lead to sudden 'insights' or produce a 'missing link' in the anamnesis."

Around 2:15 am, the senior *jhākri* picks up the *mālās* and bell bandolier, while one of the junior *jhākris* starts pounding the drum in a slow, steady beat. All three chant in unison asking the gods on the altar to give them strength for the task ahead. The senior *jhākri* puts on the two bell bandoliers and places the *rudrācche mālā* round the neck of one junior *jhākri* and the *riṭṭho mālā* around the neck of the other. He wraps another *riṭṭho mālā* around his own wrist, takes the drum along with one of the *phurbas* from the altar in the same hand, and begins drumming and chanting. After about 15 minutes, he stands up, dances around the altar, drumming and singing, bells jingling, and goes over to the patient.

The patient rises on cue and moves up and sits on the floor in front of the altar. The *jhākri* walks around him, drumming, whistling, making mumbling sounds, and touches the patient's shoulders and four directions on the floor around him with the point of the drum handle. One of the junior *jhākris* carrying some rice in the palm of his right hand gestures to the four directions around the patient and tosses the rice at him. This is to feed the host of evil spirits attracted to him due to the neighbor's spells (*bheda*). Beating the drum slowly, whistling, and chanting "aah-aahhah, ohh-ohh-ohh, *om ma hūm*" the senior *jhākri* continues to walk around the patient.

Theatricality replaces narrative as a communicative channel as he begins to tremble, mumble incomprehensively shaking his head left to right, face contorted. He runs around the room, returns, circles the patient, and points to his chest with the tip of the drum handle. He embodies numerous evil spirits that have converged upon the patient and must expel them from the room using the strength, or *śakti*, of his tutelary spirits. He races outside the house, whistling, mumbling "bleba-bleba-bleba, balalalala, blalalalala, hh-hat, hhhat, hhaahaa," stands in the darkness pounding his drum, dancing, bells jingling, as the evil is dispersed into the darkness of the night. In the meantime, the patient returns to his place in the back of the room. After several minutes outside, the *jhākri* returns to the room, slamming the door shut to prevent the evil spirits expelled from returning. He skips, jumps, and dances, pounding his drum, shouting "hhey, hhhat, hhey, hhhat." Clinching his jaw and shaking his head left to right, he continues to mumble, "bleba-bleba-bleba, balalalala, blalalalala, hhhat, hhhat, hhaahaa, *om ma hūm*! "

Then he begins singing alone, returning to figurative language he starts elaborating upon the patient's condition, when he became ill and his symptoms, how he has suffered, mentions the causes of his affliction, and the peril facing him. He continues singing and beating the drum and then suddenly throws his head back slightly, stops drumming, and remains motionless with eyes closed as he once again projects his spirit into Yama Lok. His body quivering lightly, bells jingling, he remains in this state for several minuets. Then suddenly, eyes wide open, he shouts, "hheyy," and resumes pounding the drum. He announces, "Ho, I have seized the patient's death flag. Ho, I have destroyed it." The junior *jhākris*, who seem very pleased, throw rice on the altar as offerings to the gods.

At around 3:00 am, the senior *jhākri* beckons Gorkhānath Guru, "a reincarnation of Lord Śiva," according to Shukra Bahādur, to possess him. Meanwhile an assistant sprinkles a little holy water on the floor next to the altar, places a charcoal ember on the ground on top of which he puts a piece of *gājā* (ganja, resinous marijuana), a drug much favored by Śiva and his devotees. While incarnating the god, the *jhākri* leans over and inhales the rising *gājā* smoke, and resumes drumming. Smoking the *gājā* is a way of tangibly demonstrating the presence of the deity and acquiring his *śakti*, or power. While still incarnating Śiva, the *jhākri* invites other gods, spirits, and ghosts to appear once more. All three begin chanting in unison. One of the junior *jhākris* throws rice on the altar. A break follows around until 3:20 am. The three *jhākris* consume more alcohol and cigarettes.

Then one of the junior *jhākris* and the assistant begin preparations for summoning Yamarāja and cutting the thread of ill fate to negate *daśā garah*. A banana sapling, a physical link or conduit between the room where the *jhākris* are and Yama Lok, is placed upright on the floor before the altar, the ground is sprinkled with holy water, and one of the *jhākris* begins creating a representation of Yamarāja using white and red paint powder. Below the image, four circles mark the place for the patient to sit.

In reference to the discussion of shamanic art, petroglyphs/cave paintings, and trance states, it should be noted that although this is a somber moment, the shaman artist is not in a trance or ASC. The image is drawn in ordinary waking consciousness according to established artistic conventions passed on from teacher to student. The picture conveys symbolic messages connected to the ritual drama and is not a medium for the representation of the shaman's visions or hallucinations

This is a point of high tension and danger. The sacred image invokes strong emotions because the deity manifests himself in the painting, bringing it to life. Everyone in the room now comes into direct contact with the god through the sacred art. It is another moment of high drama. Riboli's (1995: 85) comments are relevant:

> While creating a godhead image the shaman-artist feels danger or even death coming closer. Even only watching the shaman at work during the sessions, it is possible to feel this deep dramatic involvement in each line he traces, in each movement he makes. During the artistic phase, the man has to face not only the godheads, but also himself, his strength, his life and death. The result is, a high, deep dramatic work of art, full of meaning; a work in which you can feel an art without boundaries, and art freely expressed and even exasperated.

Once the image is complete, a betel nut (seed of the palm tree *Areca cat-echu*) which the *jhākris* say is the symbol of evil spirits, is placed over it as an offering, and red *ṭikā* marks are placed on the banana sapling as a sign of reverence for the evil spirits. A coin is also inserted into the sapling as an offering. The blade of the *khukuri* knife near the altar also receives *ṭikā* marks in honor of the Bishwakarma, the deity who blessed humans with the art of metallurgy. The *daśī garah* plate is positioned next to the sapling and a mat laid down for the patient to sit on at the feet of Yamarāja's image. As these activities take place, the other junior *jhākri* begins drumming, while the assistant produces a chicken and holds it over the incense burner next to the altar.

The senior *jhākri* then takes the chicken and all three *jhākris* begin chanting, asking the gods for success. He sprinkles the chicken with a pinch of rice from the altar and then pours some holy water over it. The patient is directed to sit on the mat near the image of Yamarāja and a cotton string is used to connect him to the sapling.

The *jhākris* through their orchestrations during the preceding hours have, bit by bit, analyzed, redefined, and symbolically expressed the patient's problem in terms of the group's cosmology in the context of the ritual space under their control. These activities now reach a climax as the patient sits in a precisely defined position, his relationship to the godhead menacing him symbolically represented by the thread connecting them. This, as Riboli (1995: 85) observes, "is the highest artistic point of the session: the music, the singing, the dances and the drawing, which were single independent elements until now, begin to form a 'beautiful, harmonious' [union]."

Around 4:00 am, the senior *jhākri*, still holding the chicken, gets up and begins chanting and dancing around the patient, and summons Yamarāja saying, "I have betel nut, food, incense, and a chicken for you, please come." The process of clarification continues through the chant, which relates the patient's problems, details the reasons for *daśī garah*, how Yamarāja and the other gods intervene in the life of human beings, the patient's critical situation, and how *jhākris* cure diseases. The chant also addresses Yamarāja, asking him to accept the life of the chicken as a substitute for that of the patient.

Moving into action, the senior *jhākri* brushes the patient's body with the chicken symbolically transferring the affliction into the bird. He says the mantra, "let the disease of the sick man come into this." He then addresses the god, saying, "I have transferred the diseases of the sick man to this chicken and I am offering this to you." Then, with face contorted, he begins to shake, whistle, and with bells jingling hops around the patient, raising one leg off the ground, and then the other as he goes around. With the chicken still in one hand, the *jhākri* next picks up the egg from the altar and rubs the patient's head and body with it, repeating the above mantra.

Next, he picks up a small bowl containing rice, a mixture of wheat, barely, corn, chili peppers, iron and gold particles, and pieces of the patient's clothes, hair, finger and toenail clippings, a symbolic offering that is a substitute for the patient. Taking some of the mixture in the palm of his hands, he waves it over the patient's head and throws it into the leaf cups representing the planets at the foot of the banana sapling, repeating the procedure several times. These are offerings for Yamadūta, the minions of the Lord of Death. The *jhākri* does the same thing using holy water. Meanwhile, the patient sits quietly in a contemplative mood, eyes toward the floor.

After completing these procedures, the *jhākri* throws the chicken out the door, follows it outside, grabs it, and tears the head off with his hands. He then returns to the room holding the dead chicken, its wings still flapping. He places the head on the altar, and dabs each of the dough images and the banana sapling with blood. Sacrificial blood is poured on the leaf cups in which the *jhākri* also places some chicken feathers. The chicken's blood serves as a substitute for the patient's blood (cf. Riboli 1995: 86). Crushing the egg, the *jhākri* throws it into the leaf cups as well. As an offering to vegetarian deities, the *jhākri* also sprinkles the dough images, banana sapling, and the leaf cups with liquefied rice.

At approximately 4:30 am, the senior *jhākri* sits in front of the banana sapling facing the patient and begins chanting and drumming. Lit wicks are placed on either side of the image of Yamarāja as offerings to the deity who is now inside the painting. An intense possession event follows as the *jhākri* embodies the god Dolakha Bhimsen Guru for a showdown with Yamarāja and the Yamadūta. He stands up, shouting "hheyy," begins dancing around the patient, alternatively raising each leg off the ground and holding it up for a few seconds as he dances. He continues dancing, his gestures suggesting that he is fighting pugnacious invisible beings. It is a cosmic battle between the *jhākri*, struggling for his patient's life, and the menacing forces intent on taking that life. The adversaries, one visible, the others invisible, tussle back and forth for several minuets. Then suddenly, the *jhākri* succumbs and collapses on the floor. Eyes closed, body seemingly lifeless, he remains motionless for about five minutes. Everyone's attention is on the unfolding drama. This is because there is a strong possibility that the

Figure 10.4.   The *jhākri* succumbs and collapses on the floor (Photo by H. Sidky)

Lord of Death and his soldiers may have triumphed and the *jhākri* is dead. However, as suddenly as he collapsed, the *jhākri* gets up, shouting "hheyy," whistling, and resumes dancing and pounding his drum. The *jhākri* and Bhimsen prevail. The Yamadūta have scattered, but their master remains.

After a few minutes, the *jhākri* hands over the drum to one of the junior *jhākris* who begins playing. The senior *jhākri* then bows to the altar, starts chanting, and picks up the *khukuri* knife with his right hand and a *phurba* with the left. Thus armed, he moves around the patient, performing *mudrās*, symbolic mystical gestures made with the hand and fingers that generate power and focus concentration.

He begins chanting, "Yamarāja, I have come to fight you! With sword, *khukuri*, and flags in my hand, I have come to fight you!" He continues dancing around the patient, making cutting motions in the air with his knife as he moves. Around 4:55 am, the intensity of the performance heightens as the *jhākri* begins shaking, his expression turns fierce, and he powerfully slashes the air with his knife, shouting *om ma hu˜m, om ma hu˜m*. He whistles and moves around the patient, slashing the air over his head and shoulders. He is in fierce combat with Yamarāja. Everyone in the room is intently watching the performance as the blade moves back and forth, sometimes dangerously close to the onlookers' heads. The battle intensifies and continues for about ten minutes. Then suddenly the *jhākri* falls to the ground, but this time, his eyes remain open and he quickly leaps up and resumes the battle, slashing with the knife and *phurba*, whistling, and dancing. He nearly falls down once again, but this time only staggers a bit and remains standing. He then takes some grains of rice in the same hand in which he is holding the *phurba* and throws them over the patient and the image of Yamarāja.

He continues dancing and fighting, grimacing and shouting *om ma hūm, om ma hūm, phhhet*, and begins striking the clay floor around the banana sapling with his blade, sending chunks of mud flying about. Dropping the *phurba* on the altar, the *jhākri* picks up more rice, which he throws over the image on the ground, and continues to dance. After about ten minutes of combat, he positions himself next to the banana sapling and begins quietly uttering mantras. He then slashes the sapling with the knife, slicing it into several pieces, thus "cutting away the evil fate," or *khargo kaṭāunu*, as well as the conduit linking the world of the living and Yama Lok. The force of the blow not only severs the sapling, but also cuts the string connecting it to the patient. The symbolic connection between the patient and the menacing God of Death is thus cut with the blow of the *jhākri*'s blade. The patient takes the section of the string in his hand, ties it around his neck in the manner of a Buddhist protection knot, and an onlooker swiftly escorts him to the back of the room out of Yamarāja's gaze.

The *jhākri* now destroys the betel nut over the image of Yamarāja with the point of his knife and begins erasing the image on the ground using his feet, chanting:

Om ma hūm, om ma hūm
I have locked the golden, silver and iron doors
I have blocked all the directions
You cannot return
Om ma hūm
In the name of Gauri Pārbati
Please return to your own golden palace
We have locked our golden, silver and iron doors
We have blocked all the directions
Please return to your own golden palace
Om ma hūm, om ma hūm
phhhet!

He does all of this very rapidly because the god is very dangerous and as soon as the necessary procedures are completed, the image is to be obliterated and the deity dispatched from the house and village (cf. Riboli 1995: 81, 83).

The main task of the ritual, to sever the patient's ill fate, is now accomplished. But the *jhākris* are far from ready to terminate their activities, which is illuminating with respect to suggestions that these practitioners are insincere and are merely play-acting or going through the motions. Comments made by Mastromattei (1989: 230) are relevant in this connection:

what most leads me to believe that, even at this. . . stage of the séance, the *jhākri* is not in a [an ordinary state of consciousness] . . . is his stupefying resistance, entirely unrelated to age and physical condition [to] ending a rite which, from the point of view of its public value for the benefit of third parties, should have been finished sometime before.

Indeed, instead of bringing the proceedings to a close after reaching the high point of the ritual, the activities become even more explicitly theatrical and intense (Mastromattei 1989: 230).

A break follows around 5:20 am. Household women serve tea and then go on to sweep the area where a short time ago Yamarāja was present. Around 5:30 am, the *jhākris* resume their position behind the altar and begin the treatment phase of the ritual. One of the junior *jhākris* takes up drumming.

The senior *jhākri* then picks up a *phurba* and goes over to the hearth where his assistant has set up a boiling cauldron of water. He utters secret mantras and dips the *phurba* into the bubbling water. He repeats this several times. Then he displays his power by dipping his hand into the cauldron, holds it there for several seconds, and removes it unscathed. With his *śakti* demonstrated, he directs the patient to take off his shirt and once again sit on the mat in front of the altar.

The *jhākri* next takes a bundle of leafy branches, dips it in the pot of boiling water on the fire, utters mantras so that the boiling liquid does not

Figure 10.5. Cutting the thread of fate that links the patient to the banana sapling and Yamarājā's image on the ground (Photo by H. Sidky)

cause harm, and approaches the patient to administer treatment (*sorah pānile jhārphuke gareko*). He circles him and sweeps his body with the leaves, and then flicks the water in the direction of the open door. Dipping the leaves in boiling water once more, the *jhākri* repeats the procedure. The patient sits quietly staring at the ground. The *jhākri* is using the metaphor of cleansing and discarding, which is a known feature of shamanic healing (cf. Moerman 1979: 60; Madsen 1955: 51). After undergoing this procedure three times, the patient returns to the back of the room. The *jhākri* then administers the same treatment to the patient's wife and other family members. Finally, he uses the leaves to sprinkle everyone else in the room as well as the animals in the buffalo shed adjacent to the house. A sense of connection, or unity, Turner's *communitas*, is thus established among all those present, feelings that are essential to well-being.

He returns to the room and all three *jhākris* chant together. The senior *jhākri* now picks up a bundle of dried wheat stalks and sets one end on fire, making a smoking torch to administer fire treatment (*agani jwālā jhārphuke*). Holding the torch in one hand, he takes a handful of rice flour in the other hand. The patient with his shirt back on and covering his head and shoulders with a blanket comes to the front of the room once again and sits on the mat. The *jhākri* extends the flaming torch over him, chanting *om ma hūm* and shouting "phhhet" throws the flour at the fire, producing a spectacular flare. The patient, eyes closed and grimacing, shakes the blanket throwing off the embers. The *jhākri* creates the pyrotechnic effect three more times. The patient's wife and family members also undergo treatment by fire. Then he goes out once again to the adjacent animal shed and repeats the procedure over the buffalos. Upon his return, he also repeats the procedure in four corners of the room and then throws the remainder of the torch out the door and utters a mantra.

Around 6:30 am, the *jhākris* summon the patient to the front of the room one more time. The senior *jhākri* then sets fire to the *daśā garah* plate representing the nine planets, or as the *jhākris* put it, "to burn down the sick man's *daśā garah*." Taking a burning stick from the leaf cups, he waves it around the patient's head. Then the three *jhākris* sprinkle the fiery object with rice and holy water. A few moments later, assistants take the burning leaf cups outside and throw them in a river west of the patient's house. Fire dramatically destroys the patient's linkages with the planets. Thus neutralizing the destructive cosmic forces, the *jhākri* symbolically destroys the association between the patient and the planets.

We may note that stage by stage through the ritual, the *jhākri* have taken the patient from the status of a sick person, through a stage of liminality, to ritual liberation from the impinging evil forces, ritual purification, and finally transformation. The patient emerges from the experience with a new course in life and a new fate before him.

Household women then sweep the floor clean. Finally, one of the junior *jhākris* sacrifices a goat at an altar set up outside the house. This is an offering to the deities who assisted the shamans during the night. For the moment, it seems that the shaman has triumphed. Evil is at bay. However, the elaborate procedures of the preceding night did not destroy evil. Evil remains, leaving the need for *jhākris* and their rituals intact.

Figure 10.6.   Fire treatment (*agani jwālā jhārphuke*) (Photo by H. Sidky)

With the performance at an end, the shaman seals the spiritually charged ritual space created at the start of the ceremony. It is time for all the spirits summoned to go back to where they belong lest they linger behind and cause havoc. The last segment of the nightlong ritual to be completed is the dismissal of the divinities. The senior *jhākri* returns to his seated position behind the altar and begins chanting and drumming:

> By the oath of my guru
> East, West, North, South
> Therai, Nepal Valley
> Village, home, where you belong
> Rock, log, slate, copper plate, tree
> Where you belong
> Running water, seven oceans, sky
> Where you belong
> Moon and Sun
> Where you belong
> Earth
> Where you belong
> O my gurus, go back
> Go back to your own place
> By the oath of my guru
> Go back

The altar is then ceremoniously dismantled, the wheat is swept up and placed in a container, and the *tormas* are decapitated and neutralized and then cut up to be served along with the rest of the food offerings (*prasād*) and the flesh of the sacrificial animals. The food is for everyone present, including a few who joined the proceedings that morning. However, the patient cannot consume the flesh of the chicken into which his illness was transferred. The meal is cooked and served, with the feast ending by 10:30 am. The *cintā* is complete.

As the materials presented in this chapter indicate, the *cintā*, to use Mastromattei's (1989: 230) phrase, is "a complex ritual construction," or a dynamic and dramatic performance involving the manipulation of numerous symbols and intense theatrical devices. There are many similarities between the ceremony described here and the healing rites of Siberian shamans (cf. Jochelson 1926: 210–211). An important question is: how precisely does such a performance affect the participants, especially the patient? By what means, if any, do the procedures described enable people to undergo transformative changes that are the basis for healing? The patient seems relieved, happier, and more confident than before. But what does this signify? These are questions addressed in the next chapter.

11

Shamanic Healing

Keeping the *cintā* described in chapter 10 in mind, we may address the question: How does shamanic healing work? This question, which has long fascinated anthropologists, as Morris (2006: 40) has pointed out, is another way of asking: "Whence the power of the shaman?" Anthropologists have approached this problem in terms of the influence of symbols, or "symbolic healing" (Dow 1986; Moerman 1997: 241; Romanucci-Ross 1997: 215). Medical anthropologist Cecil Helman (2001: 277) defines symbolic healing as:

> healing that does not rely on any physical or pharmacological treatments for its efficacy, but rather on language, ritual and the manipulation of powerful cultural symbols.

The exact psychophysiological mechanisms through which symbolic healing works are not yet fully understood (Helman 2001: 280). What we know is that in a number of cases, the manipulation of symbols and imagery seems to affect recovery. In other words, the complex psychosocial factors brought into play by the shaman's dramatic symbolic evocations and enactments as described in the previous chapter—essentially the use of symbols to convey important information and elicit emotional and cognitive responses—have a direct effect upon human biology by triggering a psychoneuroimmunological response. As anthropologist Daniel Moerman (1979: 62) has put it:

> there are substantial pathways which link physiological and cognitive states . . . these two realms of human existence, body and mind, are linked and

moreover . . . these pathways are the stage on which metaphoric concepts of performance may (indeed *must*) "be effective," that is, influence biological processes.

Laughlin et al. (1992: 193) suggest that, "ritualized practices of evocation or dramatic performance of metaphor" are techniques that use symbols to activate neurognostic structures (archetypes) present in the human brain toward specific intentional objectives, such as healing. Practices of evocation include music, imagery, words, figures of speech, and gestures, employed individually, or in various combinations, as in the context of the *cintā*.

The symbolism of ritual performances derives from the culture's mythological system, such as, for example, the "death flag" with the patient's name found near the palace of Yamarāja, the God of Death. The *jhākri* directs his efforts in making the patient accept "a particularization of the general mythic world" as a valid model of his experience that, as described in chapter 10, is achieved through theatricality and rhetorical techniques (cf. Helman 2001: 279).

One of the classic studies emphasizing the central place of myth in symbolic healing is anthropologist Claude Lévi-Strauss's analysis of the song used in cases of difficult childbirth by shamans among the Cuna Indians of Panama:

> That the mythology of the shaman does not correspond to an objective reality does not matter. The [patient] believes in the myth and belongs to a society which believes in it. The tutelary spirits and malevolent spirits, the supernatural monsters and magical animals, are all part of a coherent system on which the native conceptions of the universe is founded. The [patient] accepts these mythological beings, or, more accurately, she has never questioned their existence. What she does not accept are the incoherent and arbitrary pains, which are an alien element in her system but which the shaman, calling upon the myth, will re-integrate within a whole where everything is meaningful. . . . Once she understands, however, she does more than resign herself; she gets better. (Lévi-Strauss 1967: 192–193)

In such performances, the shaman relies on metaphor and draws parallels between the events or scenarios in the myth and the patient's physiological conditions (Dow 1986: 60). In other words, patients receive images through which to comprehend their own somatic sensations. For this reason, Samuel (1995: 254) refers to this approach as the "analogic model of healing," meaning that the healer works using analogies. The shifting back and forth between mythical and physiological themes throughout the performance operates to blur in the patient's mind the distinction between the mythic and the real (Lévi-Strauss 1967: 188). In this way, the patient comes to accept the mythical scenario the shaman is presenting as a valid model of his own experience (Dow 1986: 61).

Oppitz's (1993) analysis of how Magar *jhākris* in central Nepal deal with difficult childbirths is comparable to Lévi-Strauss's study. The Magar shaman's therapy, like that of the Cuna healer and the *jhākris* described in the previous chapter, relies exclusively upon the use of symbols to produce therapeutic cognitive and behavioral changes. He does not use medications, herbal treatments, massage, or obstetric manipulations. The healing, Oppitz notes, involves "a psychological manipulation of the patient" (cf. Lévi-Strauss 1967: 187).

The Magar shaman sings mythical chants that relate stories in which the protagonist in the narrative is undergoing the same condition as the patient. However, what is different between the two examples is that the Magar story is "over dramatized" in that the condition of the protagonist in the mythical story is much worse than that of the patient. According to Oppitz, this makes the patient first identify and then "dis-identify" with her mythical counterpart in the shaman's scenario, with the expectation of a happy conclusion for herself compared to the terrible ending always in store for the protagonist in the myth. Oppitz sees the process of dis-identification from the mythical figure as the mechanism through which the patient undergoes cognitive and behavioral changes, or grasps cognitively and reinterprets her symptoms, and successfully gives birth.

In both of these example, we find that the healer distills from the general schema of the culture's mythology a story or scenario that is suited to the case at hand within which he frames the patient's malady (Dow 1986: 60). However, the shaman not only constructs the mythic scenario, but he also projects, dramatizes, and makes it real for the patient through performance (Dow 1986: 61). As we have seen, dramatic extratextual theatricality accompanies the chants and narratives. The symbolic imagery employed functions as a communication link between mind and body. As anthropologist James Dow (1986: 63) has put it:

> It is possible to affect processes in the self and unconscious-somatic systems through the manipulation of symbolic parameters at the social level. For this process to work there must be codes in which messages can be sent. *The mythic world contains the symbols that couple the social system to the self system of the patient.*

The assumption here is that mythological symbolism brought to bear upon neurocognitive systems that mediate sensorial experiences produces transformations of somatic systems that do not mediate sensorial experiences (cf. Achterberg 1987: 104; Laughlin et al. 1992: 193).

Maskarinec's approach to the *jhākri*'s healing rituals also falls in the category of symbolic healing. Maskarinec (1995: 116–152) suggests that it is through the manipulation of words, transformed into movement and portrayed in action, that the shaman is able to reorder events in the world and affect a cure. From the opening lines of the performance, which refers to the creation of the world, the *jhākri* shifts the ritual from the present age of corruption and decay back into mythic time, or the Golden Age. This is when the world was pristine and orderly, when the gods were responsive to intercession, and when the primordial *jhākris* were at the height of their powers (Maskarinec 1995: 120). Afflictions as well as cures go back to the original intercessors and original afflictive agents (Maskarinec 1995: 123).

References to "sacred archetypes" to invoke supernatural powers whose nature and functions are depicted in the oral texts are intended to establish connections to the mythic past. References in the narratives to actual places in this world are also a device to incorporate the present into the sacred order of mythic time. Thus, continuity emerges between the actions of the present-day shaman and those of the original *jhākri*. A cure is affected by pushing the present back into its original orderliness (Maskarinec 1995: 118). The altered states of consciousness, as expressed in the "spectacular possessions" of the *jhākri*, are a means of keeping the patient and spectators engaged in what the *jhākri* is trying to achieve by "manipulating linguistic worlds" (Maskarinec 1995: 118).

The *jhākri*'s song which describes the origins of diseases, the reasons why people become sick, how protagonists stricken by particular illnesses have recovered, and his discussions of mythical themes converge with the patient's condition, giving his symptoms cosmic significance (cf. Lévi-Strauss 1967: 193–194). For example, dramatically announcing the discovery of the patient's death flag in Yamarāja's abode, which the *jhākri* is able to retrieve during his spiritual journey to the land of the dead, achieves this effect. Peters (1995: 59) suggests that this creates a "near-death-experience" for the patient, which in Jungian terms is necessary in order to facilitate radical transformation and transpersonal experience. The shaman brings about such a transformation when he captures the patient's death flag and physically cuts the cotton string, the string of fate that symbolically links the patient to the banana sapling.

The *jhākri*'s performance amounts to restating the patient's unspecified condition/symptoms and experience in forms accessible to conscious thought. In other words, the illness is expressed through basic ideas and concepts understandable to the patient, for example, *daśā garah*, Yama Lok, death flag, witchcraft, and so on. Thus, what the shaman really does is to provide the sick person "with a *language*, by means of which unexpressed and otherwise inexpressible, psychic states can be immediately expressed" (Lévi-Strauss 1967: 193). What takes place is a "cognitive reinterpretation of symptoms" and this can make the experience more bearable and is a strategy also used in pain clinics in the West (see Smith et al. 1980). The shaman's suggestive techniques transform the patient's thought patterns and behavior in a manner not possible for the patient himself to achieve (Dow 1986: 58).

> The cure [involves] making explicit a situation originally existing on the emotional level and in rendering acceptable to the mind pains which the body refuses to tolerate. (Lévi-Strauss 1967: 192)

Patients emerge from the healing experience with a new and clear comprehension of their circumstances, past, present, and future, aware of not only why they became ill, but also how they have come back to a state of normalcy (cf. Kleinman 1980: 372).

One of the criticisms of Lévi-Strauss's analysis of the Cuna shamanic song (and by extension similar approaches) is that the patients generally do not comprehend the fine points of the song and therefore cannot employ the imagery in the exact and systematic manner suggested (Sherzer 1989). If patients cannot understand the chant with such precision, they cannot utilize its imagery to transform their experience. Among the things that hamper a patient's comprehension of chants and songs are the linguistic characteristics of the shaman's narratives, which sometimes include idiosyncratic, nonindigenous, specialized, or archaic language or terminologies, as well as the acoustics of the room and noise levels.

Anthropologist Michael Brown's (1988) critique of Lévi-Strauss's analysis is along similar lines. He points out that when the social and political contexts of the healing session are taken into account the interaction appears polyphonic rather dyadic in nature. Through textual analysis of rhetoric and counter-rhetoric in an Aguaruna healing session in Peru, Brown points out that unlike Lévi-Strauss's romanticized construal of shamanistic healing, the patient is not a passive subject. Instead, the patients along with the participants vie with the shaman in shaping the ritual's discursive contours through verbal exchanges at various points in the ceremony, rather than accepting the shaman's assessment as unquestioned orthodoxy. According to Brown (1988: 115), this "dissident subtext" also reveals the contested nature of shamanic practice and the ambivalence with which shamanism is regarded, a practice that people must rely upon to negate acts of harmful magic due to the handiwork of shaman-sorcerers, thereby validating the very system (shaman-sorcerer complex) that menaces them. Brown (1988: 111, 116), however, acknowledges that an "orthodox" symbolic interpretation supports the view that the healing discourse does create order by assuring patients that their suffering will soon terminate and that his analysis intentionally downplays the ways in which the ritual contributes to social solidarity and is an expression of social cohesiveness.

During my interactions with people attending *cintās*, it was perfectly clear that generally those in attendance had a firm understanding of *jhākri* recitals and often commented on subtle variations in the texts and other details of the proceedings. Maskarinec (1995: 127–128), who encountered similar circumstances with respect to the comprehension of shaman texts, found that villagers are able to reproduce the recitals "word for word." Maskarinec (1995: 127–128) concluded that excessive familiarity rather than disinterest accounts for lack of audience attentiveness during *jhākri* performances.

Moreover, as analyses of symbolic or analogic healing elsewhere indicate, even if there is only partial comprehension of the narratives, this does not necessarily impede the patient's use of the imagery because there is no one correct interpretation (Samuel 1995: 254). Ritual symbols, as Turner (1977: 44, 50) noted, are multivocalic, that is, they possess multiple meanings. Patients and participants in the ritual construct an understanding appropriate or relevant to their own circumstances from the array of meanings, rather than internalizing a predetermined model (Samuel 1995: 255).

Nor does the comprehension of symbolic imagery have to occur at a conscious level. As Laughlin et al. (1992: 191) have pointed out:

> Symbolic penetration does not . . . require mediation of conscious networks. Symbols penetrate directly to unconscious intentionalities, and far from being impossible or unlikely, this process is common and characteristic of the ongoing functioning of the nervous system.

Höfer (1985: 26) says something along the same line, pointing out that Tamang shaman ritual texts operate at "a sub-rational (rather than unconscious) level and is thus related to the . . . effectiveness of symbols."

As in the case of the Aguaruna healing session, the *cintā* also has a subtext that emerges through exchanges between the shaman and his interlocutors, although it is far more subtle and indirect in nature. Thus, aside from the *jhākri's* chants, patients are able to draw upon the subtext that emerges through the interactions between onlookers and the *jhākri*, as noted in the previous chapter. It is in the context of these interchanges during breaks throughout the various stages of the *cintā* that a concurrence of opinion emerges regarding the patient's prospects. This consensus regarding the shaman's diagnosis is an important element of shamanic healing (Sagant 1988: 23).

Drawing upon this subtext, the patient, searching his own past and tapping knowledge of previous cases of shamanic healings of other villagers, seeks what is meaningful in the association of his particular condition to the particular supernatural agency designated by the *jhākri*. Healing, thus, involves the shaman interrelating and creating transitions between the patterns of social relationships around and between individuals, or among and between the patient's body, society, and the spirits (Samuel 1995: 256; Sagant 1988: 29; Walsh 1996: 101). Höfer's (1994: 41) observations are relevant in this connection:

> The [patient] is drawn into a discourse (with and about him) which is not free from paradoxes and imponderabilities, and which thus provides him with a chance of stepping out, again and again, from the entrenchment of his own subjectivity . . . the staged and unstaged, said and unsaid, the private and the public interact in such a way that the patient comes to perceive himself from different angles and with the eyes of the others so as to relativize his own self by experiencing his present as something already past or as the others' present.

Along slightly different lines, McClenon (2002: 79; 2006) interprets the shamanistic healing process in terms of the hypnotic response. He suggests that hypnotic mechanisms enable healers to associate people's emotions with transactional symbols and the manipulation of those symbols provides waking hypnotic suggestions that facilitate transformative states among hypnotizable subjects. Peters (1995: 60) believes that during the liminal phase of the healing ceremony, patients experience altered states of consciousness facilitated by rapid drumming, a technique that has been shown to produce such effects (see chapter 6). As a result, the patient undergoes a "transpersonal experience" in which the sense of self extends to wider dimensions of psyche and cosmos. This, according to Peters (1995: 53), accounts for the efficacy of shamanic healing rituals.

Many anthropologists writing about shamanism take the efficacy of the shaman's therapies for granted. However, what efficacy means exactly is not always clear. What seems to be the case most often is that various writers know of particular instances in which the patient has recovered or has reported relief of symptoms following the shaman's curative ritual. Twenty-nine patients in the forty-seven *jhākri* healing ceremonies I videotaped reported some positive results. The question is, what does this signify? The assumption among some writers is that shamans cure diseases. However, without systematic objective assessments using double-blind testing it is not possible to conclude that a cure has taken place in a clinical sense, regardless of the whether one is assessing shamanic therapies or biomedical treatments (Beyerstein 1997). This is because, as Beyerstein (1997) has put it, "personal testimonials offer no basis on which to judge whether a putative therapy has, in fact, cured a disease."

I have found no evidence in the literature that anyone has conducted such an assessment of shamanistic healing in the ethnographic context.

What we find are studies based primarily upon anecdotal evidence (i.e., stories and personal testimonials), small sample sizes, problematic sampling techniques, or claims of paranormal healing that are nonreplicable (e.g., Csordas and Kleinman 1990; Kleinman and Sung 1979; Kaja 1985; Frank 1973; Benor 1990). While I am by no means dismissing the shaman's therapeutic approach (I have documented numerous cures), I object to the mystification of the shaman's ingenious healing practices. My point is that unless we first understand the phenomena in question scientifically we are hardly in a position to make qualitative judgments, much less make claims about miracle healing and paranormal powers.

Many writers influenced by the New Age mysticism and the "will to believe," which has lamentably also influenced scholars, as Hamayon (2001: 1) has pointed out, are uncritical of the data and are keen to accept miraculous cures, no matter how dubious the evidence (Beyerstein and Sampson 1996). The authors of a recent book on Nepalese shamanism write, for example:

> many ethnologists are under the false impression that shamanism is a form of symbolic healing. Shamanism is a direct intervention into reality. It is only the performance and tools that have a symbolic meaning—for the audience. (Müller-Ebeling et al. 2002: 194)

There is no evidence to justify this kind of supernaturalism. Such inexcusable gullibility and sensationalism merely mystify the phenomenon in question and deter ethnographic understanding. Yet a number of anthropologists have naively accepted as miraculous simple sleight-of-hand tricks and other illusions (Turner 1993; Stoller 1986: 55; Jackson 1989: 13; for a critique see Lett 1997: 71–72) known to and easily reproducible by any stage magician or conjurer with a modicum of skill (Lett 1997b: 71–72; Randi 1997: 191). While it may be true that "the postmodernist turn among the humanities has . . . weakened the old certainties" and many might regard shamanism as a "serious competitor to science" (Samuel 1995; 253), this has been a detriment to the discipline's credibility. Anthropologists who have adopted such credulous perspectives have become nothing more than, to use Arens's (1979: 7) expression once again, the "erudite purveyors of attractive pedestrian myths."

Beyerstein's (1997) critique of "complementary" or alternative medicine, which the discussion below draws upon, is particularly relevant in the context of the anthropological treatment of shamanic healing and the dangers of mystification (see also Beyerstein 1999a; 1999b). As Beyerstein (1997) points out, when evaluating whether or not a therapeutic procedure has been successful, it is necessary to differentiate between the concepts of illness and disease (Eisenberg 1977; Helman 1981). Illness refers to the subjective perceptions of being sick, such as sensations of weakness, discomfort, pain, and the feeling that something is not quite right. Disease pertains to organic physiological conditions that are the result of viral and bacterial infections, tissue damage, cancerous growths, arterial blockages, or introduction of toxins into the system (Beyerstein 1997). The experience of illness is shaped by psychological and cultural factors, such as expectations, folk explanatory models, subjective biases, and even self-delusion (Beyerstein 1997; Kleinman and Sung 1979; Kleinman 1988b; Green et al. 2002).

Benefits that the "sick role" confers on the patient can cause and perpetuate illness by means of implicit psychosocial mechanisms, without the involvement of disease. Many such illnesses involve somatization, psychological disorders expressed in a language of distress as physiological symptoms that are unrelated to an organic medical condition (Beitman et al. 1982; Helman 2001: 267; Holder-Perkins and Wise 2001). The anthropological literature suggests that spiritual healing most frequently comes into play in cases that are primarily psychosomatic in nature (Bourguignon 1976b: 18; McClenon 2002: 64–67). These illnesses often respond well to social support, attention, sense of inclusion, and comfort that the shaman's healing rituals can provide (Eisenberg 1977). Thus, in evaluating shamanic therapy, one must establish whether the malady in question is organic or psychosomatic in nature (Beyerstein 1997), otherwise it is impossible to evaluate if a therapy has effectively cured a disease.

There are several other possibilities for the efficacy of shamanic healing. The human body tends to heal itself and therefore many diseases are self-limiting (Klein 1997). Given enough time, the patient recovers. To prove that the cure stems from the shaman's therapy and not because the disease has run its natural course, we need evidence that meaningful numbers of patients have been cured by the purported shamanic procedure at significantly higher and faster rates than patients without any form of therapeutic intervention (Beyerstein 1997).

Another important factor is the cyclical nature of various diseases, such as, for example, arthritis, multiple sclerosis, allergies, and various gastrointestinal ailments (Beyerstein 1997). Symptoms fluctuate markedly, with flare-ups followed by remission of symptoms. Under these circumstances, an ineffective therapy applied during a period of flare-up, a time when people ordinarily seek help, will be followed by an inevitable improvement (Beyerstein 1997). This gives the impression that the therapy has been successful, even though improvement would have occurred anyway.

Shamanistic healing may be effective in helping the patient psychologically cope better with an illness, without necessarily affecting the disease itself. In the case of pain, as Beyerstein (1997) has pointed out, such therapies can reduce anxiety by making the patient cognitively reinterpret his symptoms. This can affect the emotional component of pain and can psychologically relieve suffering. Shamanic healing may also uplift the patient's mood and expectation (as it appears to have done in the case discussed in the previous chapter), reduce stress, and this sort of psychological elevation can have a positive effect on the immune system and the body's natural ability to recuperate (cf. Mestel 1994).

Another factor that may convey the perception of improvement stems from the "demand characteristics" of the therapeutic setting that influence patient response to treatment (Orne 1962). The patient subliminally picks up the expectations of the enthusiastic therapist, who confidently believes in the efficacy of his procedures, and then responds in a manner that meets the therapist's desired expectations by overestimating the perceived benefits of therapy (Beyerstein 1997).

Finally, perceived improvements following a therapy may be due to the placebo effect. The placebo effect refers to measurable changes in symptoms after treatments that are the result of expectations, beliefs, enthusiasm, and encouragement of the therapist rather than the therapy itself. Placebo, as psychiatrist Arthur Shapiro (1959: 298) put it,

> [refers to] the psychological, physiological or psychophysiological effect of any medication or procedure given with therapeutic intent, which is independent of or minimally related to the pharmacological effect of the medication or to the specific effects of the procedure, and which operates through a psychological mechanism.

A placebo can be an inert pill, or bogus surgery, or psychotherapy. Central to the effect are the beliefs in the efficacy of the placebo substance/procedure by the recipient and/or the administrator of that substance/procedure (Helman 2001: 196). Thus, any seemingly credible treatment may have positive results because of the placebo effect (Klein 1997). The effect is "culture-bound," meaning that it takes place in particular cultural settings that endorse the placebo and the therapist administering it (Helman 2001: 197), such as a *cintā* in Nepal, or a physician's examination room in the United States.

If beliefs can have positive effects, they can also cause harm. Stress resulting from culturally instilled beliefs can produce the "nocebo effect," which is the opposite of the placebo effect (Helman 2001: 304). An extreme example of the nocebo effect is what anthropologists call "magical death," or "voodoo death," a phenomenon for which there is some documentation (Hahn and Kleinman 1983; Eastwell 1982; Lex 1974; Lester 1972; Cannon 1942). In such cases, individuals learn that they have been the target of spells or curses, become highly emotionally agitated, lose a sense of control, rapidly sicken, and die (Helman 2001: 306–309). As Hahn and

Kleinman (1983: 3) have put it, "belief kills; belief heals." As a side note it should be stressed that as in the case of claims of miraculous shamanic cures, one must treat the evidence for voodoo or magical death with equal caution because the data consist of recycled personal testimonials and eyewitness accounts with an absence of statistically sound controlled comparative data.

The negative effects of diagnostic labels illustrate another way in which cultural beliefs result in the nocebo effect. Patients told by their doctors that they have high blood pressure, cancer, or heart problems will exhibit symptoms and behaviors culturally associated with those illnesses even if they do not suffer from those conditions (Helman 2001: 306). The label alone suffices to trigger the effect. Diagnostic labels may also lead family members and friends to respond in ways deemed culturally appropriate for dealing with patients suffering from the disease in question. A label may in fact result in physiological responses associated with the disease, even when there is no organic basis for the diagnosis.

While the nocebo effect may account for the force imputed to witches, sorcerers, spells, and curses in some cultures, and it may explain the fear some *jhākri*s arouse, it is the positive or placebo effect of beliefs that underlies successful shamanistic healings. The placebo effect operates within the context of biomedical therapies as well. It occurs in the context of clinical trials of new drugs as well as in surgery (for an overview see Harrington 2002). Clinical trials in the West have shown that approximately one-third of patients improve in response to placebo treatments, such as pharmacologically inert pills and sham surgical procedures (Helman 2001: 200). As in shamanistic healing, in these settings the patient's expectations of a cure and a firm conviction in the efficacy of the procedures employed are highly significant. The ability of the physician to establish his authority and knowledge convincingly is equally important. It has been shown that the physician's authority can be employed to alter the patient's motives and expectations to increase, decrease, or even reverse drug effects (Helman 2001: 190). This is why the *jhākri* finds it necessary to demonstrate his paranormal powers by performing extraordinary feats, such walking on hot coals, eating lit wicks, and immersing his hands in boiling liquids (cf. Peters 1995: 57). With his *śakti* tangibly demonstrated the healer's authority is reinforced and his credentials as a practitioner visibly validated.

The healer's own belief in and enthusiasm for the therapeutic procedures employed is crucial as well. For example, angina pectoris, the chest pain due to coronary arteriosclerosis and constricted blood supply, responds not only to small quantities of nitroglycerine, but also to placebo treatments (Moerman 1997: 243; 2002). During the 1950s and 1960s, enthusiastic doctors were achieving 70 to 90 percent success in treating angina pectoris, with patients exhibiting measurable increases in endurance, decrease in nitroglycerine intake, and better electrocardiogram readings. These successful surgical procedures proved to be ineffective and were abandoned following controlled trials by skeptics (Helman 2001: 201). This sheds light on why the *jhākri*'s self-confidence in his performance, which generates concurrence of opinion among the participants in the *cintā* that patients draw upon in contemplating their condition, is an important element of shamanic healing. An enthusiastic healer and a believing audience, whether nurses and lab technicians or onlookers at a *cintā*, can obtain positive results from practically any plausible therapy.

The effect of patient expectation has also been documented in clinical trials in the West. In one test, patients anticipating relief receiving saline solution injections reacted as if they received morphine, producing painkilling endorphins, or endogenous opiates. The empirical reality of this response was demonstrated when the analgesic effects of the endorphins generated could be reversed by an injection of naloxone, an opiate antagonist (Levine et al. 1978; Moerman 1992: 76; 2002). Similar results were recorded in a study of ultrasound treatment for swelling following "wisdom teeth" extraction. The patients were sorted into three groups. The first group received ultrasound treatment; the second group received a placebo treatment with the machine applied without activation; while the third group received standard dental care but no ultrasound treatment. In relation to the third group, the placebo treatment reduced swelling in all cases (Moerman 1992: 76; 2002).

Aside from the context, expectations, and doctor-patient relations, other factors, such as what patients know, also influence the placebo effect. Researchers found, for example, that the color of the pill can influence patient reaction, with some conditions responding to certain colors (Helman 2001: 198). For example, the tranquilizer oxazypam in green tablets worked better than in yellow ones for anxiety symptoms. In another study, medical students were requested to take part in the test of two new drugs, a tranquilizer and a stimulant. Each student received two blue tablets or two red tablets. The pills were pharmacologically inert. Several hours later, the students responding to a questionnaire reported that the red pills acted as stimulants and the blue ones as depressants. It was also reported that two pills had greater effect than one. These findings are significant because they highlight that it is what the patient knows, rather than some personality trait, that is important in the placebo effect (Moerman 1992: 72; 2002). Americans know that according to their culture's color symbolism blue stands for cool/low and red means hot/high. In addition, two denotes a greater quantity than one. The students responded according to what they knew.

There are additional examples in clinical settings that highlight the role of the patient's knowledge in the efficacy of treatments. In one study comparing the effectiveness of aspirin and a placebo for headaches, subjects were divided into four groups. One group received a placebo that resembled generic aspirin, the second group received the brand-name drug, the third group received generic aspirin, and the fourth group got a placebo with the advertised brand name (Branthwaith and Cooper 1981). Patients reported that the brand-name pills were more effective than the generic versions. In addition, the brand-name placebo turned out to be more effective than the generic placebo. Not only did the advertisements of the brand name lead patients to believe that it was more effective than the generic variety, but also the brand name increased the effectiveness of the placebo (Moerman 1992: 73).

Jhākris seem to grasp intuitively that what patients know is important to the outcome of their healing ceremonies. This is why they pay such careful attention to the smallest and most tedious details in their procedures, layout of the altars, use of ritual paraphernalia, and symbolism, these are crucial just as the color of pills, number of tablets, or brand names are to patients in the West.

The placebo effect extends beyond the cases and conditions noted here. It has been documented in relieving a host of conditions, including depression, schizophrenia, rheumatoid arthritis, ulcers, insomnia, asthma, nausea associated with chemotherapy, and pain (Helman 2001: 196, 201; Moerman 1992: 74; 2002). Some researchers believe that 35 to 65 percent of the efficacy of Western biomedicine in general is due to the placebo effect (Moerman 1997: 24; Romanucci-Ross and Moerman 1997). Moreover, there is a symbolic or placebo dimension in all prescribed medications (Helman 2001: 198). The *jhākri* is not alone, therefore, in relying upon the placebo effect. Moreover, in recent years the biomedical establishment's view of the placebo has shifted from a perspective considering it a sham or a control agent in clinical trials toward a view of it as a therapeutic ally (Kleinman et al. 2002: 1). The genius of the shaman's therapy does not rest on magic, miracles, or mysterious supernatural forces, but in its ability to evoke the placebo response in patients using symbolic procedures, beliefs, and expectations to activate pathways connecting mental states and physiological processes to produce positive biochemical and physiological changes.

The important point here is that the placebo effect is actually a form of "non-verbal symbolic healing." Symbolic healing therefore is a component of all therapeutic systems, rather than being an exclusive attribute of shamanism. However, one cannot label all forms of symbolic healing as shamanism as this would conflate distinct specialists. For example, the various ritual intercessors in Nepal, such as the *dhāmi, mātā, jhārphuke, janne manche*, *lāmā*, and *jōtisi*, all employ symbolic healing techniques, as do psychoanalysts, voodoo priests, medicine men, and healers of all varieties from Amazonia to the Australian Outback. For this reason, one finds generic similarities in the ritual repertoires of these practitioners. This does not mean, however, that these individuals are shamans or that their practices are rooted in a once-universal Paleolithic religion. The widespread occurrence of systems of therapy centered on symbolic healing is indicative simply of a universal human psychophysiological propensity, which is that emotional and cognitive factors can trigger a psychoneuroimmunological response under appropriated circumstances. It says nothing about the universality of shamanism or its antiquity.

12

From Nepal to Siberia: Disentangling a Conceptual Morass

In this study, I have attempted to use ethnographic materials from Nepal, where a thriving and remarkable shamanistic tradition exists, to highlight and address certain problems encountered in the scholarly discourse on shamanism. In this final chapter I wish to address the problem of definition. A number of anthropologists have asserted that "there are no reliable criteria for diagnosing shamanism cross-culturally" (Klein et al. 2002; Klein and Stanfield-Mazzi 2004; Klein et al. 2005). The seeming intractability of the subject matter has led others to assert that shamanism is an "insipid" category and "an artifact of anthropological history and an illusion" (Holmberg 1989: 144–145; 1984: 697; 1983: 41). The materials presented in the previous chapters do not support these contentions.

The roots of the quandary, as I have attempted to show, are traceable to Eliade's work. In an effort to add precision to the concept of shamanism so that the shaman is not conflated with "any magician, sorcerer, medicine man, or ecstatic," Eliade offered the idea of shamanism as an "archaic technique of ecstasy" centered on soul journeys, which he considered to be a timeless universal human psychological attribute (Eliade 1964: xv, 3, 504). Although starting with a model of the archaic shaman based on Siberian materials, to bolster his contention that shamanism is an extremely ancient form of spirituality, and hence worthy of scholarly analysis, Eliade had to provide evidence of time depth. He did this by relying on the defective diffusionist postulate of geographic distribution, that is, the more widespread something is the older it must be. It was necessary for Eliade to find evidence of shamanism everywhere cross-culturally, which he did, an effort that ironically directed scholarship back to the point of labeling anyone trafficking with spirits as a shaman. The outcome of this feat of scholarly ingenuity was a thorough conceptual morass. It is unfortunate that Eliade's knotty construal not only defined the parameters for the subsequent study of the subject matter, it continues to inform the works of many writers interested in shamanism.

The concept of shamanism in its current usage is intractable because it subsumes several ontologically distinct elements: (1) a historical/ethnographic complex in Siberia; (2) a Paleolithic magicoreligious tradition based on ASC; and (3) historically/ethnographically unrelated magicoreligious beliefs/behaviors with similarities due to the propensity of the human central nervous system to display common functional attributes in ASC. Examples of (3) include phenomena such as *ban-jhākri* kidnappings and UFO abduction experiences, discussed in chapter 9. Shamanism acquires a different meaning depending on which one of these distinct elements, or combination of elements, a particular author has in mind. Solving this multifarious conceptual morass requires that we disentangle the various elements subsumed under the label and pinpoint the problems in terms of the discussions in the previous chapters.

We may begin with the historical/ethnographic complex in Siberia. Of particular relevance in this connection is the material provided by Shirokogoroff on Tungus shamanism. Shirokogoroff (1935: 269), we may recall, characterized shamans as persons who have "mastered spirits, who at their will can introduce these spirits into themselves and use their power over the spirits in their own interests, particularly helping other people, who suffer from spirits." This construal is far more nuanced than it appears. While most writers on the subject frequently cite this passage, many overlook the additional constellation of features Shirokogoroff (1935: 274) provides to qualify his characterization, without which the full meaning of what he has in mind is unclear. The shaman, according to Shirokogoroff (1935: 274):

> (1) [is] . . . a master of spirits; (2) he has a group of mastered spirits; (3) there is a complex of methods and paraphernalia recognized and transmitted; (4) there is a theoretical justification of the practice; (5) the shaman assumes a special position.

It is instructive to look at each of these categories in detail as they provide the basis for making a distinction between various types of intercessors often mistakenly labeled as shamans. Shirokogoroff (1935: 271) describes the mastery of spirits as follows:

> the master must take care of the spirits, feed them and handle them, when he wants to introduce them into himself . . . the difference between a person who is possessed by spirits (e.g., manifested in some nervous and psychic

troubles) and a shaman is also essential, for the shaman introduces spirits into himself at his own will when he wants it, i.e., the shaman uses his own body as a placing for spirits. A voluntary introduction of a spirit is . . . a characteristic of shamanism . . . the same is true about the next step, namely, the expulsion of the spirits, which is beyond the power of ordinary people. Thus among the shamans a voluntary introduction and expulsion of the spirits are particular cases of "mastering."

The nature of the shaman's interaction with spirits is at issue here. This is a key experiential and phenomenological dimension of shamanic experience, often disregarded by many, that sets it apart from other types of human-spirit interactions. Hallucinogenic or psychotropic drugs are not features of this complex because the shaman is able to shift phases of consciousness at will.

The next item is mastery of a group of spirits. Shirokogoroff (1935: 271–272) elaborates on this as follows:

the shaman must have several spirits possessing various qualities, the latter being used by the shaman when spirits are introduced. Indeed, the number of spirits possessed is subject to variation. The shaman is supposed to have at the beginning of his career, at least one spirit . . . with the help of which he may master many other spirits or at least know them . . . the more spirits [he has] the more powerful the shaman . . . the shaman must have a list of spirits.

In terms of the two criteria given above, mastery over and variety of spirits, it is possible to differentiate between shamans, mediums, oracles, or other ecstatics, as in the case of Nepalese ritual intercessors discussed in chapter 2. The shaman, we may recall, interacts with sundry classes of spirits and is able to initiate and terminate that interaction at will. Thus, defining shamanism simply as interaction with spirits using ASC for the benefit of clients or community, as many writers do, is not sufficient to differentiate a shaman from other ritual intercessors. Moreover, only a thorough misreading can lead one to use Shirokogoroff's criteria as a definition for South Asian spirit mediumship and oracular deity possession, as Smith (2006: 64) has done. The interactions between shamans and spirits are qualitatively and phenomenologically distinct from the interactions of oracles and mediums and the spirit world.

By "a complex of methods and paraphernalia recognized and transmitted," Shirokogoroff (1935: 272) means that:

the shaman must know, from learning them, a series of methods of attracting spirits, of offering them sacrifice, and, generally, of dealing with them, when they are not attracted into himself. Since the complex of spirits (their characters and needs) is a complex created through the accumulation of elements

by the previous generation of shamans, it is transmitted through the mechanism of tradition, consciously or unconsciously assimilated by the new
shamans.

The generation and transmission of the body of knowledge that forms the
basis of Nepalese shamanism amply illustrate these points.

Shirokogoroff (1935: 272) adds that the transmission of this dynamic
body of knowledge "serves as a condition for the recognition of the
shaman's ability," or the theoretical justification of his activities:

> the practicing of shamanism presumes that the shamans accept some theo-
> retical basis of shamanism, i.e., a general theory of spirits and their particu-
> lar characters, and practical possibilities of dealing with spirits. [This theory
> includes] recognition of the existence of spirits; the possibility of their re-
> moval from one placing to another, including man; the possibility of master-
> ing them in the above given sense. Naturally, every shaman must know what
> to do. The shamans must know the character of the mastered spirit and of
> those with which they have to deal. (Shirokogoroff 1935: 273)

The discussion of the *jhākri*'s cosmology in chapter 7 fully illustrates
this. There is an articulated theory of spirits that specifies the relationship
between humans and the spirit world, as well as the knowledge needed
to deal with such entities, and what is required to operate as a shaman.
This body of knowledge also provides the theoretical justification for the
jhākri's activities.

The next criterion in Shirokogoroff's list is the shaman's paraphernalia.
In this regard he adds that,

> Various paraphernalia are found used by the shamans during the perform-
> ances. It is supposed that without these paraphernalia shamanizing is im-
> possible, and therefore the persons who have no such paraphernalia cannot
> function as shamans. In this way, paraphernalia become an absolutely indis-
> pensable component of shamanistic complex. (Shirokogoroff 1935: 272)

The *jhākri*'s indispensable assemblage of equipment—the drum, headdress, metal bells, beads, and costume—which is remarkably similar to
the equipment used by Siberian practitioners, distinctly differentiates the
shaman from other classes of ritual intercessors. In terms of shamanism as
a historical/ethnographic complex the presence or absence of this assemblage becomes an important diagnostic feature.

Finally, in addition to the above stated criteria, acknowledgment by
members of the community is another diagnostic feature:

> The candidates are required practically to show what use they can make of
> the spirits, and the shamanistic methods; how deep their general knowledge

is; whether they satisfy the moral requirements of the community or not. This may be shown in a series of performances for helping people in distress and confirmed by the general opinion of the moral character of the candidate. (Shirokogoroff 1935: 273)

The *jhākri's* social position, as noted in chapter 4, is dependent upon public consensus. Mastery of spirits and knowledge of techniques alone are insufficient. The *jhākri* has a well-defined and unique social position, a "transcendental persona," which is also highly ambivalent (Hitchcock 1974b: 153; Maskarinec 1995: 113; Riboli 2000: 65–66), characteristics also true of Siberian shamans.

Taken together, Shirokogoroff thus provides us with a precise set of diagnostic criteria that, with some amendments, can be employed to differentiate shamanistic practices as a historical/ethnographic complex from other forms of magicoreligious practices/behaviors. This is the sense in which I have used the terms *shaman* and *shamanism* in the context of the present study. Shirokogoroff diagnostic attributes certainly closely fit the Nepalese ethnographic setting. Moreover, the material from Nepal allows further refinement of those attributes.

What Shirokogoroff does not explicitly mention, although it is certainly implied in his work, is the nature of the shaman's calling and his repertoire. When these elements are included, we obtain the following construal of shamanism as an historical/ethnographic complex:

> The shaman is a socially recognized part-time ritual intercessor, a healer, problem solver, and interpreter of the world, whose calling is involuntary and involves a transformative initiatory crisis. His repertoire consists of dramatic public performances involving drumming, singing, and dancing in which he is the musicant. He has the ability to access ASC at will (without drugs) and enters into a distinctive mode of interaction with paranormal beings of various classes. The embodiment (adhesion) of spirits does not result in the replacement of the shaman's consciousness. He has mastery over spirit helpers and uses that power for the benefit of clients. The shaman has distinctive specialized paraphernalia: the drum, costume, headdress, metal bells, and beads. Finally, he commands a body of specialized knowledge transmitted orally from teacher to pupil according to tradition.

I shall refer to this formulation base on Tungus and Nepalese shamanic practices as the *historical/ethnographic complex* definition of shamanism.

We have just dealt with the first component in the concept of shamanism as currently understood by most writers. Further conceptual issues that need clarification include the idea of shamanism as a magicoreligious tradition dating back to the Paleolithic, and the place of historically/ethnographically unrelated magicoreligious beliefs/behaviors that are similar because of functional similarities of the human central nervous system in ASC.

Eliade (1964: 495–500) considered Tungus shamanism as a distorted variant of the genuine pristine configuration he envisioned, that is, a soul-journeying enterprise dating back to the Paleolithic period. However, there is no evidence anywhere to support the notion of soul-journeying shamanism as the pristine form of the practice. The ethnographic material from Nepal clearly suggests that the binarism between soul-journeying and spirit possession, endlessly repeated by other writers, is simplistic and misleading. As we have seen, the manner in which Nepalese shamans interact with spirits is highly complex and defies classification as either one or the other kind. *Jhākris* not only embody spirits, they also undertake spirit-journeys and travel to other worlds to interact with divinities, as well as simply summoning spirits for the purpose of interrogation. More-over, as discussed in chapter 6, the shaman's incorporation of spirits is completely different from that of other ritual intercessors, such as medi-ums or oracles, because the embodied spirits seldom replace the shaman's consciousness, a fact that attests to the shaman's mastery over spirits and the altered state of consciousness (Böckman and Hultkrantz 1978: 25; Mi-trani 1992: 154; Torrance 1994: 138). For this reason, I have suggested the use of "spirit adhesion" in place of "spirit possession" when referring to the shaman's interactions with supernatural beings.

As for the antiquity of shamanism, although the anthropological litera-ture is replete with statements regarding the extreme age of shamanism, and there are numerous treatises on shamanism as humankind's oldest religious tradition, tangible scientific evidence for this claim is sorely lack-ing. Remarkably, its status as a concrete fact seems to stem from its end-less reiteration in the literature. The history of shamanism in Siberia does not go beyond the sixteenth century and its antiquity is unknown. Argu-ments for the antiquity of shamanism in general based on ethnographic analogies are highly questionable as well, as noted in chapter 1. Cave paintings depicting costumed figures that are open to numerous equally plausible interpretations do not constitute conclusive evidence that can serve as the basis for positing the existence of an entire magicoreligious system in prehistoric times. Even working with the most general, am-biguous, and analytically problematic definition of shamanism as "the use of ASC for the benefit of others," cave paintings and rock art do not supply tangible evidence to infer the use of trance in prehistory. The sug-gestion that it is possible to identify entoptics in rock art and hence estab-lish the artist's trance state is ingenious but highly speculative, method-ologically unsound, and nonfalsifiable.

Finally, the purported widespread distribution of shamanism and the prevalence of its basic ideas are highly problematic as a basis for estab-lishing chronology. First, the geographical scope of shamanism varies depending on how the phenomenon is defined. Second, the assumption that the more widespread a cultural trait is the older it must be is flawed.

Therefore, there are no reasons to consider Tungus shamanism as described by Shirokogoroff as a decadent or distorted version of an alleged pristine and possibly nonexistent Paleolithic prototype. This also means that the diagnostic criteria Shirokogoroff provides for defining what the shaman is and does, with the amendments made above, offers a valid approach for looking at shamanism as a historical/ethnographic complex.

The final elements of the conceptual morass under discussion relate to the historically/ethnographically unrelated magicoreligious beliefs/behaviors that are similar because of the propensity of the human central nervous system to display common functional attributes in ASC. For Eliade (1964: xv, 504) the shaman's ecstatic experience was a universal aspect of human psychology rather than the product of historical or cultural factors. Ecstasy represents the manifestation of a timeless "sacred." This has become the inspiration for the development of "spatiotemporally free" neurophysiological and neuropsychological models of shamanism (Jones 2006: 7), which draw upon, among other ideas, Jungian archetypes, or neurognostic structures, and the collective unconscious.

Spatiotemporally free models tend to label anyone who uses ASC to commune with spirits for the benefit of clients or community as a shaman. Similarities in how the human nervous system operates in ASC are treated as shamanistic. Thus, a neurophysiological human universal is classified in terms of an idiographic temporal ethnographic category. Such a construal of shamanism, as noted in chapter 2, results in the conflation of ethnographically distinct ritual intercessors. Moreover, the category "shaman" becomes so ambiguous that it loses its analytical utility. *Ban-jhākri* abductees, UFO abductees, people who have had near-death experiences, mediums, oracles, prophets, messiahs, voodoo priests, and healers of all varieties from Amazonia to the Australian Outback become "shamans."

Because of the accretion of different simultaneous meanings, (1) a historical/ethnographic complex in Siberia, (2) a religious heritage from the Paleolithic, (3) historically/ethnographically unrelated but similar magicoreligious beliefs/behaviors, as it stands, shamanism as an analytical concept is hopelessly flawed. Hutton (1993: 16–17) has recognized the problems with respect to the relationship between (1) and (3):

If shamanism is defined as what went on in Siberia . . . then it was practiced in a relatively few areas of the world. . . . If, on the other hand, shamans are any people who are expert in entering trance and dealing with the spirit world, then the Siberian examples are not typical of the whole but an extreme and unusually elaborate variety of it.

The association between (1) and (2) is dubious at best because of an absence of compelling evidence. Moreover, (1) and (3) cannot be conflated because (1) encompasses only a specific range of the spectrum of ASC. This is evident from the differences between the *jhākri's* ASC and the medium's psychic interactions with divinities, as discussed in chapter 2. Shamanism as a historical/ethnographic complex represents a set of behaviors and beliefs related to the utilization of the potentials of one category of ASC. Because humans have the propensity for ASC and the human central nervous system displays common functional attributes in altered states of consciousness we encounter cross-cultural similarities in the domain of religious behavior. Using shamanism as a blanket label for all of these, that is, equating (1) and (3) really adds nothing to the discussion and in fact muddles what is in its own right an extremely interesting and important area of research relating to human consciousness, spirituality, and religious behavior.

Are we any closer to a resolution of the problem? Distinguishing shamanism as an historical/ethnographic complex from magicoreligious beliefs/behaviors with similarities based on common neurophysiological and neuropsychological factors will take us a long way in clarifying the difficulties associated with the concept of shamanism as currently understood and used. This, I submit is possible using the *historical/ethnographic complex* definition of shamanism provided above. Using this approach, it becomes evident that the Tungus shaman and the Nepalese *jhākri* demonstrably belong in an analytical category different from *yagé*-imbibing Amazonian healers or African spirit mediums. One can also use these diagnostic criteria to differentiate between various local categories of ritual intercessors, as I have shown in the context of Nepal.

I am not going to advocate the introduction of new terminology, or the use of suitable local words beyond the source area of the historical/ethnographic complex as a substitute for "shaman" and "shamanism," as others have (e.g., Bahn 2001: 57). What I am recommending, based on the material presented in this book, is that more attention be devoted to the detailed empirical and phenomenological attributes of different magicoreligious practitioners, so that we do not needlessly conflate distinct intercessors. I have shown that this is possible in the context of Nepal. Such an approach enhances analytical understanding as well as clarifying appropriate categories for the purpose of cross-cultural comparison. It is my contention that the subject matter is not intractable and anthropologists have needlessly, and unjustifiably disengaged from the debate on shamanism. As a final statement, I reiterate the point made by Jones (1976a: 53), which is that anthropology has a great deal to offer to the study of shamanism, and empirical ethnographic analysis (not self-referential particularistic narratives) can rectify many of the erroneous notions forwarded regarding the subject matter.

Bibliography

Abu-Lughod, Lila. 1991. Writing Against Culture. In *Recapturing Anthropology.* Richard Fox (ed.). Santa Fe, NM: School of American Research Press (distributed by the University of Washington Press). Pp. 37–62.

Acharya, B. K. 1994. Nature Cure and Indigenous Healing Practices in Nepal: A Medical Anthropological Perspective. In *Anthropology of Nepal: People, Problems and Processes.* Michael Allen (ed.). New York: State Mutual Book & Periodical Service. Pp. 234–244.

Achterberg, Jeanne. 2002. *Imagery in Healing: Shamanism and Modern Medicine.* Boston: Shambhala.

———. 1987. The Shaman: Master Healer in the Imaginary Realm. In *Shamanism: An Expanded View of Reality.* Shirley Nicholson (ed.). Wheaton, IL: Theosophical Publishing House. Pp. 103–124.

Ackerknecht, E. 1943. Psychopathology, Primitive Medicine, and Primitive Culture. *Bulletin of the History of Medicine* 14:30–67.

Alcock, James. 1999. Alternative Medicine and the Psychology of Belief. *The Scientific Review of Alternative Medicine* 3, no. 2. http://www.sram.org/0302/bias.html.

Allen, Nicholas. 1976a. Shamanism Among the Thulung Rai. In *Spirit Possession in the Nepal Himalayas.* John Hitchcock and Rex Jones (eds.). Warminster, England: Aris and Phillips. Pp. 124–140.

———. 1976b. Approaches to Illness in the Nepalese Hills. In *Social Anthropology and Medicine.* J. B. Loudon (ed.). London: Academic Press. Pp. 500–552.

———. 1974. The Ritual Journey, a Pattern Underlying Certain Nepalese Rituals. In *Contributions to the Anthropology of Nepal.* Christoph von Fürer-Haimendorf (ed.). Warminster, England: Aris and Phillips Ltd. Pp. 6–22.

Alper, Harvey (ed.). 1989. *Understanding Mantras.* Albany: State University of New York Press.

213

Alper, Matthew. 2003. Drug-Induced God. In *NeuroTheology: Brain, Science, Spirituality, Religious Experience*. R. Joseph (ed.). San Jose: University Press. Pp. 409–410.

Amnesty International. 2004. *Amnesty International Media Briefing: Making Violence Against Women Count*. AI Index: ACT 77/036/2004 (Public) News Service No: 051, http://news.amnesty.org/library/Index/ENGACT770362004.

An-Che, Li. 1948. Bon: The Magico-Religious Belief of the Tibetan-Speaking Peoples. *Southwestern Journal of Anthropology*, 4 (1):31–42.

Appell, G. N. 1989. Facts, Fiction, Fads, and Follies: But Where Is the Evidence? *American Anthropologist* 91 (1): 195–198.

Appelle, Stuart, Steven Lynn, and Leonard Newman. 2000. Alien Abduction Experiences. In *Varieties of Anomalous Experience: Examining the Scientific Evidence*. E. Cardeña, S. Lynn, and S. Krippner (eds.). Washington, DC: American Psychological Association. Pp. 253–282.

Arens, William. 1979. *The Man-Eating Myth: Anthropology and Anthropophagy*. New York: Oxford University Press.

Arnott, W. Geoffrey. 1989. Nechung: A Modern Parallel to the Delphic Oracles? *Greece & Rome* 36 (2): 152–157.

Atkinson, Jane. 1992. Shamanisms Today. *Annual Review of Anthropology* 21: 307–330.

Atran, Scott. 2006. The Cognitive and Evolutionary Roots of Religion. In *Where God and Science Meet: How Brain and Evolutionary Studies Alter Our Understanding of Religion*. Patrick McNamara (ed.). Westport, CT: Praeger. Vol. 1, pp. 181–208.

———. 2002. *In Gods We Trust: The Evolutionary Landscape of Religion*. Oxford: Oxford University Press.

Bahn, Paul. 2001. Save the Last Trance for Me: An Assessment of the Misuse of Shamanism in Rock Art Studies. In *The Concept of Shamanism: Uses and Abuses*. Henri-Paul Francfort, Roberte Hamayon, and Paul Bahn (eds.). Budapest: Akadémiai Kiadó. Pp. 51–93.

Bahn, Paul, and Jean Vertut. 1997. *Journey Through the Ice Age*. Berkeley: University of California Press.

Balzer, Marjorie. 1997. Introduction. In *Shamanic Worlds: Rituals and Lore of Siberia and Central Asia*. M. Balzer (ed.). Armonk, NY: M. E. Sharpe. Pp. xiii–xxxii.

———. 1996. Shamanism. In *Encyclopedia of Cultural Anthropology*. David Levinson and Melvin Ember (eds.). New York: Henry Holt. Vol. 4, pp. 1182–1185.

———. 1990. Introduction. In *Shamanism: Studies of Traditional Religion in Siberia and Central Asia*. M. Balzer (ed.). New York: M. E. Sharpe. Pp. vii–xviii.

Barušs, Imants. 2003. *Alterations of Consciousness: An Empirical Analysis for Social Scientists*. Washington, DC: American Psychological Association.

———. 1996. *Authentic Knowing: The Convergence of Science and Spiritual Aspiration*. West Lafayette, IN: Purdue University Press.

Basil, Robert (ed.). 1988. *Not Necessarily the New Age: Critical Essays*. Buffalo: Prometheus Books.

Basilov, Vladimir. 1997. Chosen by the Spirits. In *Shamanic Worlds: Rituals and Lore of Siberia and Central Asia*. M. Balzer (ed.). Armonk, NY: M. E. Sharpe. Pp. 3–48.

Baumer, Christoph. 2002. *Bön: Tibet's Ancient Religion*. Trumbull, CT: Weatherhill.

Beaune, Sophie de. 1998. Chamanisme et Préhistoire. *L'Homme* 147:203–219.

Bednarik, Robert, J. D. Lewis-Williams, and Thomas Dowson. 1990. On Neuropsychology and Shamanism in Rock Art. *Current Anthropology* 31 (1): 77–84.

Beitman B., H. Featherstone, L. Kastner, W. Katon, and A. Kleinman. 1982. Steps Toward Patient Acknowledgment of Psychosocial Factors. *The Journal of Family Practice* 15:1119–1126.

Benor, Daniel. 1990. Survey of Spiritual Healing Research. *Complementary Medical Research* 4(1):9-33.

Berglie, Per-Arne. 1978. On the Question of Tibetan Shamanism. In *Tibetan Studies: Presented at the Seminar of Young Tibetologists, Zurich, June 26–July 1, 1977*. Martin Brauen and Per Kværne (eds.). Zürich: Völkerkundemuseum der Universität Zürich. Pp. 39–51.

Berman, Morris. 2000. *Wandering God: A Study in Nomadic Spirituality*. Albany: State University of New York Press.

Beyerstein, Barry. 2002. Anomalous Perceptual Experiences: Is Believing is Seeing is Believing. *The Scientific Review of Alternative Medicine*. 6(2): 19–28.

———. 1999a. Pseudoscience and the Brain: Tuners and Tonics for Aspiring Superhumans. In *Mind Myths: Exploring Everyday Mysteries of the Mind and Brain*. S. Della Sala (ed.). Chichester, UK: John Wiley and Sons. Pp. 59–82.

———. 1999b. Psychology and "Alternative Medicine": Social and Judgmental Biases That Make Inert Treatments Seem to Work. *The Scientific Review of Alternative Medicine* 3 (2), http://www.sram.org/0302/bias.html.

———. 1997. Why Do Bogus Therapies Seem to Work? *The Skeptical Inquirer*. September/October. 21:29–34.

———. 1996a. Altered States of Consciousness. In *Encyclopedia of the Paranormal*. G. Stein (ed.). Amherst, NY: Prometheus Books. Pp. 8–16.

———. 1996b. Dissociation, Possession, and Exorcism. In *Encyclopedia of the Paranormal*. G. Stein (ed.). Amherst, NY: Prometheus Books. Pp. 544–552.

———. 1988. Neuropathology and the Legacy of Spiritual Possession. *The Skeptical Inquirer*. 12:248–262.

Beyerstein, B., and W. Sampson. 1996. Traditional Medicine and Pseudoscience in China. *Skeptical Inquirer* 20 (4): 18–26.

Bista, Dor Bahadur. 1987. *People of Nepal*. Kathmandu: Ratna Pustak Bhandar.

Blackmore, Susan. 1994. Alien Abduction: The Inside Story. *The New Scientist* 19: 29–31.

Blustain, Harvey. 1976. Levels of Medicine in a Central Nepali Village. *Contributions to Nepalese Studies* 3:83–105.

Böckman, Louise, and Åke Hultkrantz. 1978. *Studies in Lapp Shamanism*. Stockholm Studies in Comparative Religion 16. Stockholm: Almqvist and Wiksell.

Boddy, Janice. 1994. Spirit Possession Revisited: Beyond Instrumentality. *Annual Review of Anthropology* 23:407–434.

Bogoras, Waldemar. 1909. *The Chukchee*. Memoirs of the American Museum of Natural History 11.

Bourguignon, Erika. 1976a. *Possession*. San Francisco: Chandler and Sharp.

———. 1976b. The Effectiveness of Religious Healing Movements: A Review of the Literature. *Transcultural Psychiatric Research Review* 13:5–21.

———. 1974. *Culture and the Varieties of Consciousness*. Reading, MA: Addison-Wesley.

———. 1973. Introduction: A Framework for the Comparative Study of Altered States of Consciousness. In *Religion: Altered States of Consciousness, and Social Change*. E. Bourguignon (ed.). Columbus: Ohio State University Press. Pp. 3–38.

———. 1968. *Cross-Cultural Study of Disassociational States*. Columbus: Ohio State University Press.

Bourguignon, E., and T. Evascu. 1977. Altered States of Consciousness Within a General Evolutionary Perspective: A Holocultural Analysis. *Behavior Science Research* 12 (3): 197–216.

Bower, Bruce. 2005. Night of the Crusher: The Waking Nightmare of Sleep Paralysis Propels People into a Spirit World. *Science News* 168 (2): 27.

Bowie, Fiona. 2000. *The Anthropology of Religion: An Introduction*. Oxford: Blackwell.

Branthwaite, A., and P. Cooper. 1981. Analgesic Effects of Branding in Treatment of Headache. *British Medical Journal* 282:1576–1578.

Breuil, A. Henri. 1952. *Four Hundred Centuries of Cave Art*. Montignac [France]: Centre d'études et de documentation préhistoriques.

Brown, Michael. 1989. Dark Side of the Shaman. *Natural History* 98 (11): 8–10.

———. 1988. Shamanism and Its Discontents. *Medical Anthropology Quarterly* 2 (2): 102–120.

Brugger, Peter. 2001. From Haunted Brain to Haunted Science: A Cognitive Neuroscience View of Paranormal and Pseudoscientific Thought. In *Hauntings and Poltergeists: Multidisciplinary Perspectives*. J. Houran and R. Lange (eds.). Jefferson, NC: McFarland. Pp. 195–213.

Bulbulia, Joseph. 2006. Nature's Medicine: Religiosity as an Adaptation for Health and Cooperation. In *Where God and Science Meet: How Brain and Evolutionary Studies Alter Our Understanding of Religion*. Patrick McNamara (ed.). Westport, CT: Praeger. Vol. 1, pp. 87–121.

Bullard, Thomas. 2000. Forward: UFOS—Folklore of the Space Age. In *UFOs and Popular Culture: An Encyclopedia of Contemporary Myth*. James Lewis (ed.). Santa Barbara, CA: ABC-CLIO. Pp. ix–xxv.

Bureau of Democracy, Human Rights, and Labor. 2004. Country Reports on Human Rights Practices: Nepal. http://www.state.gov/g/drl/rls/hrrpt/2004/41742.htm.

———. 2005. Country Reports on Human Rights Practices: Nepal. http://www.state.gov/g/drl/rls/hrrpt/2005/61709.htm.

Cannon, Walter. 1942. Voodoo Death. *American Anthropologist* 44 (2): 169–181.

Cardeña, Etzel. 1996. "Just Floating on the Sky:" A Comparison of Hypnotic and Shamanic Phenomena. In *Jahrbuch für Transkulturelle Medizin und Psychotherapie*. D. Eigner and R. van Guekelbherge (eds.). Berlin: VWB, Verlag für Wissenschaft und Bildung. Pp. 85–98.

———. 1994. The Domain of Dissociation. In *Dissociation: Clinical and Theoretical Perspectives*. S. Lynn and J. Rhue (eds.). New York: Guilford Press. Pp. 15–31.

Carroll, Robert. 1999. Humans Are Not Being Abducted by Aliens. In *UFOs*. William Dudley (ed.) San Diego, CA: Greenhaven Press. Pp. 79–87.

Castillo, Richard. 2004. Review of "Shamanism: A Neural Ecology of Consciousness and Healing." *Journal of Ritual Studies* 18 (1): 101–104.

———. 1994a. Spirit Possession in South Asia, Dissociation or Hysteria? Part 1: Theoretical Background. *Culture, Medicine and Psychiatry* 18:1–21.

———. 1994b. Spirit Possession in South Asia, Dissociation or Hysteria? Part 2: Case Histories. *Culture, Medicine and Psychiatry* 18: 142–162.

Cerroni-Long, E. L. 1996. "Human Science." *Anthropology Newsletter* 37 (1): 50, 52.

Chang, Garma. 1977. *The Hundred Thousand Songs of Milarepa: The Life-Story and Teaching of the Greatest Poet-Saint Ever to Appear in the History of Buddhism.* Boulder, CO: Shambhala.

Cheyne, J. Allen. 2001. The Ominous Numinous: Sensed Presence and "Other" Hallucinations. *Journal of Consciousness Studies* 8:133–150.

Claus, Peter. 1997. Ritual Performances in India. In *Anthropology of Religion: A Handbook.* Stephen Glazier (ed.). Westport, CT: Praeger. Pp. 191–209.

———. 1979. Spirit Possession and Spirit Mediumship from the Perspective of Tulu Oral Traditions. *Culture, Medicine and Psychiatry* 3:29–52.

Clifford, James. 1986. Introduction: Partial Truths. In *Writing Culture: The Poetics and Politics of Ethnography.* James Clifford and George Marcus (eds.). Berkeley: University of California Press. Pp.1–26.

Clottes, Jean, and J. David Lewis-Williams. 2001. *Les Chamanes de la Préhistoire: Transe et Magie Dans les Grottes Ornées.* Paris: Maison des Roches.

———. 1998. *The Shamans of Prehistory: Trance and Magic in the Painted Caves.* New York: Abrams.

Conton, Leslie. 2005. Encounters with Ban Jhankri: Shamanic Initiation by Abduction in Nepal. *Shamanism* 18 (1/2): 26–36.

Csordas, Thomas, and Arthur Kleinman. 1990. The Therapeutic Process. In *Medical Anthropology: A Handbook of Theory and Method.* Thomas Johnson and Carolyn Sargent (eds.) Westport, CT: Greenwood. Pp. 11–25.

Crapanzano, Vincent. 1977. Introduction. In *Case Studies in Spirit Possession.* V. Crapanzano and V. Garrison (eds.). New York: Wiley. Pp. 1–40.

Czaplicka M. A. 1914. *Aboriginal Siberia: A Study in Social Anthropology.* Oxford: Clarendon Press.

D'Andrade, Roy. 1999. Culture is not Everything. In *Anthropological Theory in North America.* E. L. Cerroni-Long (ed.). Westport CT: Bergin and Garvey. Pp. 85–103.

D'Aquili, Eugene, and Andrew Newberg. 2000. The Neuropsychology of Aesthetic, Spiritual, and Mystical States. *Zygon* 35 (1): 39–51.

———. 1999. *The Mystical Mind: Probing the Biology of Religious Experience.* Minneapolis: Fortress Press.

———. 1998. The Neuropsychological Basis of Religions, or Why God Won't Go Away. *Zygon* 33 (2): 187–201.

Dás, Sarat. 1881. Dispute Between a Buddhist and a Bon-Po Priest for the Possession of Mt. Kailas and the Lake of Manasa. *Journal of the Asiatic Society of Bengal* 1:206–211.

Davenport, Demorest, and Michael Jochim. 1988. The Scene in the Shaft at Lascaux. *Antiquity* 62 (236): 558–562.

Dawes, Robyn. 2001. *Everyday Irrationality: How Pseudo-Scientists, Lunatics, and the Rest of Us Systematically Fail to Think Rationally.* Boulder, CO: Westview.

DeMause, L. 2002. The Evolution of Psyche and Society. *Journal of Psychohistory* 29: 238–285.

De Sales, Anne. 1991. *Je Suis né de vos Jeux de Tambours: La Religion Chamanique des Magar du Nord.* Nanterre: Société d'ethnologie.

Desjarlais, Robert. 1992. *Body and Emotion: The Aesthetics of Illness and Healing in the Nepal Himalayas.* Philadelphia: University of Pennsylvania Press.

———. 1989. Healing Through Images: The Magical Flight and Healing Geography of Nepali Shamans. *Ethos* 17:289–307.

Devereux, George. 1961. Shamans as Neurotics. *American Anthropologist* 63: 1088–1090.

Dhakal, Sanjaya. 2003. Women Victims of Witch-Hunts in Nepal. *Worldwide Religious News.* April 3. http://www.wwrn.org/article.php?idd=5414&sec=73&con=24.

Díaz-Andreu, Margarita. 2001. An All-embracing Universal Hunter-Gatherer Religion? Discussing Shamanism and Spanish Levantine Rock-Art. In *The Concept of Shamanism: Uses and Abuses.* Henri-Paul Francfort, Roberte Hamayon, and Paul Bahn (eds.). Budapest: Akadémiai Kiadó. Pp. 118–134.

Dickson, Bruce. 1990. *The Dawn of Belief: Religion in the Upper Paleolithic of Southwestern Europe.* Tucson: University of Arizona Press.

Dietrich, Angela. 1998. *Tantric Healing in the Kathmandu Valley: A Comparative Study of Hindu and Buddhist Spiritual Healing Traditions in Urban Nepalese Society.* Delhi: Book Faith India.

Diószegi, Vilmos. 1996. The Problem of Ethnic Homogeneity of Tofa (Kargas) Shamanism. In *Folk Beliefs and Shamanistic Traditions in Siberia.* V. Diószegi and M. Hoppál (eds.). Budapest: Akadémiai Kiadó. Pp. 181–235.

———. 1960. *Tracing Shamans in Siberia: The Story of an Ethnographical Research Expedition.* New York: Humanities Press.

Dougherty, Linda. 1986. Sita and the Goddess: A Case Study of a Woman Healer in Nepal. *Contributions to Nepalese Studies* 14 (1): 25–36.

Dow, James. 1986. Universal Aspects of Symbolic Healing: A Theoretical Synthesis. *American Anthropologist* 88 (1): 56–69.

Eastwell, Harry. 1982. Voodoo Death and the Mechanism for Dispatch of the Dying in East Arnhem, Australia. *American Anthropologist* 84 (1): 5–18.

Eigner, Dagmar. 2001. Becoming a Shaman: Two Stories from Nepal. *Shamanism: The Newsletter of the Foundation for Shamanic Studies* 4 (2): 24–30.

Eisenberg, L. 1977. Disease and Illness: Distinctions between Professional and Popular Ideas of Sickness. *Culture, Medicine and Psychiatry* 1:9–23.

Ekvall, Robert. 1964. *Religious Observances in Tibet: Patterns and Functions.* Chicago: University of Chicago Press.

Eliade, Mircea. 1981. *Autobiography.* Vol. II: 1937–1960. Chicago: University of Chicago Press.

———. 1978. *A History of Religious Ideas, Volume 1: From the Stone Age to the Eleusinian Mysteries.* Chicago: University of Chicago Press.

———. 1964. *Shamanism: Archaic Techniques of Ecstasy.* Princeton, NJ: Princeton University Press.

———. 1961. Recent Works on Shamanism: A Review. *History of Religions* 1 (1): 152–186.

———. 1951. *Le chamanisme et les techniques archaïques de l'extase.* Paris: Payot.

Ellingson-Waugh, Ter. 1974. Magical Flight in Tibet. *Asian Music* 5 (2): 3–44.

Evans, Hilary. 2001. The Ghost Experience in a Wider Context. In *Hauntings and Poltergeists: Multidisciplinary Perspectives.* J. Houran and R. Lange (eds.). Jefferson, NC: McFarland. Pp. 41–61.

Evans-Pritchard, Edward. 1937. *Witchcraft, Oracles and Magic Among the Azande.* Oxford: Clarendon.

Farthing, G. William. 1992. *The Psychology of Consciousness.* Englewood Cliffs, NJ: Prentice Hall.

Fernandez, James. 1991. *Beyond Metaphor: The Theory of Tropes in Anthropology.* Stanford: Stanford University Press.

Firth, Raymond. 1967. *Tikopia Ritual and Belief.* Boston: Beacon Press.

Flaherty, Gloria. 1992. *Shamanism and the Eighteenth Century.* Princeton, NJ: Princeton University Press.

Foucault, Michel. 1973. *The Birth of the Clinic: An Archaeology of Medical Perception.* London: Tavistock.

Fournier, Alan. 1978. The Role of the Priest in Sunuwar Society. In *Himalayan Anthropology: The Indo-Tibetan Interface.* James Fisher (ed.). The Hague: Mouton. Pp. 167–178.

———. 1976. A Preliminary Report on the Puimbo and the Ngiami: The Sunuwar Shamans of Sabra. In *Spirit Possession in the Nepal Himalayas.* John Hitchcock and Rex Jones (eds). Warminster, England: Aris and Phillips. Pp. 110–123.

Fox, C. 2000. The Search for Extraterrestrial Life. *Life* (March): 46–51, 54, 56.

Francfort, Henri-Paul. 2001a. Prehistoric Section: An Introduction. In *The Concept of Shamanism: Uses and Abuses.* Henri-Paul Francfort, Roberte Hamayon, and Paul Bahn (eds.). Budapest: Akadémiai Kiadó. Pp. 31–49.

———. 2001b. Art, Archaeology and the Prehistory of Shamanism in Inner Asia. In *The Concept of Shamanism: Uses and Abuses.* Henri-Paul Francfort, Roberte Hamayon, and Paul Bahn (eds.). Budapest: Akadémiai Kiadó. Pp. 243–276.

Francfort, Henri-Paul, Roberte Hamayon, and Paul Bahn (eds.). 2001. *The Concept of Shamanism: Uses and Abuses.* Budapest: Akadémiai Kiadó.

Frank, Jerome. 1973. *Persuasion and Healing.* Baltimore: Johns Hopkins University Press.

Fukui, Katsuyoshi. 1994. The Relation Between Symbolism and Ecology. In *Circumpolar Religion and Ecology: An Anthropology of the North.* Takashi Irimoto and Takako Yamada (eds.). Tokyo: University of Tokyo Press. Pp.137–140.

Fürer-Haimendorf, Christoph von. 1974. Introduction. In *Contributions to the Anthropology of Nepal.* Christoph von Fürer-Haimendorf (ed.). Warminster, England: Aris and Phillips. Pp. 1–5.

Fürer-Haimendorf, Christoph von (ed). 1974. *Contributions to the Anthropology of Nepal.* Warminster, England: Aris and Phillip Ltd.

Furst, Peter. 1977. The Roots and Continuities of Shamanism. In *Stones, Bones and Skin: Ritual and Shamanic Art.* A. Brodzky, R. Danesewich, and N. Johnson (eds.). Toronto: Society for Art Publications. Pp. 1–28.

———. 1976. *Hallucinogens and Culture.* San Francisco: Chandler & Sharp.

Furst, Peter (ed.). 1990. *Flesh of the Gods: The Ritual Use of Hallucinogens.* Prospect Heights, IL: Waveland Press.

Gaborieau, Marc. 1976. Preliminary Report on the God Mastā. In *Spirit Possession in the Nepal Himalayas.* John Hitchcock and Rex Jones (eds). Warminster, England: Aris and Phillips. Pp. 217–243.

Gallegos, Eligio. 1987. *The Personal Totem Pole: Animal Imagery, the Chakras, and Psychotherapy.* Santa Fe: Moon Bear Press.

Ganaway, G. 1989. Historical Truth versus Narrative Truth: Clarifying the Role of Exogenous Trauma in the Etiology of Multiple Personality Disorder and Its Variants. *Dissociation* 2:205–220.

Gargett, Robert. 1989. Grave Shortcomings: The Evidence for Neanderthal Burial. *Current Anthropology* 30 (2): 157–190.

Geertz, Clifford. 1973. *The Interpretation of Cultures*. New York: Basic Books.

———. 1966. Religion as a Cultural System. In *Anthropological Approaches to the Study of Religion*. Michael Banton (ed.). London: Tavistock Publications. Pp. 1–46.

Gellner, David. 1994. Priests, Healers, Mediums and Witches: The Context of Possession in the Kathmandu Valley, Nepal. *Man* 29 (1): 27-48.

Gellner, Ernest. 1992. *Postmodernism, Reason and Religion*. London: Routledge.

Gibson, Todd. 1997. Note on the History of the Shamanic in Tibet and Inner Asia. *Numen* 44 (1): 39–59.

Giedion, Sigfried. 1962. *The Eternal Present: A Contribution on Constancy and Change*. Bollingen Series: 35.6.1. The A. W. Mellon Lectures in the Fine Arts, 1957. New York: Bollingen Foundation.

Gilberg, R. 1984. How to Recognize a Shaman among Other Religious Specialists? In *Shamanism in Eurasia*. M. Hoppál (ed.). Gottingen: Herodot. Pp. 21–27.

Ginzburg, Carlo. 1990. *Ecstasies: Deciphering the Witches' Sabbath*. London: Hutchinson Radius.

Glavatskaya, Elena. 2001. The Russian State and Shamanhood: The Brief History of Confrontation. In *Shamanhood: Symbolism and Epic*. Juha Pentikäinen (ed.). Budapest: Akadémiai Kiadó. Pp. 237–248.

Glosecki, Stephen. 1989. *Shamanism and Old English Poetry*. New York: Garland.

Glover, Jessie. 1972. The Role of the Witch in Gurung Society. *Eastern Anthropologist* 25 (3): 221–226.

Gombrich, Richard. 1988. *Theravada Buddhism: A Social History from Ancient Benares to Modern Colombo*. New York: Routledge and Kegan Paul.

Gorf, Christina, and Stanislav Gorf. 1986. Spiritual Emergency: The Understanding and Treatment of Transpersonal Crises. *ReVision* 8:7–20.

Gorf, Stanislav. 1998. *The Cosmic Game: Explorations of the Frontiers of Human Consciousness*. Albany: State University of New York Press.

Green, Alexander, J. Emilio Carrillo, and Joseph Betancourt. 2002. Why the Disease-Based Model of Medicine Fails Our Patients. *Western Journal of Medicine* 176 (2): 141–143.

Green, J. Timothy. 1998. Near-Death Experiences, Shamanism, and the Scientific Method. *Journal of Near-Death Studies* 16 (3): 205–222.

Greve, Reinhard. 1989. The Shaman and Witch: An Analytical Approach to Shamanic Poetry in the Himalayas. In *Shamanism Past and Present*. M. Hoppál and O. von Sadovszky (eds.). Budapest: Hungarian Academy of Sciences. Pp. 219–223.

———. 1981. A Shaman's Concept of Illness and Healing Ritual in the Mustang District, Nepal. *Journal of the Nepal Research Center* (5–6): 99–124.

Grim, John. 1983. *The Shaman: Patterns of Siberian and Ojibway Healing*. Norman: University of Oklahoma Press.

Groesbeck, C. J. 1997. C. G. Jung and the Shaman's Vision. In *The Sacred Heritage: The Influence of Shamanism on Analytical Psychology*. Donald Sandner and Steven Wong (eds.). New York: Routledge. Pp. 29–43.

Gross, Paul, and Norman Levitt. 1994. *Higher Superstition: The Academic Left and Its Quarrels with Science*. Baltimore: Johns Hopkins University Press.

Guthrie, Stewart. 2004. Review of "Shamanism: A Neural Ecology of Consciousness and Healing." *Journal of Ritual Studies* 18 (1): 97–100.

Hahn, R., and A. Kleinman. 1983. Belief as Pathogen, Belief as Medicine: "Voodoo Death" and the "Placebo Phenomenon" in Anthropological Perspective. *Medical Anthropology Quarterly* 14 (4): 16–19.

Halifax, Joan. 1991. *Shamanic Voices: A Survey of Visionary Narratives*. New York: Arkana.

———. 1982. *Shaman: The Wounded Healer*. New York: Crossroad.

Hamayon, Roberte. 2001. Shamanism: Symbolic System, Human Capability and Western Ideology. In *The Concept of Shamanism: Uses and Abuses*. Henri-Paul Francfort, Roberte Hamayon, and Paul Bahn (eds.). Budapest: Akadémiai Kiadó. Pp. 1–27

———. 1998. "Ecstasy" or the West-Dreamt Siberian Shaman. In *Tribal Epistemologies: Essays in the Philosophy of Anthropology*. Helmut Wautischer (ed.). Brookfield: Ashgate. Pp. 175–187.

———. 1995. Le Chamanisme Sibérien: Réflexions sur un Médium. *La Recherche* 275:416–422.

———. 1993a. Shamanism and Pragmatism in Siberia. In *Shamans and Cultures*. M. Hoppál and K. Howard (eds.). Budapest: Akadémiai Kiadó. Pp. 200–205.

———. 1993b. Are "Trance," "Ecstasy," and Similar Concepts Appropriate in the Study of Shamanism? *Shaman: An International Journal for Shamanistic Research* 1 (2) :3–25.

———. 1990. *La Chasse à L'âme: Esquisse d'une Théorie du Chamanisme Sibérien*. Nanterre: Société d'Ethnologie.

Harner, Michael. 1999. Science, Spirits, and Core Shamanism. *Shamanism* Spring/Summer 12 (1): 1–4. http://www.shamanism.org/articles/article10.html.

———. 1980. *The Way of the Shaman: A Guide to Power and Healing*. San Francisco: Harper & Row.

———. 1972. *The Jívaro: People of the Sacred Waterfalls*. Garden City, NY: Natural History Press.

———, (ed) 1973. *Hallucinogens and Shamanism*. New York: Oxford University Press.

Harner, Michael, and Gary Doore. 1987. The Ancient Wisdom in Shamanic Cultures. In *Shamanism: An Expanded View of Reality*. Shirley Nicholson (ed.). Wheaton, IL: Theosophical Publishing House. Pp. 3–16.

Harner, Sandra, and Warren Tyron. 1996. Psychological and Immunological Responses to Shamanic Journeying with Drumming. *Shaman* 4:89–97.

Harrington, Anne. 2002. Seeing the Placebo Effect: Historical Legacies and Present Opportunities. In *The Science of the Placebo: Toward an Interdisciplinary Research Agenda*. H. Guess, A. Kleinman, J. Kusek, and L. Engel (eds.). London: BMJ Books. Pp. 35–52.

Hastings, Arthur. 1990. The Effects of Marijuana on Consciousness. In *Altered States of Consciousness*. Charles Tart (ed.). San Francisco: Harper. Pp. 407–431.

Hayden, Brian. 2003. *Shamans, Sorcerers, and Saints: A Prehistory of Religion*. Washington: Smithsonian Books.

Hedges, Ken. 1992. Shamanistic Aspects of California Rock Art. In *California Indian Shamanism*. L. Bean (ed.). Menlo Park, CA: Ballena Press. Pp. 67–88.

Heinze, Ruth-Inge. 1991. *Shamans of the 20th Century*. New York: Irvington Publishers.

Helman, Cecil. 2001. *Culture, Health, and Illness: An Introduction for Health Professionals*. London: Hodder Arnold.

———. 1981. Disease versus Illness in General Practice. *Journal of the Royal College of General Practitioners* 31:548–552.

Helvenstone, P. A., and P. G. Bahn. 2004. Waking the Trance-Fixed. *Cambridge Archaeological Journal* 14 (1): 90–100.

———. 2003. Testing the "Three Stages of Trance" Model. *Cambridge Archaeological Journal* 13 (2): 213–224.

Herzfeld, Michael. 2001. *Anthropology: Theoretical Practice in Culture and Society*. Oxford: Blackwell.

Heusch, Luc de. 1965. Possession et Chamanisme: Essai d'Analyse Structurale. In *Les Religions Africaines Traditionnelles*. Paris: Éditions du Seuil. Pp. 139–170.

Hinton, Devon, Vuth Pich, Dara Chhean, and Mark Pollack. 2005. "The Ghost Pushes You Down": Sleep Paralysis-Type Panic Attacks in a Khmer Refugee Population. *Transcultural Psychiatry* 42:46–77.

Hitchcock, John. 1976a. Aspects of Bhujel Shamanism. In *Spirit Possession in the Nepal Himalayas*. John Hitchcock and Rex Jones (eds). Warminster, England: Aris and Phillips. Pp. 165–196.

———. 1976b. Introduction. In *Spirit Possession in the Nepal Himalayas*. John Hitchcock and Rex Jones (eds). Warminster, England: Aris and Phillips. Pp. xii–xxviii.

———. 1974a. A Nepali Shaman's Performance as Theater. *Artscanada*. 30th Anniversary Issue. 74–80.

———. 1974b. A Shaman's Song and Some Implications for Himalayan Research. In *Contributions to the Anthropology of Nepal*. Christoph von Fürer-Haimendorf (ed.). Warminster, England: Aris and Phillips. Pp. 150–158.

———. 1967. Nepalese Shamanism and the Classical Inner Asian Tradition. *History of Religions* 7 (2): 149–158.

Hitchcock, John, and Rex Jones (eds.). 1976. *Spirit Possession in the Nepal Himalayas*. Warminster, England: Aris and Phillips Ltd.

Hodgson, Derek. 2006. Altered States of Consciousness and Palaeoart: An Alternative Neurovisual Explanation. *Cambridge Archaeological Journal* 16 (1): 27–37.

Höfer, András. 1994. *A Recitation of the Tamang Shaman in Nepal*. Bonn: VGH Wissenschaftsverlag.

———. 1985. Tamang Ritual Texts, Notes on the Interpretation of an Oral Tradition of Nepal. *Journal of the Royal Asiatic Society of Great Britain and Ireland* 1:23–28.

———. 1981. *Tamang Ritual Texts: Preliminary Studies in the Folk-Religion of an Ethnic Minority in Nepal*. 2 vols. Wiesbaden: Franz Steiner.

———. 1975. Urgen Pema und Tusur Bon: Eine Padmasambhava-Legend der Tamang. In Hermann Berger (ed.). *Mündliche Uberlieferungen in Südasien*. Wiesbaden: Franz Steiner. Pp. 1–70.

———. 1974a. A Note on Possession in South Asia. In *Contributions to the Anthropology of Nepal*. Christoph von Fürer-Haimendorf (ed.). Warminster, England: Aris and Phillips. Pp. 159–167.

———. 1974b. Is the *Bombo* an Ecstatic? Some Ritual Techniques of Tamang Shamanism. In *Contributions to the Anthropology of Nepal*. Christoph von Fürer-Haimendorf (ed.), Warminster, England: Aris and Phillips. Pp. 168–180

Höfer, A., and B. P. Shrestha. 1972. Ghost Exorcism among the Brahmans of Central Nepal. *Central Asiatic Journal* 17 (1): 51–77.

Hoffmann, Helmut. 1979. *The Religions of Tibet.* Westport, CT: Greenwood Press.

Holder-Perkins, Vicenzio, and Thomas Wise. 2001. Somatization Disorder. In *Somatoform and Factitious Disorders.* K. Phillips (ed.). Washington, DC: American Psychiatric Publications. Pp. 1–26.

Holmberg, David. 1989. *Order in Paradox: Myth, Ritual, and Exchange among Nepal's Tamang.* Ithaca, NY: Cornell University Press.

———. 1984. Ritual Paradoxes in Nepal: Comparative Perspectives on Tamang Religion. *Journal of Asian Studies* 43 (4): 697–722.

———. 1983. Shamanic Soundings: Femaleness in the Tamang Ritual Structure. *Signs: Journal of Women in Culture and Society* 9 (1): 40–58.

Hoppál, Mihály. 1992. Shamanism: An Archaic and/or Recent System of Beliefs. In *Studies on Shamanism.* Anna-Leena, Siikala, and Mihály, Hoppál, eds. Budapest: Akadémiai Kiadó, Pp. 117–130.

Houran, J. 2000. Toward a Psychology of "Entity Encounter Experiences." *Journal of the Society for Psychical Research* 64:141–158.

Houran, J., and M. Thalbourne. 2001. Further Study and Speculation of the Psychology of "Entity Encounter Experiences." *Journal of the Society for Psychical Research* 65:26–37.

Howells, William. 1962. *The Heathens: Primitive Man and His Religions.* New York: Doubleday.

Hufford, David. 2005. Sleep Paralysis as Spiritual Experience. *Transcultural Psychiatry* 42:11–45.

———. 2001. An Experience-Centered Approach to *Hauntings.* In *Hauntings and Poltergeists: Multidisciplinary Perspectives.* J. Houran and R. Lange (eds.). Jefferson, NC: McFarland.Pp. 62–81.

———. 1995. Beings Without Bodies: An Experience-Centered Theory of the Belief in Spirits. In *Out of the Ordinary: Folklore and the Supernatural.* Barbara Walker (ed.). Logan: Utah State University Press. Pp. 11–45.

———. 1982. *The Terror That Comes in the Night: An Experience-Centered Study of Supernatural Assault Traditions.* Philadelphia: University of Pennsylvania Press.

Hultkrantz, Åke. 2001. Shamanism: Some Recent Findings from a Comparative Perspective. In *Shamanhood: Symbolism and Epic.* Juha Pentikäinen (ed.). Budapest: Akadémiai Kiadó. Pp. 1–10.

———. 1998a. On the History of Research in Shamanism. In *Shamans.* J. Pentikäinen, T. Jaatinen, I. Lehtinen, and M. Saloniemi (eds.). Tampere, Finland: Tampere Museum. Pp. 51–70.

———. 1998b. The Meaning of Ecstasy in Shamanism. In *Tribal Epistemologies: Essays in the Philosophy of Anthropology.* Helmut Wautischer (ed.). Brookfield: Ashgate. Pp. 163–174.

———. 1998c. Rejoinder. In *Tribal Epistemologies: Essays in the Philosophy of Anthropology.* Helmut Wautischer (ed.). Brookfield: Ashgate. Pp. 188–190.

———. 1991. The Drum in Shamanism: Some Reflections. In *The Saami Shaman Drum: Based on Papers Read at the Symposium on the Saami Shaman Drum Held at Åbo, Finland, on the 19th-20th of August 1988.* Tore Ahlbäck and Jan Bergman (eds.). Åbo, Finland: Donner Institute for Research in Religious and Culture History. Pp. 9–27.

———. 1989. The Place of Shamanism in the History of Religion. In *Shamanism: Past and Present.* M. Hoppál and O. von Sadovszky (eds.). Budapest: Ethnographic Institute, Hungarian Academy of Sciences. Pp. 43–52.

———. 1988. Shamanism: A Religious Phenomenon? In *Shaman's Path: Healing, Personal Growth and Empowerment*. Gary Doore (ed.). Boston: Shambhala. Pp. 33–41.

———. 1978. Ecological and Phenomenological Aspects of Shamanism. In *Studies in Lapp Shamanism*. L. Backman and A. Hultkrantz (eds.). Stockholm: Almqvist and Wiksell. Pp. 9–35.

———. 1973. A Definition of Shamanism. *Temenos* 9:25–37.

Humphrey, Caroline. 1994. Shamanic Practice and the State in Northern Asia: Views from the Center and Periphery. In *Shamanism, History, and the State*. N. Thomas and C. Humphrey (eds.). Ann Arbor: University of Michigan Press. Pp. 191–228.

Humphrey, Caroline, and Urgunge Onon. 1996. *Shamans and Elders: Experience, Knowledge and Power Among the Daur Mongols*. Oxford: Clarendon Press.

Huntington, John. 1975. The Phur-Pa, Tibetan Ritual Daggers. *Artibus Asiae. Supplementum*, 33: pp. III-. VII+1–76+I-LXIII.

Hutton, Ronald. 2001. *Shamans: Siberian Spirituality and the Western Imagination*. London: Hambledon and London.

———. 1993. *The Shamans of Siberia*. Glastonbury, England: Isle of Avalon Press.

Irimoto, Takashi, and Takako Yamada (eds.). 1994. *Circumpolar Religion and Ecology: An Anthropology of the North*. Tokyo: University of Tokyo Press.

Jackson, Michael. 1989. *Paths Toward a Clearing: Radical Empiricism and Ethnographic Enquiry*. Bloomington: Indiana University Press.

Jacobson, Esther. 2001. Shamans, Shamanism, and Anthropomorphizing Imagery in Prehistoric Rock Art of the Mongolian Altay. In *The Concept of Shamanism: Uses and Abuses*. Henri-Paul Francfort, Roberte Hamayon, and Paul Bahn (eds.). Budapest: Akadémiai Kiadó. Pp. 277–294.

Jakobsen, Merete. 1999. *Shamanism: Traditional and Contemporary Approaches to the Mastery of Spirits and Healing*. Oxford: Berghahn Books.

Jochelson, Waldemar. 1908. *The Koryak*. Leiden: E. J. Brill.

———. 1926. *The Yukaghir and the Yukaghirized Tungus*. Leiden: E. J. Brill.

Jolly, Pieter. 2005. On the Definition of Shamanism. *Current Anthropology* 46 (1): 127–128.

Jones, Peter. 2006. Shamanism: An Inquiry into the History of the Scholarly Use of the Term in English-Speaking North America. *Anthropology of Consciousness* 17 (2): 4–32.

Jones, Rex. 1976a. Limbu Spirit Possession and Shamanism. In *Spirit Possession in the Nepal Himalayas*. John Hitchcock and Rex Jones (eds). Warminster, England: Aris and Phillips. Pp. 29–55.

———. 1976b. Spirit Possession and Society in Nepal. In *Spirit Possession in the Nepal Himalayas*. John Hitchcock and Rex Jones (eds). Warminster, England: Aris and Phillips. Pp. 1–20.

Joseph, Rhawn. 2003a. Paleolithic Spiritual Evolution. In *NeuroTheology: Brain, Science, Spirituality, Religious Experience*. R. Joseph (ed.). San Jose: University Press. Pp. 315–356.

———. 2003b. Possession and Prophecy. In *NeuroTheology: Brain, Science, Spirituality, Religious Experience*. R. Joseph (ed.). San Jose: University Press. Pp. 527–554.

Jung, Carl. 1978. *Flying Saucers: A Modern Myth of Things Seen in the Skies*. Princeton, NJ: Princeton University Press.

———. 1967. *Alchemical Studies*. Bollingen Series, 20: The Collected Works of C. G. Jung, Vol. 13. Princeton, NJ: Princeton University Press.

Kaja, Finkler. 1985. *Spiritualist healers in Mexico*. New York: Praeger.

Kakar, Sudhir. 1982. *Shamans, Mystics, and Doctors: A Psychological Inquiry into India and Its Healing Traditions*. New York: Knopf.

Kalweit, Holger. 2000. *Shamans, Healers, and Medicine Men*. Boston: Shambhala.

Kehoe, Alice. 2000. *Shamans and Religion: An Anthropological Exploration in Critical Thinking*. Prospect Heights, IL: Waveland.

———. 1997. Eliade and Hultkrantz: The European Primitivism Tradition. *American Indian Quarterly* 20 (3/4): 377–392.

Kirchner, Horst. 1952. Ein Archäologischer Beitrag zur Urgeschichte des Schamanismus. *Anthropos* 47:244–286.

Kirmayer, Laurence. 1994. Pacing the Void: Social and Cultural Dimensions of Dissociation. In *Dissociation: Culture, Mind, and Body*. David Spiegel (ed.). Washington, DC: American Psychiatric Press. Pp. 91–122.

Klaniczay, G. 1984. Shamanistic Elements in Central European Witchcraft. In *Shamanism in Eurasia*. M. Hoppál (ed.). Göttingen: Edition Herodot. Pp. 404–422.

Klein, Cecilia, Eulogio Guzmán, Elisa Madell, and Maya Stanfield-Mazzi. 2002. The Role of Shamanism in Mesoamerican Art: A Reassessment. *Current Anthropology* 43 (3): 383–419.

Klein, Cecilia, and Maya Stanfield-Mazzi. 2004. On Sharpness and Scholarship in the Debate on "Shamanism." *Current Anthropology* 45 (3): 404–406

Klein, Cecilia, Eulogio Guzmán, and Maya Stanfield-Mazzi. 2005. On the Definition of Shamanism. *Current. Anthropology* 46 (1): 127–128.

Klein, Donald. 1997. Control Groups in Pharmacotherapy and Psychotherapy Evaluations. Treatment. http://journals.apa.org/treatment/vol1/97_a1.html#3.

Kleinman, Arthur. 1988a. *Rethinking Psychiatry*. New York: Free Press.

———. 1988b. *The Illness Narrative: Suffering, Healing and the Human Condition*. New York: Basic Books.

———. 1980. *Patients and Healers in the Context of Culture: An Exploration of the Borderland Between Anthropology, Medicine, and Psychiatry*. Berkeley, CA: University of California Press.

Kleinman, Arthur, and L. H. Sung. 1979. Why do Indigenous Practitioners Successfully Heal? A Follow-up Study of Indigenous Practice in Taiwan. *Social Science and Medicine* 13: 7-26.

Kleinman, Arthur, Leon Eisenberg, and Byron Good. 1978. Culture, Illness, and Care: Clinical Lessons from Anthropological and Cross-Cultural Research. *Annals of Internal Medicine* 88:251–258.

Kleinman, A., Harry Guess, and Joan Wilentz. 2002. Explanatory Mechanisms for Placebo: Cultural Influences and the Meaning of Response. In *The Science of the Placebo: Toward an Interdisciplinary Research Agenda*. H. Guess, A. Kleinman, J. Kusek, and L. Engel (eds.). London: BMJ Books. Pp. 1–32.

Knecht, Peter. 2003. Aspects of Shamanism: An Introduction. In *Shamans in Asia*. C. Chilson and P. Knecht (eds.). London: Routledge Curzon. Pp. 1–30.

Krader, Lawrence. 1978. Shamanism: Theory and History in Buryat Society. In *Shamanism in Siberia*. Vilmos Diószegi and Mihály Hoppál (eds.). Budapest: Akadémiai Kiadó. Pp. 181–236.

Krippner, Stanley. 2002. Conflicting Perspectives on Shamans and Shamanism: Points and Counterpoints. *American Psychologist* (November): 962–977.

———. 2000. The Epistemology and Technologies of Shamanic States of Consciousness. *Journal of Consciousness Studies* 7 (11–12): 93–118.

———. 1997. The Varieties of Dissociative Experience. In *Broken Images, Broken Selves: Dissociative Narratives in Clinical Practice.* S. Krippner and S. Powers (eds.). Washington, DC: Brunner/Mazel. Pp. 336–361.

———. 1994. Cross-cultural Treatment Perspectives on Dissociative Disorders. In *Dissociation: Clinical and theoretical perspectives* S. J. Lynn and J. W. Rhue (eds.). New York: Guilford. Pp. 338-361.

Krippner, Stanley, and A. Combs. 2002. The Neurophenomenology of Shamanism: An Essay Review. *Journal of Consciousness Studies* 9 (3): 77–82.

Kroeber, Alfred. 1940. Psychotic Factors in Shamanism. *Character and Personality* 8: 204–215.

Kuznar, Lawrence. 1997. *Reclaiming a Scientific Anthropology.* Walnut Creek, CA: AltaMira.

Kværne, Per. 2001. *The Bön Religion of Tibet: The Iconography of a Living Tradition.* Boston: Shambhala.

La Barre, Weston. 1979. Shamanic Origins of Religion and Medicine. *Journal of Psychiatric Drugs* (2): 1–2, 7–12.

———. 1972a. *The Ghost Dance: Origins of Religion.* New York: Delta.

———. 1972b. Hallucinogens and the Shamanic Origins of Religion. In *Flesh of the Gods: The Ritual Use of Hallucinogens.* Peter Furst (ed.). New York: Praeger Publishers. Pp. 261–278.

Lane, James, S. Kasian, J. Owens, and G. Marsh. 1998. Binaural Auditory Beats Affect Vigilance Performance and Mood. *Physiology and Behavior* 63 (2): 240–252.

Laufer, Berthold. 1917. Origin of the Word Shaman. *American Anthropologist* 19: 169–371.

Laughlin, Charles, John McManus, and Eugene d'Aquili. 1992. *Brain, Symbol and Experience: Toward a Neurophenomenology of Human Consciousness.* New York: Columbia University Press.

Layton, Robert. 2000. Shamanism, Totemism and Rock Art: Les Chamanes de la Prâehistoire in the Context of Rock Art Research. *Cambridge Archaeological Journal* 10 (1): 18.

Lechler, George. 1951. The Interpretation of the "Accident Scene" at Lascaux. *Man* 51:165–167.

Le Quellec, Jean-Loïc. 2001. Shamans and Martians: The Same Struggle? In *The Concept of Shamanism: Uses and Abuses.* Henri-Paul Francfort, Roberte Hamayon, and Paul Bahn (eds.). Budapest: Akadémiai Kiadó. Pp. 135–159.

Leroi-Gourhan, André. 1987. Le Préhistorian et le Chamane. *L'Ethnographie* 74–75 (2): 19–15.

Leroi-Gourhan, Arlette. 1975. The Flowers Found with Shanidar IV, a Neanderthal Burial in Iraq. *Science* 190 (4214): 562–564.

Lester, David. 1972. Voodoo Death: Some New Thoughts on an Old Phenomenon. *American Anthropologist* 74 (3): 386–390.

Lett, James. 1997a. *Science, Reason, and Anthropology: The Principles of Rational Inquiry.* Lanham, MD: Rowman and Littlefield.

———. 1997b. Science, Religion, and Anthropology. In *Anthropology of Religion: A Handbook*. Stephen Glazier (ed.). Westport, CT: Praeger. Pp. 103–120.

Levine, J., N. Gordon, and H. Fields. 1978. The Mechanism of Placebo Analgesia. *Lancet* 2:645–647.

Levine, Nancy. 1982. Belief and Explanation in Nyinba Women's Witchcraft. *Man* 17 (2): 259–274.

Lévi-Strauss, Claude. 1967. *Structural Anthropology*. Garden City, NY: Anchor Books.

Lewis, Ioan M. 2003. Trance, Possession, Shamanism and Sex. *Anthropology of Consciousness* 14 (1): 20–39.

———. 1984. What Is a Shaman? In *Shamanism in Eurasia*. Mihály Hoppál (ed.). Göttingen: Herodot. Pp. 3–12.

———. 1971. *Ecstatic Religion: An Anthropological Study of Spirit Possession and Shamanism*. Harmondsworth: Penguin Books.

Lewis, James (ed.). 1995. *The Gods Have Landed: New Religions from Other Worlds*. Albany: State University of New York Press.

Lewis-Williams, J. David. 2004. On Sharpness and Scholarship in the Debate on "Shamanism." *Current Anthropology* 45 (3): 404.

———. 2003. Putting the Record Straight: Rock Art and Shamanism. *Antiquity* 77 (295): 5.

Lewis-Williams, J. David, and Thomas Dowson. 1988. The Signs of All Times: Entroptic Phenomena in Upper Paleolithic Art. *Current Anthropology* 29 (2): 201–245.

Lex, Barbara. 1974. Voodoo Death: New Thoughts on an Old Explanation. *American Anthropologist* 76 (4): 818–823.

Lindholm, Charles. 1997. Shaman, Shamanism. In *The Dictionary of Anthropology*. Thomas Barfield (ed.). Oxford: Blackwell. Pp. 424–425.

Lommel, Andreas. 1967. *Shamanism: The Beginnings of Art*. New York: McGraw-Hill.

Long, D. J., and R. Tipping. 2001. The Use of Henbane (Hyoscyamus Niger L.) as a Hallucinogen at Neolithic "Ritual" Sites: A Re-Evaluation. *Antiquity* 74 (283): 49–53.

Lot-Falck, Éveline. 1961. A Propos d'un Tambour de Chaman Toungouse. *L'Homme: Revue Française d'Anthropologie* 1 (2): 23–50.

Ludwig, Arnold. 1990. Altered States of Consciousness. In *Altered States of Consciousness*. Charles Tart (ed.). San Francisco: Harper. Pp. 18–33.

Lynn, Steven, and Judith Rhue. 1994. Introduction: Dissociation and Dissociative Disorders in Perspective. In *Dissociation: Clinical and Theoretical Perspectives*. S. Lynn and J. Rhue (eds.). New York: Guilford Press. Pp. 1–14.

Macdonald, Alexander. 1997. Foreword. In *Faith-Healers in the Himalaya: An Investigation of Traditional Healers and Their Festivals in the Dolakha District of Nepal*. Casper Miller. Delhi: Book Faith India. Pp. xix–xxii.

———. 1976a. Preliminary Report on Some Jhākri of the Muglan. In *Spirit Possession in the Nepal Himalayas*. John Hitchcock and Rex Jones (eds.). Warminster, England: Aris and Phillips. Pp. 309–341.

———. 1976b. Sorcery in the Nepalese Code of 1853. In *Spirit Possession in the Nepal Himalayas*. John Hitchcock and Rex Jones (eds.). Warminster, England: Aris and Phillips. Pp. 367–384.

———. 1975. Healers in the Nepalese World. In *Essays on the Ethnology of Nepal and South Asia*. A. Macdonald (ed.). Kathmandu: Ratna Pustak Bhandar. Pp. 113–128.

Macfarlane, Alan. 1981. Death, Disease and Curing in a Himalayan Village. In *Asian Highland Societies in Anthropological Perspective*. Christoph von Fürer-Haimendorf (ed.). New Delhi: Sterling Publishers. Pp. 79–131.

MacLean, Paul. 1990. *The Triune Brain in Evolution: Role in Paleocerebral Functions*. New York: Plenum Press.

———. 1973. *A Triune Concept of the Brain and Behaviour*. Toronto: University of Toronto Press.

Madsen, W. 1955. Shamanism in Mexico. *Southwestern Journal of Anthropology* 11: 48–57.

Majupuria, Trilok Chandra. 1991. *Sacred Animals of Nepal and India: With Reference to Gods and Goddesses of Hinduism and Buddhism*. Gwalior, India: M. Devi.

Mandel, Arnold. 1980. Toward a Psychobiology of Transcendence: God in the Brain. In *The Psychobiology of Consciousness*. R. J. Davidson and J. M. Davidson (eds). New York: Plenum. Pp. 379–479.

Maquet, Jacques. 1981. Introduction: Scholar and Shaman. In *Ecstasy and Healing in Nepal: An Ethnopsychiatric Study of Tamang Shamanism*. Larry Peters. Malibu: Undena Publications. Pp. 1–6.

Marcus, George. 1986. Afterword: Ethnographic Writing and Anthropological Careers. In James Clifford and George Marcus (eds.). *Writing Culture: The Poetics and Politics of Ethnography*. Berkeley: University of California Press. Pp. 262–266.

Maskarinec, Gregory. 1998. *Nepalese Shaman Oral Texts*. Cambridge, MA: Harvard University Press.

———. 1995. *The Rulings of the Night: An Ethnography of Nepalese Shaman Oral Texts*. Madison: University of Wisconsin Press.

———. 1993. Flatter, Promise, Threaten, Kill: A Discursive Analysis of Shamanic Mantar. In *Anthropology of Tibet and the Himalaya*. C. Ramble, M. Brauen, B. Miller, and G. Toffin (eds.). Zurich: Ethnological Museum of the University of Zurich. Pp. 198–207.

———. 1992 . A Shamanic Etiology of Affliction from Western Nepal. *Social Science & Medicine* 35 (5): 723–34.

———. 1989. A Shamanic Semantic Plurality: Dhamis and Jhakris of Western Nepal. In *Shamanism: Past and Present*. M. Hoppál and O. von Sadovszky (eds.), Budapest: Ethnographic Institute, Hungarian Academy of Sciences. Pp. 219–223.

Mastromattei, Romano. 1989. Shamanism in Nepal: Modalities of Ecstatic Experience. In *Shamanism: Past and Present*. M. Hoppál and O. von Sadovszky (eds.). Budapest: Ethnographic. Institute, Hungarian Academy of Sciences. Pp. 225–251.

Maurer, R., V. K. Kumar, L. Woodside, and R. Pekala. 1997. Phenomenological Experience in Response to Monotonous Drumming and Hypnotizability. *American Journal of Clinical Hypnosis* 40 (2): 130–145.

Maxfield, Melinda. 1994. The Journey of the Drum. *ReVision* 16:157–163.

McClenon, James. 2006. The Ritual Healing Theory: Therapeutic Suggestion and the Origin of Religion. In *Where God and Science Meet: How Brain and Evolution-*

ary Studies Alter Our Understanding of Religion. Patrick McNamara (ed.). Westport, CT: Praeger. Vol. 1, pp. 135–158.

———. 2002. *Wondrous Healing: Shamanism, Human Evolution, and the Origin of Religion*. DeKalb: Northern Illinois University Press.

———. 2001. Sociological Investigation of Haunting Cases. In *Hauntings and Poltergeists: Multidisciplinary Perspectives*. J. Houran and R. Lange (eds.). Jefferson, NC: McFarland. Pp. 62–81.

———. 1995. Supernatural Experience, Folk Belief, and Spiritual Healing. In *Out of the Ordinary: Folklore and the Supernatural*. Barbara Walker (ed.) Logan: Utah State University Press. Pp. 107–121.

McHugh, Ernestine. 1992. Dialogue, Structure, and Change in Himalayan Anthropology. *Comparative Studies in Society and History* 34 (3): 552–559.

McNally, R. J., and S. A. Clancy. 2005. Sleep Paralysis, Sexual Abuse, and Space Alien Abduction. *Transcultural Psychiatry* 42 (March): 113–122.

McNamara, Patrick (ed.). 2006. *Where God and Science Meet: How Brain and Evolutionary Studies Alter Our Understanding of Religion*. Westport, CT: Praeger. 3 vols.

Meredith, Georgette. 1967. The "Phurbu": The Use and Symbolism of the Tibetan Magic Dagger. *History of Religions* 6 (3): 236–253.

Messerschmidt, Donald. 1976. Ethnographic Observations of Gurung Shamanism in Lamjung District. In *Spirit Possession in the Nepal Himalayas*. John Hitchcock and Rex Jones (eds.). Warminster, England: Aris and Phillips. Pp. 197–216.

Mestel, R. 1994 . Let Mind Talk Unto Body. *The New Scientist* (July): 26–31.

Métraux, Alfred. 1967. Le Chamanisme Araucan. In *Religions et Magies Indiennes d'Amérique du Sud*. Paris: Gallimard. Pp. 177–147.

Michl, Wolf. 1976. Notes on the Jhākri of Ath Parbat/Dhaulagiri Himalaya. In *Spirit Possession in the Nepal Himalayas*. John Hitchcock and Rex Jones (eds.). Warminster, England: Aris and Phillips. Pp.153–164.

Miller, Casper. 1997. *Faith-Healers in the Himalaya: An Investigation of Traditional Healers and Their Festivals in the Dolakha District of Nepal*. Delhi: Book Faith India.

Mironov, N. D., and S. Shirokogoroff. 1924. Sramana Shaman: Etymology of the Word "Shaman." *Journal of the Royal Asiatic Society, North China Branch* (Shanghai) 55: 105–130.

Mithen, Steven. 1996. *The Prehistory of the Mind: A Search for the Origins of Art, Religion and Science*. London: Thames and Hudson.

Mitrani, Philippe. 1992. A Critical Overview of the Psychiatric Approaches to Shamanism. *Diogenes* 40:145–164.

Moerman, Daniel. 2002. Explanatory Mechanisms for Placebo: Cultural Influences and the Meaning of Response. In *The Science of the Placebo: Toward an Interdisciplinary Research Agenda*. H. Guess, A. Kleinman, J. Kusek, and L. Engel (eds.). London: BMJ Books. Pp. 77–107.

———. 1997. Physiology and Symbols: The Anthropological Implications of the Placebo Effect. In *The Anthropology of Medicine: From Culture to Method*. L. Romanucci-Ross, D. Moerman, and L. Tancredi (eds.). Westport, CT: Bergin and Garvey. Pp. 240–253.

———. 1992. Minding the Body: The Placebo Effect Unmasked. In *Giving the Body Its Due*. Maxine Sheets-Johnstone (ed.). Albany: State University of New York Press. Pp. 69–84.

————. 1979. Anthropology and Symbolic Healing. *Current Anthropology* 20 (1): 59–80.

Morris, Brian. 2006. *Religion and Anthropology: A Critical Introduction*. Cambridge: Cambridge University Press.

Müller-Ebeling, Claudia, Christian Rätsch, and Surendra Shahi. 2002. *Shamanism and Tantra in the Himalayas*. Rochester, VT: Inner Traditions.

Mumford, Stan. 1989. *Himalayan Dialogue: Tibetan Lamas and Gurung Shamans in Nepal*. Madison: University of Wisconsin Press.

Myerhoff, Barbara. 1997. *Peyote Hunt: The Sacred Journey of the Huichol Indians*. Ithaca, NY: Cornell University Press.

Nadel, Siegfried. 1965. Study of Shamanism in the Nuba Hills. In *Reader in Comparative Religion: An Anthropological Approach*. W. Lessa and E. Vogt (eds.). New York: Harper and Row. Pp. 464–479.

Narby, Jeremy, and Francis Huxley (eds.). 2001. *Shamans Through Time: 500 Years on the Path to Knowledge*. London: Thames & Hudson.

Narr, Karl. 1959. Bärenzeremoniell und Schamanismus in der Älteren Steinzeit Europas. *Saeculum* 10 (3): 233–272.

Nebesky-Wojkowitz, René de. 1956. *Oracles and Demons of Tibet: The Cult and Iconography of the Tibetan Protective Deities*. Gravenhage: Mouton.

Neher, Andrew. 1990. *The Psychology of Transcendence*. New York: Dover.

————. 1962. A Physiological Explanation of Unusual Behavior in Ceremonies Involving Drums. *Human Biology* 34:151–160.

Nichols, David, and Benjamin Chemel. 2006. The Neuropharmacology of Religious Experience: Hallucinogens and the Experience of the Divine. In *Where God and Science Meet: How Brain and Evolutionary Studies Alter Our Understanding of Religion*. Patrick McNamara (ed.). Westport, CT: Praeger. Vol. 3, pp. 1–34.

Nickell, Joe. 2001. Phantoms, Frauds, or Fantasies? In *Hauntings and Poltergeists: Multidisciplinary Perspectives*. J. Houran and R. Lange (eds.). Jefferson, NC: McFarland. Pp. 214–224.

Nicoletti, Martino. 2004. *Shamanic Solitudes: Ecstasy, Madness and Spirit Possession in the Nepal Himalaya*. Kathmandu: Vajra Publications.

Niraula, Bhanu. 1994. Use of Health Services in Hill Villages in Central Nepal. *Health Transition Review* 4:151–166.

Noel, Daniel. 1999. *The Soul of Shamanism: Western Fantasies, Imaginal Realities*. New York: Continuum.

Noll, Richard. 1985. Mental Imagery Cultivation as a Cultural Phenomenon. *Current Anthropology* 6: 443–451.

————. 1983. Shamanism and Schizophrenia: A State-Specific Approach in the "Schizophrenia Metaphor" of Shamanic States. *American Ethnologist* 10 (3): 443–459.

Oakley, D., and L. Eames. 1985. The Plurality of Consciousness. In *Brain and Mind*. D. Oakley (ed.). London: Methuen.

Okada, Ferdinand. 1976. Notes on Two Shaman-Curers in Kathmandu. *Contributions to Nepalese Studies* 3:107–112.

Oppitz, Michael. 1993. Who Heals the Healer? Shaman Practice in the Himalayas. *Psychotherapie, Psychosomatik, medizinische Psychologie* 43 (11): 387–395.

————. 1992. Drawings on Shamanic Drums: Nepal. *Anthropology and Aesthetics* 22: 63–81.

———. 1991. Die magische Trommel rē. In *Hungrige Geister und rastlose Seelen: Texte zur Schamanismusforschung*. Michael Kuper (ed.). Berlin: D. Reimer Verlag. Pp. 77–107.

———. 1981. *Schamanen im Blinden Land: Ein Bilderbuch aus dem Himalaya*. Frankfurt am Main: Syndikat.

———. 1968. *Geschichte und Sozialordnung der Sherpa*. Insbruck: Universitats Verlag. Pp. 217–251.

Orne, M. T. 1962. Implications for Psychotherapy Derived from Current Research on the Nature of Hypnosis. *American Journal of Psychiatry* 118:1097–1103.

Ortner, Sherry. 1995. The Case of the Disappearing Shaman, or No Individualism, No Relationalism. *Ethos* 23 (3): 355–399.

Ott, Jonathan. 1993. *Pharmacotheon: Entheogenic Drugs, Their Plant Sources and History*. Kennewick, WA: Natural Products Company.

Pandian, Jacob. 1991. *Culture, Religion, and the Sacred Self: A Critical Introduction to the Anthropological Study of Religion*. Englewood Cliffs, NJ: Prentice Hall.

Paul, Robert. 1976. Some Observations on Sherpa Shamanism. In *Spirit Possession in the Nepal Himalayas*. John Hitchcock and Rex Jones (eds.). Warminster, England: Aris and Phillips. Pp. 141–151.

Pearson, James. 2002. *Shamanism and the Ancient Mind: A Cognitive Approach to Archaeology*. Walnut Creek, CA: AltaMira Press.

Persinger, Michael. 2003. Experimental Simulation of the God Experience. In *NeuroTheology: Brain, Science, Spirituality, Religious Experience*. R. Joseph (ed.). San Jose: University Press. Pp. 279–292.

———. 1989. "The Visitor" Experience and the Personality: The Temporal Lobe Factor. In *Cyberbiological Studies of the Imaginational Component of the UFO Contact Experience*. D. Stillings (ed.). St. Paul: Archaeus Project. Pp. 157–171.

———. 1987. *Neuropsychological Bases of God Beliefs*. New York: Praeger.

———. 1983. Religious and Mystical Experiences as Artifacts of Temporal Lobe Function: A General Hypothesis. *Perceptual and Motor Skills* 57:1255–1262.

Peter, Prince of Greece and Denmark. 1978. Tibetan Oracles in Dharamsala. In *Proceedings of the Csoma de Korös Memorial Symposium*. L. Ligeti (ed.). Budapest: Akadémiai Kiadó. Pp. 327–334.

Peters, Larry. 2005. The Yeti: Spirit of the Himalayan Forest Shaman. *Shamanism* 18 (1/2): 37–59.

———. 1996. The Contributions of Anthropology to Transpersonal Psychiatry. In *Textbook of Transpersonal Psychiatry and Psychology*. B. Scotton, A. Chinen, and J. Battista (eds.). New York: Basic Books. Pp. 207–216.

———. 1995. Karga Puja: A Transpersonal Ritual of Healing in Tamang Shamanism. *Alternative Therapies* 1 (5): 53–61.

———. 1987. Tamang Shamanism in Nepal. In *Shamanism: An Expanded View of Reality*. Shirley Nicholson (ed.). Wheaton, IL: Theosophical Publishing House. Pp. 161–180.

———. 1982. Trance, Initiation, and Psychotherapy in Tamang Shamanism. *American Ethnologist* 9 (1): 21–46.

———. 1981. *Ecstasy and Healing in Nepal: An Ethnopsychiatric Study of Tamang Shamanism*. Malibu: Undena Publications.

———. 1979. Shamanism and Medicine in Developing Nepal. *Contributions to Nepalese Studies* 1 (2): 27–43.

Peters, Larry, and Douglass Price-Williams. 1980. Toward an Experiential Analysis of Shamanism. *American Ethnologist* 7 (3): 397–418.

Pigg, Stacy. 1996. The Credible and the Credulous: The Question of Villagers' Belief in Nepal. *Current Anthropology* 11 (2): 160–201.

———. 1995. The Social Symbolism of Healing in Nepal. *Ethnology* 34 (1): 17–38.

Pignède, Bernard. 1966. *Les Gurungs*. Paris: Mouton.

Pinker, Steven. 1997. *How the Mind Works*. New York: W. W. Norton.

Price, Neil. 2001. An Archaeology of Altered States: Shamanism and Material Culture Studies. In *The Archaeology of Shamanism*. Neil Price (ed.). New York: Routledge. Pp. 3–16.

———, (ed.). 2001. *The Archaeology of Shamanism*. New York: Routledge.

Price, T. Douglas, and James Brown (eds.). 1985. *Prehistoric Hunter-Gatherers: The Emergence of Cultural Complexity*. New York: Academic Press.

Price-Williams, Douglass, and Dureen Hughes. 1994. Shamanism and Altered States of Consciousness. *Anthropology of Consciousness* 5 (2): 1–15.

Putnam, F. 1989. *Diagnosis and Treatment of Multiple Personality Disorder*. New York: Guilford.

Pyakurel, Amit. 2006. Nepal "Witches" Targets of Brutal Wrath. Accusations from Ignorance Can Lead to Torture, Murder. *Ohmynews*. February 26. http://english.oh mynews.com/articleview/article_view.asp?menu=c10400&no=276134&rel_no=1.

Rai, Shiba, Ganesh Rai, Ayako Abe, and Yoshimi Ohno. 2001. The Health System in Nepal—An Introduction. *Environmental Health and Preventive Medicine* 6:1–8.

Randi, James. 1997. *An Encyclopedia of Claims, Frauds, and Hoaxes of the Occult and Supernatural*. New York: St. Martin's Griffin.

Rank, Gustav. 1967. Shamanism as a Research Subject. In *Studies in Shamanism*. Carl-Martin Edsman (ed.). Stockholm: Almqvist and Wiksell. Pp. 15–22.

Reed, Graham. 1988. *The Psychology of Anomalous Experience: A Cognitive Approach*. Buffalo, NY: Prometheus Books.

Reinhard, Johan. 1976. Shamanism and Spirit Possession: The Definitional Problem. In *Spirit Possession in the Nepal Himalayas*. John Hitchcock and Rex Jones (eds.). Warminster, England: Aris and Phillips. Pp. 12–22.

Reyna, S. P. 1994. Literary Anthropology and the Case against Science. *Man* 29: 555–581.

Riboli, Diana. 2000. *Tunsuriban: Shamanism in the Chepang of Southern and Central Nepal*. Kathmandu: Mandala Book Point.

———. 1995. Shamanic Visual Arts in Nepal. In *Shamanism in Performing Arts*. T. Kim, M. Hoppál, and O. von Sadovszky (eds.). Budapest: Akadémiai Kiadó. Pp. 76–88.

Richards, Douglas. 1991. Subjective Psychic Experiences and Dissociative Experiences. *Dissociation* 4: 83–91.

Ring, Kenneth. 1989. Near-Death and UFO Encounters as Shamanic Initiations: Some Conceptual and Evolutionary Implications. *ReVision: The Journal of Consciousness and Change* 11 (3): 14–22.

———. 1980. *Life at Death: A Scientific Investigation of the Near-Death Experience*. New York: Coward, McCann and Geoghegan.

Ripinsky-Naxon, Michael. 1998. Shamanistic Knowledge and Cosmology. In *Tribal Epistemologies: Essays in the Philosophy of Anthropology*. Helmut Wautischer (ed.). Brookfield: Ashgate. Pp. 119–162.

———. 1993. *The Nature of Shamanism: Substance and Function of a Religious Metaphor*. Albany: State University of New York Press.

———. 1992. Shamanism: Religion or Rite? *Journal of Prehistoric Religion* (6): 37–44.

Roberts, Thomas. 2006. Chemical Input, Religious Output: Entheogens: A Pharmatheology Sampler. In *Where God and Science Meet: How Brain and Evolutionary Studies Alter Our Understanding of Religion*. Patrick McNamara (ed.). Westport, CT: Praeger. Vol. 3, pp. 235–268.

Rock, Joseph, Georg Jayme, and M. Harders-Steinhäuser. 1963. *The Life and Culture of the Na-khi Tribe on the China-Tibet Borderland*. Wiesbaden: Franz Steiner.

Rogers, Spencer. 1982. *The Shaman: His Symbols and His Healing Power*. Springfield, IL: Charles C. Thomas.

Romanucci-Ross, Lola. 1997. The Impassioned Knowledge of the Shaman. In *The Anthropology of Medicine: From Culture to Method*. L. Romanucci-Ross, D. Moerman, and L. Tancredi (eds.). Westport, CT: Bergin and Garvey. Pp. 214–223.

Romanucci-Ross, Lola, and Daniel Moerman. 1997. The Extraneous Factor in Western Medicine. In *The Anthropology of Medicine: From Culture to Method*. L. Romanucci-Ross, D. Moerman, and L. Tancredi (eds.). Westport, CT: Bergin and Garvey. Pp. 351–368.

Ross, C., and S. Joshi. 1992. Paranormal Experiences in the General Population. *Journal of Nervous and Mental Disease* 180:357–361.

Rouget, Gilbert. 1985. *Music and Trance: A Theory of the Relations Between Music and Possession*. Chicago: University of Chicago Press.

Ruck, Carl, and J. Bigwood., D. Staples, J. Ott, and R. G. Wasson. 1979. Entheogens. *Journal of Psychedelic Drugs* 11 (1–2): 145–146.

Sagant, P. 1988. The Shaman's Cure and the Layman's Interpretation. *Kailash* 14 (1/2): 5–40.

———. 1982. Le Chamane et le Grele. *L'Ethnographie* 78:87–88, 163–174.

———. 1976. Becoming a Limbu Priest: Ethnographic Notes. In *Spirit Possession in the Nepal Himalayas*. J. Hitchcock and R. Jones (eds.). Warminster, England: Aris and Phillips. Pp. 56–99.

Samuel, Geoffrey. 1995. Performance, Vision and Transformation in Shamanic Ritual: Healers, Clients and Societies. In *Shamanism in Performing Arts*. T. Kim, M. Hoppál, and O. Sadovszky (eds.). Budapest: Akadémiai Kiadó. Pp. 253–262.

———. 1993. *Civilized Shamans: Buddhism in Tibetan Societies*. Washington, DC: Smithsonian Institution Press.

Sandner, Donald. 1997. Introduction: Analytical Psychology and Shamanism. In *The Sacred Heritage: The Influence of Shamanism on Analytical Psychology*. Donald Sandner and Steven Wong (eds.). New York: Routledge. Pp. 3–17.

Sangren, Steven. 1988. Rhetoric and the Authority of Ethnography: "Postmodernism" and the Social Reproduction of Texts. *Current Anthropology* 29 (3): 405–435.

Sargant, William. 1973. *The Mind Possessed: A Physiology of Possession, Mysticism, and Faith Healing*. Philadelphia: Lippincott.

———. 1957. *Battle for the Mind: A Physiology of Conversion and Brain-washing*. London: Heinemann.

Saver, J., and J. Rabin. 1997. The Neural Substrates of Religious Experience. *Journal of Neuropsychiatry and. Neuroscience* 9:498–510.

Schmid, Toni. 1967. Shamanistic Practice in Northern Nepal. In *Studies in Shamanism*. Carl-Martin Edsman (ed.). Stockholm: Almqvist and Wiksell. Pp. 82–89.

Schultes, Richard. 1998. Antiquity of the Use of New World Hallucinogens. *The Heffter Review of Psychedelic Research* 1:1–17.

Schultes, Richard, and Albert Hofmann. 1992. *Plants of the Gods: Their Sacred, Healing, and Hallucinogenic Powers*. Rochester, VT: Healing Arts Press.

Shaara, Lila, and Andrew Strathern. 1992. A Preliminary Analysis of the Relationship between Altered States of. Consciousness, Healing, and Social Structure. *American Anthropologist* 94 (1): 145–160.

Shapiro, Arthur. 1959. The Placebo Effect in the History of Medical Treatment: Implications for Psychiatry. *American Journal of Psychiatry* 116:298–304.

Sherzer, Joel. 1989. *Namakke, Sunmakke, Kormakke*: Three Types of Cuna Speech Event. In *Explorations in the Ethnography of Speaking*. R. Bauman and J. Sherzer (eds.). Cambridge: Cambridge University Press. Pp. 263–283.

Shiba, K., R. Ganesh, K. Hirai, A. Abe, and Y. Ohno. 2001. The Health System in Nepal—An Introduction. *Environmental Health and Preventive Medicine* 6 (1): 1–8

Shirokogoroff, Sergei. 1923. General Theory of Shamanism Among the Tungus. *Journal of the North China Branch of the Royal Asiatic Society* 54:246–249.

———. 1924. What Is Shamanism? *The China Journal of Sciences and Arts* 2 (3–4): 275–279, 328–371.

———. 1935. *Psychomental Complex of the Tungus*. London: K. Paul, Trench, and Trubner.

Shneiderman, Sara, and Mark Turin. 2005. Thangmi, Thami, Thani: Remembering a Forgotten People. *Himalayan Culture* 5 (1): 5–21.

Sidky, H. 2006. Cultural Materialism, Scientific Anthropology, Epistemology, and "Narrative Ethnographies of the Particular." In *Marvin Harris's Cultural Materialism and Its Legacy*. Lawrence A. Kuznar and Stephen K. Sanderson (eds.). Boulder, CO: Paradigm Publishers. Pp. 66–77.

———. 2004. *Perspectives on Culture: A Critical Introduction to Theory in Cultural Anthropology*. Englewood Cliffs, NJ: Prentice Hall.

———. 2003a. *A Critique of Postmodern Anthropology: In Defense of Disciplinary Origins and Traditions*. Lewiston, NY: Edwin Mellen Press.

———. 2003b. Shamanism, Islam. In *South Asian Folklore: An Encyclopedia*. Margaret Mills and Peter Clause (eds.). New York: Routledge. Pp. 544–546.

———. 1997. *Witchcraft, Lycanthropy, Drugs and Disease: An Anthropological Study of the European Witch Persecutions*. New York: Peter Lang.

———. 1994. Shamans and Mountain Spirits in Hunza. *Asian Folklore Studies* 53:67–96.

———. 1990. Malang, Sufis, and Mystics: An Ethnographic and Historical Study of Shamanism in Afghanistan. *Asian Folklore Studies* 49 (2): 275–301.

Sidky, H., J. Subedi, and J. Hamill. 2002. *Halfway to the Mountain: The Jirels of Eastern Nepal*. Kathmandu: Tribhuvan University Press.

Siikala, Anna-Leena. 1992a. Siberian and Inner Asian Shamanism. In *Studies on Shamanism*. Anna-Leena Siikala, and Mihály Hoppál (eds.). Budapest: Akadémiai Kiadó, Pp. 1–14.

———. 1992b. The Interpretation of Siberian and Inner Asian Shamanism. In *Studies on Shamanism*. Anna-Leena Siikala, and Mihály Hoppál (eds.). Budapest: Akadémiai Kiadó, Pp. 15–25.

Siikala, Anna-Leena, and Mihály Hoppál (eds.). 1992. *Studies on Shamanism*. Budapest: Akademiai Kiado.

Silverman, Julian. 1967. Shamans and Acute Schizophrenia. *American Anthropologist* 69:21–31.

Skafte, Peter. 1992. Called by the Spirits: Three Accounts of Shamanic Initiation From Nepal. *Shaman's Drum* 27 (1): 46–52.

———. 1990. Lessons with a Nepalese Shaman: Where Rivers Meet. *Shaman's Drum* 19 (2): 54–59.

Smith, Frederick. 2006. *The Self Possessed: Deity and Spirit Possession in South Asian Literature and Civilization*. New York: Columbia University Press.

Smith, W. Lynn, Harold Merskey, and Steven Gross (eds.). 1980. *Pain: Meaning and Management*. Jamaica, NY: Spectrum Publications.

Smith, Noel. 1992. *An Analysis of Ice Age Art: Its Psychology and Belief System*. New York: Peter Lang.

Snellgrove, David, and Hugh Richardson. 1968. *A Culture History of Tibet*. New York: Fredrick A. Praeger.

Sokal, A., and J. Bricmont. 1998. *Fashionable Nonsense: Postmodern Intellectuals' Abuse of Science*. New York: Picador.

Sokolova, Z. P. 1989. A Survey of Ob-Ugrian Shamanism. In *Shamanism: Past and Present*. M. Hoppál and O. von Sadovszky (eds.). Budapest: Ethnographic Institute, Hungarian Academy of Sciences. Pp. 155–164.

Solecki, Ralph. 1971. *Shanidar: The First Flower People*. New York: Knopf.

Sommer, Jeffrey. 1999. The Shanidar IV "Flower Burial:" A Re-evaluation of Neanderthal Burial Ritual. *Cambridge Archaeological Journal* 9 (1): 127–129.

Spencer, Robert. 1968. Review of *Studies in Shamanism*. Carl-Martin Edsman (ed.). *American Anthropologist* 70 (2): 396–397.

Srinivas, Smriti. 1998. *The Mouths of People, the Voice of God: Buddhists and Muslims in a Frontier Community of Ladakh*. Delhi: Oxford University Press.

Stein, R. A. 1972. *Tibetan Civilization*. Stanford: University of California Press.

Steinmann, Brigitte. 1987. *Les Tamang du Népal: Usages et Religion, Religion de l'Usage*. Paris: Editions Recherche sur les Civilisations.

Stevenson, Ian. 1980. *Twenty Cases Suggestive of Reincarnation*. Charlottesville: University Press of Virginia.

———. 1966. *Twenty Cases Suggestive of Reincarnation*. Charlottesville: University Press of Virginia.

Stiles, Daniel. 1992. The Hunter-Gatherer "Revisionist" Debate. *Anthropology Today* 8 (2): 13–17.

Stoller, Paul. 1986. The Reconstruction of Ethnography. In *Discourse and the Social Life of Meaning*. Phyllis P. Chock and June Wyman (eds.). Washington, DC: Smithsonian Institution Press. Pp. 51–74.

Stone, Linda. 1976. Concepts of Illness and Curing in a Central Nepal Village. *Contributions to Nepalese Studies* 3:55–80.

Subedi, Ganga Prasad. 2004. Nepal: The Power of Superstition. *International Humanist News*. February 1, http://www.iheu.org/node/992.

Subedi, Janardan, H. Sidky, and J. Hamill. 2000. Health and Healthcare in Jiri. *Contributions to Nepalese Studies*. (The Jirel Issue): 97–104.

Sullivan, Lawrence. 1994. The Attributes and Power of Shamans: A General Description of the Ecstatic Care of the Soul. In *Ancient Traditions: Shamanism in Central Asia and the Americas.* Gary Seaman and Jane Day (eds.). Niwot, CO: University of Colorado Press. Pp. 29–45.

Swanson, Guy. 1964. *The Birth of the Gods: The Origin of Primitive Beliefs.* Ann Arbor: University of Michigan Press.

Tart, Charles. 1999. Altered States of Consciousness. *Journal of Consciousness Studies-Online.* http://www.paradigm-sys.com/ctt_articles2.cfm?id=22#ptop.

———. 1986 . *Waking Up: Overcoming the Obstacles to Human Potential.* Boston: New Science Library.

———. 1980. A Systems Approach to Altered States of Consciousness. In *The Psychobiology of Consciousness.* Julian Davidson and Richard Davidson (eds.). New York: Plenum Press. Pp. 243–269.

———. 1975. *States of Consciousness.* New York: E. P. Dutton.

——— (ed.). 1969. *Altered States of Consciousness: A Book of Readings.* New York: Wiley.

Taussig, Michael. 1989. The Nervous System: Homesickness and Dada. *Stanford Humanities Review* 1 (1): 44–81.

———. 1987. *Shamanism, Colonialism, and the Wild Man: A Study in Terror and Healing.* Chicago: University of Chicago Press.

TePaske, Bradley. 1997. Eliade, Jung, and Shamanism. In *The Sacred Heritage: The Influence of Shamanism on Analytical Psychology.* Donald Sandner and Steven Wong (eds.). New York: Routledge. Pp.18–28.

Thomas, Nicholas, and Caroline Humphrey. 1994. Introduction. In *Shamanism, History, and the State.* N. Thomas and C. Humphrey (eds.). Ann Arbor: University of Michigan Press. Pp. 1–11.

Thompson, Keith. 1991. *Angels and Aliens: UFOs and the Mythic Imagination.* Reading, MA: Addison-Wesley.

Thorpe, S. A. 1993. *Shamans, Medicine Men and Traditional Healers: A Comparative Study of Shamanism in Siberian Asia, Southern Africa and North America.* Pretoria: University of South Africa.

Torrance, Robert. 1994. *The Spiritual Quest: Transcendence in Myth, Religion, and Science.* Berkeley: University of California Press.

Townsend, Joan. 2001. Traditional and Invented Shamanism. In *Shamanhood: Symbolism and Epic.* Juha Pentikäinen (ed.). Budapest: Akadémiai Kiadó. Pp. 257–264.

———. 1999. Western Contemporary Core and Neo-Shamanism and the Interpenetration with Indigenous Societies. In *Proceedings of the International Congress: Shamanism and Other Indigenous Spiritual Beliefs and Practices.* Vol. 5. Moscow: Institute of Ethnology and Anthropology of the Russian Academy of Sciences. Pp. 223–231.

———. 1997. Shamanism. In *Anthropology of Religion: A Handbook.* Stephen Glazier (ed.). Westport, CT: Praeger. Pp. 427–469.

Turner, Edith. 1993. The Reality of Spirits: A Tabooed or Permitted Field of Study? *Anthropology of. Consciousness* 4 (1): 9–12.

Turner, Ralph Lilley. 1931. *A Comparative and Etymological Dictionary of the Nepali Language.* London: K. Paul, Trench, Trubner.

Turner, Victor. 1977. Symbols in African Ritual. In *Symbolic Anthropology: A Reader in the Study of Symbols and Meanings.* Janet Dolgin, David Kemnitzer, and David Schneider (eds.). New York: Columbia University Press. Pp. 183–194.

———. 1974. *Dramas, Fields, and Metaphors: Symbolic Action in Human Society.* Ithaca, NY: Cornell University Press.

———. 1969. *The Ritual Process: Structure and Anti-Structure.* Chicago: Aldine.

———. 1968. *The Drums of Affliction: A Study of Religious Processes Among the Ndembu of Zambia.* Oxford: Clarendon Press.

———. 1967. *The Forest of Symbols: Aspects of Ndembu Ritual.* Ithaca, NY: Cornell University Press.

Van Gennep, Arnold. 2001. Shamanism Is a Dangerously Vague Word (1903). In *Shamans Through Time: 500 Years on the Path to Knowledge.* Jeremy Narby and Francis Huxley (eds.). London: Thames & Hudson. Pp. 51–52.

———. 1960. *The Rites of Passage.* London: Routledge and Kegan Paul.

Van Ommeren, Mark, I. Komproe, E. Cardeña, S. Thapa, D. Prasin, J. de Jong, and B. Sharma. 2004. Mental Illness Among Bhutanese Shamans in Nepal. *The Journal of Nervous and Mental Disease* 192 (4): 313–317.

Vasilevič, G. M. 1996. The Acquisition of Shamanistic Ability Among the Evenki (Tungus). In *Folk Beliefs and Shamanistic Traditions in Siberia.* V. Diószegi and M. Hoppál (eds.). Budapest: Akadémiai Kiadó. Pp. 135–145.

Vinding, Michael, and S. Gauchan. 1977. The History of the Thakali According to the Thakali Tradition. *Kailash* 5 (2): 97–184.

Vitebsky, Piers. 1995. *The Shaman: Voyages of the Soul, Trance, Ecstasy and Healing from Siberia to the Amazon.* Boston: Little, Brown.

Voigt, V. 1984. Shamanism: Word or Person? In *Shamanism in Eurasia.* M. Hoppál (ed.). Gottingen: Herodot. Pp. 13–20.

Von Gernet, Alexander. 1993. The Construction of the Prehistoric Ideation. *Cambridge Archaeological Journal* 3 (1): 67–81.

Wallace, Anthony. 1966. *Religion: An Anthropological View.* New York: Random House.

Walsh, Roger. 2001. Shamanic Experiences: A Developmental Analysis. *Journal of Humanistic Psychology* 41 (3): 31–52.

———. 1997. The Psychological Health of Shamans: A Reevaluation. *Journal of the American Academy of Religions* 65 (1): 101–124.

———. 1996. Shamanism and Healing. In *Textbook of Transpersonal Psychiatry and Psychology.* B. Scotton, A. Chinen, and J. Battista (eds.). New York: Basic Books. Pp. 96–103.

———. 1995. Phenomenological Mapping: A Method for Describing and Comparing States of Consciousness. *Journal of Transpersonal Psychiatry* 21 (1): 1–11.

———. 1993. Phenomenological Mapping and Comparisons of Shamanic, Buddhist, Yogic, and Schizophrenic Experiences. *Journal of the American Academy of Religion* 61 (4): 739–769.

———. 1990. *The Spirit of Shamanism.* Los Angeles: J. P. Tarcher.

Walter, Damian. 2001. The Medium of the Message: Shamanism as Localised Practice in the Nepal Himalayas. In *The Archaeology of Shamanism.* Neil Price (ed.). New York: Routledge. Pp. 105–119.

Walter, Mariko, and Eva Fridman. 2004. *Shamanism: An Encyclopedia of World Beliefs, Practices, and Culture.* San Francisco: ABC-CLIO.

Watanabe, Hitoshi. 1994. The Animal Cult of Northern Hunter-Gatherers: Patterns and Their Ecological Implications. In *Circumpolar Religion and Ecology: An*

Anthropology of the North. Takashi Irimoto and Takako Yamada (eds.). Tokyo: University of Tokyo Press. Pp. 47–69.

Watters, David. 1975. Siberian Shamanistic Traditions Among the Kham Magars of Nepal. *Contributions to Nepalese Studies* 2 (1): 123–168.

Wellmann, Klaus. 1981. Rock Art, Shamans, Phosphenes and Hallucinogens in North America. *Bollettino del Centro Camuno di Studii Preistorici* 18:89–103.

West, Harry. 2007. *Ethnographic Sorcery*. Chicago: University of Chicago Press.

Whitmore, John. 1995. Religious Dimensions of the UFO Abductee Experience. In *The Gods Have Landed: New Religions from Other Worlds*. James Lewis (ed.). Albany: State University of New York Press. Pp. 65–84.

WHO. 2003. *Country Health Profiles: Nepal*. WHO South-East Asia Region. http://w3.whosea.org/cntryhealth/index.htm.

Wilbert, Johannes. 1987. *Tobacco and Shamanism in South America*. New Haven, CT: Yale University Press.

Winkelman, Michael. 2006. Cross-Cultural Assessments of Shamanism as a Biogenetic Foundation for Religion. In *Where God and Science Meet: How Brain and Evolutionary Studies Alter Our Understanding of Religion*. Patrick McNamara (ed.). Westport, CT: Praeger. Vol. 3, pp. 139–159.

———. 2004a. Shamanism as the Original Neurotheology. *Zygon* 39 (1): 193–217.

———. 2004b. Witchcraft and Sorcery in Shamanism. In *Shamanism: An Encyclopedia of World Beliefs, Practices, and Culture*. M. Walter and E. Fridman (eds.). San Francisco: ABC-CLIO. Pp. 272–274.

———. 2003. Shamanism and Innate Brain Structures: The Original Neurotheology. In *NeuroTheology: Brain, Science, Spirituality, Religious Experience*. R. Joseph (ed.). San Jose: University Press. Pp. 387–396.

———. 2002. Shamanism as Neurotheology and Evolutionary Psychology. *American Behavioral Scientist* 45 (12): 1873–1885.

———. 2000. *Shamanism: The Neural Ecology of Consciousness and Healing*. Westport, CT: Bergin and Garvey.

———. 1997. Altered States of Consciousness and Religious Behavior. In *Anthropology of Religion: A Handbook*. Stephen Glazier (ed.). Westport, CT: Praeger. Pp. 394–428.

———. 1992. *Shamans, Priests, and Witches: A Cross-Cultural Study of Magico-Religious Practitioners*. Anthropological Research Papers no. 44. Arizona State University.

Winkler, Walter. 1976. Spirit Possession in Far Western Nepal. In *Spirit Possession in the Nepal Himalayas*. J. Hitchcock and R. Jones (eds.). Warminster, England: Aris and Phillips. Pp. 244–262.

Winzeler, Robert. 2008. *Anthropology and Religion: What We Know, Think, and Question*. Lanham, MD: AltaMira.

Yamada, Takako. 1994. Animals as the Intersection of Religion and Ecology: An Ainu Example. In *Circumpolar Religion and Ecology: An Anthropology of the North*. Takashi Irimoto and Takako Yamada (eds.). Tokyo: University of Tokyo Press. Pp. 69–103

———. 1999. *An Anthropology of Animism and Shamanism*. Budapest: Akadémiai Kiadó,

Znamenski, Andrei. 2004. Adventures of the Metaphor: Shamanism and Shamanism Studies. In *Shamanism: Critical Concepts in Sociology*. A. Znamenski (ed.). London: Routledge. Pp. xix–lxxxvi.

———. 2003. *Shamanism in Siberia: Russian Records of Indigenous Spirituality*. London: Kluwer Academic Publishers.

Zornickaja, M. J. 1978. Dances of Yakut Shamans. In *Shamanism in Siberia*. V. Diószegi and M. Hoppál (eds.). Budapest: Akadémiai Kiadó. Pp. 299–307.

Zusne, Leonard, and Warren Jones. 1989. *Anomalistic Psychology: A Study of Magical Thinking*. Hillsdale, NJ: L. Erlbaum.

Index

About the Author

H. Sidky is associate professor in the Department of Anthropology at Miami University, Oxford, Ohio. He has conducted extensive ethnographic fieldwork in Afghanistan, Pakistan, Nepal, northern India, Easter Island, and Australia. His areas of interest include the anthropology of religion, ecological anthropology, anthropological theory and history of anthropological thought and ethnography and history of central Asia, Afghanistan, Pakistan, Nepal, and northern India.